Want to have a highly productive and congenial research team? Joshua Hook, Don Davis, and Daryl Van Tongeren have a deep friendship, and each of them has a research team that seems to publish something every Wednesday based on their individual and collaborative grants. They lead you through procedures that are efficient yet relationally warm. Putting this book into action will repay its reading many times over.

—**Everett L. Worthington, Jr., PhD,** Commonwealth Professor Emeritus, Virginia Commonwealth University, Richmond, VA

Highly recommended for anyone entering, or even considering, graduate study in psychology. Loaded with specific and practical suggestions, this book will help students navigate a challenging and sometimes confusing environment, especially as it pertains to conducting research. Unlike any other book (why hasn't anyone else thought of writing it?), this one should be kept within arm's reach.

—**Peter C. Hill, PhD,** Rosemead School of Psychology, Biola University, La Mirada, CA

Three creative, prolific scholars gently offer their hard-earned practical wisdom for becoming productive—or even creative and prolific. For motivated but uncertain grad students and new academics, *The Complete Researcher* is a gold mine of generative mentoring and useful advice.

—**David G. Myers, PhD,** Hope College, Holland, MI; coauthor, *Psychology, 14th Edition* and *Social Psychology, 14th Edition*

Drawing from several decades of collaboration between three highly accomplished and respected researchers, *The Complete Researcher* gives a compelling inside scoop on what really makes research tick: value-driven projects, meaningful and effective relationships, consistent attention to self-care and work habits, and the ability to weather times of adversity. The authors do a superb job describing the nuts and bolts of project design, writing, mentoring, and the transition into an academic career. This book will be a fantastic resource for faculty, graduate students, and undergraduates alike.

—**Julie J. Exline, PhD,** Professor, Department of Psychological Sciences, Case Western Reserve University, Cleveland, OH

The Complete Researcher: A Practical Guide for Graduate Students and Early Career Professionals is a must-read for any graduate student and *their mentors*. It is practical, personal, and aspirational. The authors address the existential dilemma of why to do research, while providing direct solutions to move research projects forward.

—**Jesse Owen, PhD,** Licensed Psychologist; Professor, Department of Counseling Psychology, University of Denver, Denver, CO; Editor, *Psychotherapy*

The
Complete
Researcher

The
Complete
Researcher

A Practical Guide for Graduate Students
and Early Career Professionals

Joshua N. Hook,
Don E. Davis, and
Daryl R. Van Tongeren

 AMERICAN PSYCHOLOGICAL ASSOCIATION

Copyright © 2024 by the American Psychological Association. All rights reserved. Except as permitted under the United States Copyright Act of 1976, no part of this publication may be reproduced or distributed in any form or by any means, including, but not limited to, the process of scanning and digitization, or stored in a database or retrieval system, without the prior written permission of the publisher.

The opinions and statements published are the responsibility of the authors, and such opinions and statements do not necessarily represent the policies of the American Psychological Association.

Published by
American Psychological Association
750 First Street, NE
Washington, DC 20002
https://www.apa.org

Order Department
https://www.apa.org/pubs/books
order@apa.org

Typeset in Charter and Interstate by Circle Graphics, Inc., Reisterstown, MD

Printer: Gasch Printing, Odenton, MD
Cover Designer: Gwen J. Grafft, Minneapolis, MN

Library of Congress Cataloging-in-Publication Data

Names: Hook, Joshua N., author. | Davis, Don E., author. | Van Tongeren, Daryl R., author.
Title: The complete researcher : a practical guide for graduate students and early career professionals / Joshua N. Hook, Don E. Davis, and Daryl R. Van Tongeren.
Description: Washington, DC : American Psychological Association, [2024] | Includes bibliographical references and index.
Identifiers: LCCN 2023016661 (print) | LCCN 2023016662 (ebook) | ISBN 9781433839054 (paperback) | ISBN 9781433839061 (ebook)
Subjects: LCSH: Psychology--Research--Methodology. | Psychology--Study and teaching (Higher) | Career development. | BISAC: PSYCHOLOGY / Education & Training | EDUCATION / Research
Classification: LCC BF76.5 .H66 2023 (print) | LCC BF76.5 (ebook) | DDC 150.72--dc23/eng/20230615
LC record available at https://lccn.loc.gov/2023016661
LC ebook record available at https://lccn.loc.gov/2023016662

https://doi.org/10.1037/0000371-000

Printed in the United States of America

10 9 8 7 6 5 4 3 2 1

To Dr. Ev Worthington, my mentor in graduate school, who taught me how to do research with equal measures of discipline and care.
—JOSHUA N. HOOK

At the risk of a circular dedication—to Josh, who provided a source of social modeling, by going a year ahead through everything, and to Daryl, whose humor softened the edges of training and life in general, despite the fact that he faced many very painful experiences.
—DON E. DAVIS

To my graduate school mentors who believed in me even when I didn't—Kelli Klebe, Jeff Green, and Ev Worthington—and to Josh and Donnie, who helped me realize that science— and life—is best done with your friends.
—DARYL R. VAN TONGEREN

Contents

Foreword—Everett L. Worthington, Jr.   ix
Preface   xv

    Introduction: How This Book Can Help Build Research and Leadership Skills   3

I. PRINCIPLES: BUILDING YOURSELF INTO A SUCCESSFUL RESEARCHER   9

    1. Finding and Sustaining Motivation: Connecting Your Values to the Research Process   11

    2. Building Community as You Build Your Research Career   21

    3. Building Expertise in Research   33

    4. Setting Goals for Your Research   45

    5. Developing Good Habits for Successful Research   57

    6. Cultivating Positive Beliefs to Foster Research Success   71

    7. Nurturing the Mind–Body Connection to Support Productivity   85

    8. Navigating Adversity During the Research Process   95

II. PLAN: THE RESEARCH PROJECT FROM START TO FINISH — 105

9. Choosing a Topic for Your Research Project — 107
10. Conducting a Literature Review — 115
11. Designing Your Research Project — 129
12. Planning the Method Section — 137
13. Preparing for the Proposal Meeting — 147
14. Planning for and Conducting Data Collection — 155
15. Analyzing Data and Writing Your Results — 161
16. Crafting the Discussion — 167
17. Writing the Abstract — 173
18. Making a Conference Presentation — 179
19. Preparing Your Research Project for Publication — 189

III. PROGRAM: DEVELOPING LEADERSHIP SKILLS AND JUMP-STARTING YOUR RESEARCH CAREER — 199

20. Stepping Into Leadership in Your Research Career — 201
21. Developing a Research Program — 215
22. Collaborating With Others in Research — 225
23. Making the Transition From Graduate Student to Professor — 241
24. Mentoring Students — 257
25. Balancing Cohesion and Inclusion in Teams — 269
26. Conclusion: Final Thoughts on Growing as a Researcher — 285

Appendix: Sample Timelines — *293*
References — *295*
Index — *301*
About the Authors — *321*

Foreword

EVERETT L. WORTHINGTON, JR.

I remember one day near the end of Josh's second year at Virginia Commonwealth University (VCU), which was Donnie's first year. Daryl was also in his first year, but he was in the Social Psychology program. Josh and Donnie dropped by my opened office door and said, "We have something important to talk with you about. Can we make an appointment?"

Because I never shut my door and students were encouraged to drop in at any time, this request for an appointment could strike fear into the heart of even a lion-hearted professor. What is wrong? What terrible thing has happened that needs a special appointment? My fears were not calmed when, at the time of the appointment, they arrived and pulled the door closed. Yikes! I never shut the door on student meetings unless something personal was to be discussed—like annual evaluations or a student's personal interaction with a professor, student, or client.

They got right down to it. "We have been talking. Do you think it is out of line to think we could get over 20 publications submitted during the next year?"

I swallowed my bubble gum. (Or I would have if I still chewed gum.)

"Sure!" I tried not to shout with relief. "I see no problem with you all getting 20 or more papers under review within the next year."

Then the moment of truth. One of them said, "Of course, we are going to have to count on you to first-author some of those."

That about sums up my mentoring of Josh, Donnie, and Daryl. They were superb students in a line of superb students with whom I was privileged to collaborate and sometimes provide a little practical wisdom from my experience. I have always said that I learned far more from my graduate students—and even some talented undergraduate students—than I taught.

Now, Josh, Donnie, and Daryl are sharing the fruits of their experience and learning with you in this wonderful book. I read the book in 2 days, so it will not delay your vital research to read it. And it is a goldmine of wisdom. Part I begins with some habits that you will want to develop. Part II contains practical advice and concrete examples from their experiences about how to move through a thesis or dissertation. Much of this advice is relevant for writing publishable papers or grants as well. Part III moves you beyond the graduate student years to establishing a career involved with research.

What I think these guys have done is provide a relational guide to research. Rather than simply supplying a dry task list of steps to check off toward a completed dissertation, which many books about research seem to do, this book is full of life. It is not an abstract thesis best used as a doorstop or sleep aid, but it is teeming with anecdotes and practical examples. And at the heart of the book is relationships. As a graduate student, relationships with peers, undergraduates, professors, and your graduate school research advisor are keys to success. The good humor among Josh, Donnie, and Daryl is evident. They describe meetings together—including their effort to get 50 papers published in a 2-year period. They met together regularly for good fun and focused plans for research. They made T-shirts to declare their intentions. They planned a large party at the end of their successful campaign. And they achieved their goal—with the last couple of papers being submitted at the deadline!

I think we had an excellent lab and great relationships within the lab throughout their time at VCU. All three were intellectually sharp, with different intellectual and interpersonal strengths. They shared excellence in statistical and research design, as did each of the people in the lab. I sometimes paid for special stats courses for them to build those skills, and in return, they taught me and the others in the lab the concepts they learned. They each had a keen grasp of concepts and a wide-ranging knowledge base. They brought their specialized and broader knowledge to bear on the exciting intellectual issues that they and others in our lab engaged with, people like Andrea Miller, Michael Scherer, Katie Campana, Chelsea Greer, Caroline Lavelock, Brandon Griffin, Chelsea Reid-Short (from Social Psychology like Daryl), Jackie Moloney (from Developmental Psychology), and others. I mention these lab mates because, almost without exception, they have become successful researchers, academicians, practitioners, and teachers. The lab environment was, as much as anything else, a great Petri dish of intellectual stimulation and an environment in which we all grew from each other's knowledge and virtue.

I mention virtue because we studied virtues, but I hope you will see that virtues are really at the heart of doing good research and learning to do it with excellence. As Aristotle conceived them, virtues were excellences. And this research team, of which Josh, Donnie, and Daryl were core members, practiced virtues regularly.

I see three foundational virtues as providing a three-legged support for a platform of additional virtues. One of the supporting legs is humility. General humility involves (a) an accurate awareness and portrayal of one's strengths and weaknesses, (b) teachability to correct weaknesses, (c) modesty in self-presentation, and (d) an other-orientation to build others up and not put them down. Josh, Donnie, and Daryl have written extensively about humility. One type of humility that is extremely important is intellectual humility, which is the ability to discuss one's ideas (especially emotionally laden ideas like those we might be religiously, politically, or research-wise committed to) with committed civility while still displaying the four aspects of general humility. Any successful research career must be anchored in at least some intellectual humility. In addition, cultural humility is essential, and these three scholars have done some great work on understanding and communicating about cultural humility. This is important not only because research has gone global but also because so have doctoral students, and the great research advisor must have the cultural sensitivity to understand the specific needs of each student, working with them and understanding exactly how to approach the student, taking broader culture and localized culture into account.

The second leg supporting the platform for other virtues is self-control or self-regulation. While Josh, Donnie, and Daryl do not harp on self-regulation in this book, they clearly had it in abundance, used (and continue to use) it in their own work, and commend it to you in the form of regulating your writing time, being planful in your approach to research, thinking ahead about your career, and many other ways.

The third virtue needed for success is *phronesis*, which is practical wisdom. This practical wisdom requires that you see the complexities in a research problem, have an intuitive sense of the best ways to proceed (fueled by experience in research and thoughtful reflection on your experience), and have the courage to take a step toward the goals that your intuitive sense directs you. Phronesis is needed in multiple ways. Advisors must understand the complexities of the local culture—knowing the value placed on research by the program, the value placed on research by the students, and the rewards (and costs) of becoming excellent in research within that program. Those judgments are all shrouded in uncertainty. Practical wisdom does not eliminate uncertainty. It is what is needed specifically in the face of uncertainty. Students, too, have to juggle many plates during graduate school. They must please their advisor, but they also might have clinical demands (if they are in helping professions that require an internship), assistantship demands, course demands, interpersonal demands caused by subtle (or sometimes not-so-subtle) competition among students, and the demands needed to handle prickly, ego-driven professors (of course, we had none of those at VCU, and I am sure you do not have any at your school). And there are rumors going around that graduate students actually have a life outside of the lab (scurrilous rumors, I am sure). Phronesis is absolutely necessary.

With the three supports of humility, self-regulation, and phronesis, a platform is formed. The platform supports other important, even vital, virtues for a successful career that includes research.

One of these other virtues is forgiveness. In a 5-year doctoral program (or sometimes longer), there will be opportunities galore to consider injustices, insensitivities one encounters, and hurt feelings.

Patience is also required to complete any long-term work, whether it be the entire doctoral program or just the thesis or dissertation research project. Patience involves calmness during required waiting.

Gratitude is needed. No one succeeds in research alone. Research, by its nature, is relational, which is why I was so pleased that the book began with relational stories and ended by highlighting relationships as vital. Because we are interdependent as graduate students, undergraduate students, professors, administrators, other faculty members, teachers, journal reviewers, and journal editors, we have many people to whom we owe gratitude. I fear, though, that we too often do not take the time to express the gratitude we feel.

Another essential virtue is hope. We have hope that is tied to successful goal-reaching—the hope of agency and the hope of pathways to accomplishing our goals. But we also, at times in the research enterprise, need the hope of perseverance—a hope that can keep us plodding along on a path that we might not think has much chance of revealing success. Persevering hope is the hope that rests on the humility to know that we do not have all the answers, we are fallible, but we live in a community of people who can help us toward individual and communal goals. Persevering hope also rests on self-control and energizes us to do the next right thing. (Okay, I think I watch too many kid shows. *Frozen II*'s major song is "The Next Right Thing.") Persevering hope rests firmly on phronesis. When we are mired in complexity, phronesis helps us cut through the unnecessary to find a wise path forward.

Finally, what comes through in this book, along with all the virtues I have mentioned, is one other virtue—love. Research is relational, which is to say that it functions best when at its root, it is fueled by a nonpossessive, altruistic, generous love between student and student, student and professor, and scientist and subject matter. This generous love is willing to help one's fellow researcher, especially those who are less far along in developing phronesis as applied to research. And it is especially important within a research lab.

Josh, Donnie, and Daryl do not use the mushy, gushy l-word in their brilliant and practical book. If that seems out of kilter for a foreword in a research book, please blame me, not them. But nonpossessive, generous, altruistic love is, I believe, the glue that binds together an excellent lab and contributes to empowering relationships that will jet-fuel productivity. And if you can draw on it—which I think this book will help you to do—then it will be a core of your research program, as (it seems to me) it has been for these three wise authors.

Preface

For many graduate students, learning how to do research and completing the independent research project (i.e., the thesis or dissertation) are the most challenging parts of graduate school. This was certainly Josh's experience when he started his doctoral program in Counseling Psychology at Virginia Commonwealth University (VCU). He had been successful throughout most of his schooling, including college. He had figured out how to read textbooks, complete short assignments, and do well on multiple-choice tests. He thought he had "figured it out," so to speak, and he expected graduate school would be more of the same.

It was not the same. Now, the story is slightly more complicated than that. Some of Josh's experiences in graduate school were similar to his past schooling experiences. The coursework was similar. Sure, the level of difficulty was more rigorous, but he found that many of the study skills he developed in college continued to serve him well in graduate school. The process of attending lectures, participating in discussions, reading textbooks, and studying for exams was similar in graduate school as in college. Having a job as a teaching assistant was not too difficult either. The job took up quite a few hours each week, but if he was conscientious and followed directions, he was able to keep up with the work and earn his (small) paycheck each month.

In contrast with these tasks, the one part of graduate school that was a completely different experience was the research. As a PhD student, Josh was expected to do two independent research projects: a master's thesis and doctoral dissertation. Both projects would be large, each requiring more than a hundred pages of writing and over 2 years to complete. As a new PhD student, Josh did not know where to start. He did not even know how to choose a topic, much less collect data and run fancy statistical analyses. He was totally at a loss about how he should proceed.

Luckily, Josh had a great advisor, Dr. Everett Worthington (everyone called him Ev), who walked through each step of the research process with him. By the time Josh moved to Richmond, Virginia, to attend school at VCU, Ev was nearing retirement. Ev had a successful research career and mentored numerous doctoral students over the years, so he had a lot of experience. Plus, he enjoyed mentoring and was good at it. Ev helped Josh right from the beginning and had an open-door policy, answering all his questions. (Josh had a lot of them, and most were related to research.) Because of Ev's guidance, Josh was able to develop the necessary habits and skills of a good researcher over time. Research was still hard (that did not change), but over time, Josh was able to get the hang of it. And when Josh graduated with his PhD and started his first faculty position at the University of North Texas, he was confident in his abilities to do his own research and set up his research lab.

Maybe you have felt like Josh. You were a strong undergraduate student, but you suddenly feel at a loss for how to do research. Or maybe of all the aspects of graduate school you feel least comfortable about, research tops the list. You might find yourself doing everything but research in your graduate program, hoping that one day everything will just "click," and you will catch the research bug and know how to do it effectively. Or maybe the thought of research generates an overwhelming sense of dread and panic that sends you running to your favorite coping strategy or electronic emotional pacifier (e.g., binge-watching movies, anyone?).

Not all graduate students we have met along the way felt "lucky" when it came to learning about research. Some doctoral students had mentors who were strong researchers but the relationship was difficult. They wanted more support and guidance but were unsure how to ask for it effectively. These were bright, hardworking students, but they felt stuck and did not know how to move forward or even what to ask for. They felt frustrated and wanted more step-by-step guidance. So, they floundered and struggled to make progress on their research. Other doctoral students seemed to have a different problem. Their mentors were not as focused on research themselves, and it was not a big priority for them professionally. Yet, their students still needed to finish a thesis and dissertation to graduate, and they were not getting much help from their mentors. These students also struggled to make progress on their research.

When each of us started our academic positions and connected with early-career professionals around the country, we realized even many professors had trouble with the research process. Many of them had not received good training from their mentors, and now they were expected not only to set up their own research programs but also to lead graduate students in their own research. Pressures for tenure and getting grants mounted, and everyone was experiencing a high level of stress and frustration. When we took a step back to gain perspective, we realized there was a set of habits and processes strong researchers have in common, but some people get this information, and others do not. Our goal in writing this book was to gather the information that has been most helpful in our development as researchers and organize it all in one place. Our hope is that you will find this helpful in your own journey of development as a researcher.

The
Complete Researcher

INTRODUCTION

How This Book Can Help Build Research and Leadership Skills

Learning how to do research is challenging. The purpose of this book is to help you develop the essential skills necessary to become an effective—and complete—researcher. The research requirements of a doctoral program (often a thesis and a dissertation) demand planning and persistence over a long period. Even students aiming for academic careers may feel nervous about the process because they know delays in this area are the main reason people may not graduate on time. So, students often feel daunted by the scope of a research project. They may have volunteered in a lab as an undergraduate student, perhaps doing data entry or other novice tasks, but now, starting a doctoral program, they are the lead scientist on two projects that will take years of dedicated effort. It can feel overwhelming.

Independent research is a different sort of challenge than anything a graduate student has completed before. In college, most students work in "bursts." In other words, there might be an upcoming test or a project to complete, so students work hard to complete the task and then relax until pressure from a new task begins to mount. We have never seen anyone finish a dissertation this way. Even in a team environment, with lots of help and support, it still takes 1 to 2 years to complete each project. You simply

---

https://doi.org/10.1037/0000371-001
The Complete Researcher: A Practical Guide for Graduate Students and Early Career Professionals, by J. N. Hook, D. E. Davis, and D. R. Van Tongeren
Copyright © 2024 by the American Psychological Association. All rights reserved.

cannot "cram" for a dissertation. Gaining research acumen is like training a set of endurance-related muscles. Skill and expertise build over time. A new kind of work strategy and level of discipline is needed to complete a strong research project.

Challenging goals require lots of support. Research is a team sport. You cannot develop into your full potential as a researcher if you are going at it alone. Working in teams allows us to share our strengths and skills, which makes the work stronger than what any one person could do alone. And it is much more fun to work in teams. When one person hits a barrier, someone else can help get things going again, which decreases discouragement.

The foundation of your "research team" is your relationship with your mentor. Accordingly, the quality of students' relationships with their mentors is often a major factor in their success in a doctoral program. Mentors help balance challenge with encouragement. If this relationship falters, progress can grind to a halt. We wrote this book with the mentoring relationship in mind.

Thus, the primary audience for this book is graduate students and early career professionals, who must complete their own independent research projects as a requirement of their graduate program or faculty position and also mentor others doing research. We hope the book will help mentors and students form productive relationships that feel mutually beneficial and rewarding.

Graduate students have a range of career goals. Some know they want to go into academic careers. Some know they want to become clinicians. Others want to go into industry. Many start their doctoral programs still undecided. We wrote this book for people with a broad range of career goals. Even for people who know they will only do the minimum research requirements to graduate, it is still beneficial to have a sense of the big picture and a clear vision of the purpose of research in your program and career.

We also tried to write this book in a way that would promote empathy and perspective-taking for the multiple roles that students and faculty have while engaging in research. Beginning faculty members are often in the difficult position of training new doctoral students when they have not received much education or guidance on how to do that. Much of what new faculty members learn about advising is from how their primary advisor mentored them, and they often either try to emulate that experience closely (if their mentor experience was positive) or do the opposite (if their mentor experience was negative). There is little formal training on research mentorship. Thus, the mentoring relationship requires patience and a persistent investment of energy and care.

The mentoring relationship has the potential to continue throughout your career. Over the years, we have developed helpful resources, including various step-by-step guides for many of the steps of the research process and interviews with successful researchers on a wide range of topics. Also, we are constantly updating this material to stay current. If there is something you would like help on that is not covered in this book, send us an email, and we will try to come up with a resource for it. Research can be engaging and rewarding, but it is often a struggle. Our hope is this book can help you in your journey toward not just surviving the research process but thriving!

STRUCTURE OF THE BOOK

We have divided the book into three main sections. Part I is focused on principles. In this part, we focus on personal development and talk about personal attributes and habits that are important to develop if you are going to be a successful researcher. You can have the best step-by-step plan in the world, but if you cannot get yourself to sit down at your desk and work consistently, it will not matter much. Most graduate students want to rush ahead and focus on the details of completing their research projects, and we promise we will get there in the later sections of the book—but first, we have to lay some groundwork. Throughout Part I, we use the framework of developing expertise to guide our thinking and organization. What does it take to develop our skills in research and writing? In this first section, we walk through some of the most important character qualities to work on if you want to succeed at research, such as values, goals, habits, and dealing with adversity.

We start here because the most important asset you bring to the table is you! Investing in yourself as a researcher will pay huge dividends down the road. You can know all the tips and tricks about how to do research, but if you do not have some foundational personal attributes in place, you will struggle to be successful. These qualities may seem overly basic, but trust us, they are important. We have seen incredibly bright students fail as researchers because they have not taken the time and energy to develop these attributes and habits. They are foundational.

After covering some essential information on personal development, Part II gets more into the details. In this section, we walk through the key steps for completing a research project from start to finish. We talk about things like choosing a research topic, completing a literature review, collecting data, analyzing data, and writing up your results. It is important to note that this book is not specifically about the nitty-gritty of research methods—for example, how to conduct various specialized statistical analyses. Instead, it is more about the big picture of what it takes to do research. The material we cover can be applied to any independent research project, but because many of our readers will be graduate students, we also discuss the key milestones of the thesis or dissertation process specifically, such as successfully navigating the dissertation proposal meeting. Furthermore, we discuss navigating some of the "products" of a research project, such as presenting your research at a conference and preparing your research for publication. We want to point out ahead of time that there is not one "right" way to organize a research project. Many different paths lead to the same destination. We share what has worked for us and our students. We expect you can adapt this plan to find something that will work well for you and your mentor. Also, if you are a mentor and do not have a clear step-by-step approach to help your students complete their independent research projects, this framework can be adjusted to fit your needs.

After walking through the research process from start to finish, Part III is focused on developing your research program and transitioning from graduate student to professional. For many of our readers who want research to be part of their career moving forward, it is not enough to know how to complete a single research project (although this is important). Most academic careers require scholars to develop a programmatic research agenda, which is unified by an overarching focus, comprising smaller projects making incremental progress toward the researcher's broader goal. They also need to understand concepts such as leadership and collaboration, making the transition from graduate student to professional, and engaging in different kinds of relationships such as mentoring and team building. This section is full of practical advice we have picked up along the way from both our mentors and personal experience.

Throughout this book, we have tried to keep the all-important relationship between graduate student and mentor in mind. A big part of one's success and development as a researcher has to do with one's relationship with their mentor and other students. As most of us know, however, mentoring relationships can be tricky. Mentors and students can have different expectations, goals, working styles, and communication styles. As in any relationship, it is easy for misunderstandings to develop, and when these misunderstandings are not addressed effectively, the relationship can deteriorate. So, throughout this book, we give suggestions for navigating the material with one's mentor. Specifically, at the end of each chapter, there is a section labeled Graduate Mentor Corner and Undergraduate Mentor Corner. Each section focuses on specific considerations of the current topic within the context of mentoring graduate students and undergraduate students. If you are a mentor reading this book, these sections will also give ideas for how to bring up and discuss various important topics with your students.

Although much of the framing of this book is targeted toward graduate students and their mentors, we are aware that an increasing number of undergraduate students are hoping to get involved in independent research as competition for doctoral programs continues to increase. The best way to get engaged in research is to seek mentoring relationships that approximate what occurs within doctoral training. In fact, many departments provide opportunities for undergraduate students to get involved in formal research experiences. Thus, we also provide helpful information on how to adapt the principles in this book to the undergraduate research setting. Finally, in the appendix, we have included sample timelines for completing the independent research project (e.g., thesis or dissertation) in graduate school.

MOVING FORWARD

At the end of each chapter, a Moving Forward section wraps up the material from the current chapter and helps transition the reader to the next one. Reading this book is the first step toward a larger commitment to improving your research skills. We are glad you have decided to commit to this goal (even if someone said you had to read this book). Research can be meaningful and rewarding. You can discover things that are new to science and help people flourish. However, as rewarding as research can be, we also want to start this book with an honest look at the challenge. At least for a while, it may seem like everyone is speaking a different language you will never be able to understand. Getting to the point where you feel competent as a researcher can feel so far away. Sometimes it might feel easier to quit and do something different with your life. Wherever you are in your research process, you are not alone. There are plenty of people who have faced similar struggles and have overcome them—with help. We hope this book can be one of your "helpers" as you move forward in your research journey.

CHECKING IN

Periodically throughout the different chapters of the book, there is space for you to check in and respond to discussion questions. If you are working through the material in this book with someone else, such as a classmate or mentor, or even if you are using this as a textbook for a class, this would be a great time to have a discussion about the material you are reading. Again, research is best done in the context of a supportive environment, so it can be helpful to share your reactions to the material and hear about what others are thinking. You might hear something about another person's experience that will help you in your own research journey. Consider the following prompts for discussion: Where are you right now in your research journey? What is one thing you hope to gain from reading this book? What is your biggest challenge or struggle right now in your research process?

PART I   PRINCIPLES: BUILDING YOURSELF INTO A SUCCESSFUL RESEARCHER

1
FINDING AND SUSTAINING MOTIVATION
Connecting Your Values to the Research Process

As we discussed in the Introduction, learning how to do research can be a challenging process. Finding and sustaining your motivation is not always easy. The process of striving toward a research goal, seeking feedback, and making incremental improvements is uncomfortable. It is hard work. What anchors and motivates this pursuit is our values. If we do not have clear values about why we want to learn how to do research, it will be difficult to stay motivated for the long haul. Thus, in this chapter, we talk about what values are, how to identify your values, and how to connect your values to the research process.

To put it another way, to be a successful researcher, you need to be crystal clear about your "why." You need to be able to state it, feel it, and embody it. It needs to be a part of you. Completing a research project such as a thesis or dissertation is a long, difficult process. There are parts of the research process that are rewarding, but it is not always as fun or enjoyable as other hobbies or interests might be. It is hard to sustain motivation if there is not something deep inside you that motivates you to keep going. In our experience, the best way to keep deep, sustained motivation is to align the research process with your values.

---

https://doi.org/10.1037/0000371-002
The Complete Researcher: A Practical Guide for Graduate Students and Early Career Professionals, by J. N. Hook, D. E. Davis, and D. R. Van Tongeren
Copyright © 2024 by the American Psychological Association. All rights reserved.

As you begin to think about the connection between motivation and values, consider the experience of Lindsey.[1] Lindsey was a bright graduate student who entered her doctoral program having already completed a master's degree in social work. She had earned her license as a social worker and worked in private practice for a few years. However, she wanted to gain additional experience in research, perhaps to pursue an academic job in the future, so she went back to school to get her PhD. At first, she was quite motivated to conduct her own research, but that motivation waned at some point during her first year.

We had several conversations about her struggles to stay motivated and maintain forward progress. At some point, it occurred to Lindsey that, although she thought she wanted to gain expertise in research and perhaps pursue a faculty position, when she got into the nuts and bolts of research, she did not like it very much. Furthermore, she realized what she really enjoyed doing was seeing clients—research was more a requirement than a passion. Thus, she had trouble with motivation. She was pursuing a degree that would give her added research expertise. But along the way, she decided what she really enjoyed doing was practice, which she was already doing before entering the doctoral program. So, what was the point of doing the PhD? Why struggle for several more years completing a dissertation that was not directly contributing to her career goals? Eventually, Lindsey was able to connect the research process to her values and complete her PhD, but this process took some work.

Take a few minutes to check in with yourself about your current level of motivation for completing the research project you are working on. How would you rate your current level of motivation on a scale from 1 (*not at all motivated*) to 10 (*completely motivated*)? Also, reflect on your values. What is your core "why" for learning how to do research? (If you are not sure about your "why" yet, that's okay. We will be exploring our values in more detail throughout this chapter.)

THE IMPORTANCE OF VALUES

There is a wide range of possible things that might motivate you to complete your research project, and we touch on many of them throughout this chapter. Maybe your motivation has to do with your career goals—you want to

---

[1] The names and identifying information in the student examples throughout the book have been changed. Also, in some cases, we have combined stories or changed some of the details. Our goal is to preserve the heart of the story while maintaining confidentiality.

complete your PhD and get a good job, and you have to complete your research project to do that. Or perhaps you really like learning, and you want to learn how to use research and the scientific method to answer important questions. Maybe one of your parents or relatives was in the field, and you feel pressure to follow in their footsteps. Different types of motivation are not necessarily good or bad. Everyone is different. It is important to find the factors that work to motivate you personally. As long as you are moving forward, you will keep making progress toward being the person you authentically want to become.

For students who are struggling with motivation, we have found it helpful to do some work on values. Values are the things that are most important to us. They are the things in our lives that are "nonnegotiable"—those things that we really cannot do without. For example, some of Josh's values include physical and mental health, strong relationships with family and friends, and meaningful work. If Josh did not have those things in his life, he would feel like something important was missing. Values help orient our lives and direct our decisions. And for many people, they help clarify what gives our life purpose and meaning.

When it comes to values, we like some of the ideas from acceptance and commitment therapy (ACT; Hayes et al., 1999). In ACT, the key emphasis has to do with (a) identifying your values and (b) working to align your actions and behaviors so they are consistent with your values instead of just reacting to fear or other emotions that can hijack motivation. For most of this book, we focus on that second part—helping you to implement effective behaviors regarding your research process. But in this chapter, we focus on the first part—identifying and getting in touch with your values about the research process. To maintain motivation, it is important to clarify your values and find ways to tie everything you do back to your intrinsic motivation for training as a researcher and writer. Doing so can help provide consistent motivation when this process gets difficult.

Before we start to work on identifying your values, let us say a little more to clarify what values are and what they are not. First, ACT defines *values* as ongoing directions of committed action. In other words, values are the guiding principles that keep us going in the direction we want to go. In this way, values are different from goals. Whereas a goal is something you can complete and check off your list, a value is something you can keep working toward over the course of your entire life.

A metaphor might help. If your life is like a long journey, values are the compass, and goals are the intermittent stops along the way. Maybe you are on a backpacking trip with a group of close friends. Values set the direction you are heading—for example, if you want to hike south on the Appalachian

Trail, you can keep heading south for the entire journey. Goals, however, are specific points along the way. Maybe you see a mountain in the distance, and you would like to get to the top of the mountain peak. That is a goal—you can get to the top of the mountain peak and be done with it.

When it comes to your research, completing your research project is an example of a goal. It is something you can check off your list and be done with. You can also break your research project down into small steps and have goals for completing each specific step. But values are something different. Values are broader and deeper. Most graduate students will need to connect the research process to their deeper values to maintain motivation over the long haul.

Another key distinction to understand about values is they are freely chosen. Although we might develop our values on the basis of relationships with our family of origin or other valued communities, we ultimately must internalize values for ourselves. You cannot coerce or trick someone into adopting a particular value—it does not work that way. Also, people may perform certain actions or behaviors because they feel pressure to conform to an external standard they feel has been placed on them by their parents, religion, culture, or society as a whole. Although this pressure to conform sometimes works for a while, it does not usually result in sustained internal motivation over time. Sometimes this can be a tricky point to understand; for now, just remember that values need to be freely chosen, and sometimes conformity to an external standard can disguise itself as a true value.

IDENTIFYING YOUR VALUES

Now that we know a little about what values are and are not, how might we work to identify our values that could be linked to our research process? Here, we discuss a few practical steps to clarify your values.

Free Association About Values

First, spend some time brainstorming about what is most important to you. It seems simple, but we do not usually take the time to pause from our busy lives and think about things like this, so it is often helpful to see what comes up.

- When you think about your life right now, what are the things that stand out as being most important to you?

- Most of us live busy lives. Some of our activities are core to who we believe ourselves to be, whereas other activities are more peripheral to our core mission and purpose. If you had to take a look at your life and divide your activities into two buckets—one bucket for "core" activities and one for "extra" activities—what would fall into the bucket that is essential to who you are as a person?

- When brainstorming these questions, did anything come up for you that surprised you? According to what you wrote down, what are some key values you have recognized about yourself so far?

Attend Your Own Funeral

This next exercise can seem a bit strange at first, but if you stick with us, it can be quite powerful.

- Imagine you have died, but afterward you are still able to observe things that happen here on earth. Imagine you are able to attend your own funeral. Actually picture what it would look like. Where would it be located? Who would be in attendance? What would the feeling be like in the room? Now imagine a loved one stands up and prepares to give the eulogy. They clear their throat and begin to read from a written note they have prepared ahead of time. What do you hope they say about you at the end of your life? What would capture the essence of who you hope to be?

- Now reread what you hope your loved one says about you. Is there anything you wrote that might shed light on your values? Remember, your values are those things that are most important to you. Sometimes when faced with the reality of death, the things that are most important to us come more clearly into focus. The things that are peripheral fade into the background, allowing us to see what is essential with greater focus and clarity. What might this exercise have to teach you about your values?

Schwartz's 10 Values

Sometimes it can be challenging to conceptualize your values, especially if you have not done much thinking about your values previously. There has been a lot of research conducted that has outlined some of the most commonly held values by human beings around the world. Shalom Schwartz is a psychologist who dedicated his career to studying values (Schwartz et al., 2001). He suggested there are 10 primary values that motivate and direct the behavior of human beings. The following are Schwartz's 10 values, along with the overarching goal connected to each value.

- As you read each value, think about how important the value is to you personally. Is this value a driving force in your life? Or is it not that big of a deal for you? (Complete a free online test based on Schwartz's theory at https://www.idrlabs.com/human-values/test.php.)
  - *self-direction*: The primary goal is independent thought and action—choosing, creating, and exploring.
  - *stimulation*: The primary goal is excitement, novelty, and challenge in life.
  - *hedonism*: The primary goal is pleasure or sensuous gratification for oneself.
  - *achievement*: The primary goal is personal success through demonstrating competence according to social standards.
  - *power*: The primary goal is social status and prestige and control or dominance over people and resources.
  - *security*: The primary goal is the safety, harmony, and stability of society, relationships, and the self.
  - *conformity*: The primary goal is restraint of actions, inclinations, and impulses likely to upset or harm others and violate social expectations and norms.
  - *tradition*: The primary goal is respect, commitment, and acceptance of the customs and ideas that one's culture or religion provides.
  - *benevolence*: The primary goal is preserving and enhancing the welfare of those with whom one is in frequent personal contact (the "in-group").
  - *universalism*: The primary goal is understanding, appreciation, tolerance, and protection for the welfare of all people and nature.

Take some time and reflect on each of the 10 values. Try to identify the top three that are most important to you. Spend some time journaling about these three values. Why are these values important to you? What about them is essential to how you think about living a happy and meaningful life?

PUTTING IT ALL TOGETHER

Now that you have spent some time identifying your core values, let us put it all together. What have you learned about yourself from the last three exercises? What are your most important values at this point in your life? Briefly list and describe your top three to five values.

If you are working through this book with someone else, such as a classmate or mentor, spend some time and connect over what each of you has learned from these exercises. Take some time and let the other person share their most important values with you. Feel free to ask follow-up questions about anything you would like to know more about. What values are shared between you and your discussion partner? Were there any values they had that were new and that you had not thought of?

CONNECTING YOUR VALUES TO YOUR RESEARCH

After doing some work to learn about values and identify the things in your life that are most important to you, you might be wondering how this relates to your research. "It is great that I know I value self-direction and building relationships with my family," you might say, "but how does this help me meet the next deadline for my project draft?" That is a fair question. For some of you, there might be a clear connection between your values and the research project. (If that is the case, you may not struggle much with motivation.) For example, maybe you are motivated by achievement, and finishing the research project and receiving your doctorate would mark an important achievement in your life. You see the research project as an opportunity to display your competence in research and psychology.

For others, however, the connection between your values and the research project might not be so clear. This is where we might have to do some work to make the connection. What is the thread that connects your most important values with the tasks of research and completing your project? For example, you may value relationships with friends and family, and thriving at research will help you land a job that can offer a financial means to help contribute to a good life for those you love. Or perhaps you are motivated by universalism and trying to make the world a better place, which compels you to excel at studying a research field that will benefit underserved or marginalized people. It may be that learning how to do research is instrumental in nature—you may not inherently value the research process, but it enables you to engage in values you do care about (e.g., gaining employment as a clinician). If you are working through this book with a friend or classmate, spend some time and connect over how each of you relates their values to the process of research and writing. If you are struggling to make your connection, see if anything your discussion partner says helps you to make the connection more explicit. Did anything interesting come up for you during this discussion?

GRADUATE MENTOR CORNER

When it comes to values, most faculty members have at least some core values that align with research and writing. Faculty members certainly have a range of values, just as students do. But because faculty members usually have to do quite a bit of research and writing for their jobs, they usually have strong values related to research (otherwise they would have chosen a different field). Because of this, some mentors may have unrealistic expectations for students because of their own experience. They have certainly connected the dots between their own values and work tasks (either implicitly or explicitly)—why can't the students do the same thing?

We have two suggestions for mentors regarding values and mentoring. First, it can be helpful to spend consistent time with students so mentors get to know their students at a deeper level. Sometimes students have difficulty connecting their work on research projects to their broader hopes and dreams for their lives. Sometimes people need space to share their feelings about the research and writing process. Ideally, the mentor–student relationship could be a place where students feel known, even at the level of their deepest values. When this happens, mentors can help students find the thread that connects their values to the research process.

Second, make room for students to have their own values related to research. Also, remember it may take students a long time to figure out how research fits into their future career aspirations. For example, when Josh first started working as a faculty member, he would feel frustrated if students did not have as strong values regarding research and publishing as he did. But the reality is that everyone is different. Faculty members are generally outliers in terms of motivation for research—that is why they became faculty members. Many students may have to work harder to link research to primary sources of motivation. It is important that faculty members give students room to discover their own values without feeling too much pressure to align with the values of others because this pressure can undermine a developmental process of drawing on values that can sustain the long-term process of training and career development as a psychologist. Remember, values must be freely chosen. You cannot coerce someone to adopt a certain set of values. It is better for the relationship to be differentiated. In other words, be clear about your own values, and let students be clear about their own values.

UNDERGRADUATE MENTOR CORNER

College is a time when people often clarify their values. Because undergraduate students are still formalizing their identities, it is possible that values are still coming into focus. This provides a great opportunity for undergraduate mentors to talk about the importance of values and how to prioritize a life directed by authentically pursuing values. Part of the most helpful discernment for college students might be realizing that graduate school is not the appropriate career path for them. Many students feel pressure to attend graduate school because it is often considered a mark of success for faculty members (i.e., faculty members often assume high-achieving students naturally want to do just as they did and continue on to graduate studies), they feel pressure from their friends or family, or they are unsure what to do next and see graduate school as a placeholder until they clarify what it is they actually want to do. When mentoring undergraduates, Daryl introduces the idea of the 6 a.m. test to his students: Do you want to go to graduate school so badly that you are willing to wake up at 6 a.m. each weekday for the next 5 years (and probably longer!) to study your chosen topic and gain proficiency in that discipline? If not, what is the one thing that gets you excited to get out of bed in the morning? Students do not often take time to think about what they want because they have often developed the skill of doing what has been asked or expected of them.

For students who are serious about graduate school, getting at the why—the meaning and purpose—that motivates their decision can help them clarify the kinds of programs they would enjoy and would best fit their end goal, as well as provide them a frame for thriving while in graduate school. In advising meetings, Daryl often asks students what career they would want and then works backward with them to see if graduate school is even necessary, and if it is, what kinds of programs would offer paths toward that destination.

MOVING FORWARD

In this first chapter, we talked about values, the things that are most important to us. Our values provide the energy and motivation for our actions and behaviors. Graduate school is hard for most people. If you are doing something that is directly in line with your values, energy and motivation often help translate that difficulty into more of a flow experience and help you sustain the long slog of graduate school and research. If you are doing something inconsistent with your values, however, things feel even more difficult and discouraging. It can feel like trying to push a boulder uphill in the mud. In this chapter, we encouraged you to think about your core values and to see if you could connect your core values to the process of research and writing. In the next chapter, we talk about another factor that is essential to being a successful researcher: finding and maintaining a supportive community.

2 BUILDING COMMUNITY AS YOU BUILD YOUR RESEARCH CAREER

As you begin to think about developing your research skills, it is important to recognize we cannot do research alone. It is essential to have support along the way. Because of the importance of support, in this chapter, we focus on the importance of finding community—both professional and personal—as you go through your graduate school career. In some ways, research can feel like an individual endeavor. As a researcher, you spend a lot of time alone—reading journal articles, analyzing data, and writing manuscripts. But we have a strong conviction that finding communities you can turn to for help, support, and guidance is one of the most important aspects of being a successful researcher for the long haul. In fact, it may be that this is important because research can sometimes feel like a lonely endeavor. Thus, in this chapter, we discuss why building a strong community is important for your research career and offer some thoughts about how to do this effectively.

It is likely that to make it through graduate school in one piece (emotionally and spiritually speaking), you will need to find multiple communities to plug into and receive support. A doctoral program is a marathon, not a sprint. You are engaging in a training process that requires a great deal of time and energy. Most graduate students will spend 5 to 6 years (or perhaps

https://doi.org/10.1037/0000371-003
The Complete Researcher: A Practical Guide for Graduate Students and Early Career Professionals, by J. N. Hook, D. E. Davis, and D. R. Van Tongeren
Copyright © 2024 by the American Psychological Association. All rights reserved.

more) in intensive learning and training. Many beginning graduate students tend to focus on some of the major research tasks, such as finishing their dissertation or developing a research program if they want to pursue an academic position. But perhaps the more challenging task involves the intellectual and emotional development that will occur as you are acculturated into a new community—a pluralistic community that, at least in theory, should involve representation from all parts of society.

It can be helpful to take a step back and think about why this process could be challenging. We all grow up with a particular family or cultural upbringing. We are taught a set of beliefs, values, and attitudes—a way of thinking about the world and our place in it. If we are not purposeful about engaging with diversity, the natural tendency is to surround ourselves with people who share our identities and believe the same things that we do. In doing so, we receive consensual validation for our beliefs and values—in other words, when other people believe the same thing we do, we have more confidence that our beliefs and values are correct. The advent of social media has exacerbated this natural tendency. As social media algorithms learn your likes and preferences, you are more likely to see posts of things you agree with. Again, this creates a false sense of agreement. We are not as likely to be exposed to attitudes that are different from ours because they do not show up in our feed.

The field of psychology aspires to be different because there is an explicit value on diversity and openness to different perspectives and worldviews (Hook, Davis, et al., 2017; Sue et al., 1992). Expanding our ability to engage diversity with openness helps us become better researchers—we are more likely to be exposed to and engage with different groups, individuals, and ideas that can help us expand our research program and collaborative relationships. In addition, a broader and more diverse range of ideas and viewpoints tends to strengthen research and improve science. Myopia is a barrier to scientific progress, but widening our perspectives gives way to countless intellectual advances. As psychologists, we are working to develop a greater cultural span—the ability to earn trust and engage productively with a broad range of cultural groups while also maintaining a sense of personal integrity and connection with our family and cultural communities we call home. However, it is important to put these values into action.

The idea of differentiation of self (Bowen, 1978) can be helpful as we think through what this journey might mean for us. Differentiation of self involves (a) having a clear sense of our beliefs and values, (b) allowing other people to believe differently, yet (c) remaining emotionally connected to ourselves and others in the midst of these differences. The field of psychology may expose you to cultural differences that can weaken connections to your family of origin or other formative communities. This process gives you an opportunity to consider broadening your worldview, but this process is not easy, and it sometimes comes with a cost.

Take stock of where you are right now in your development as a researcher and psychologist. How connected do you feel with the community of psychologists as a whole? Has it been easy or challenging to feel "at home" in the psychology community? Have you noticed any changes in your relationships with or feelings toward your family of origin or formative cultural communities as you have developed as a psychologist? How has engaging with different types of communities affected your ideas about research? When you think of your community, are you intentionally cultivating relationships with people who think differently from you?

MAKE COMMUNITY A PRIORITY

For many beginning graduate students, their studies are the top priority. They may have a clear goal—such as finishing their PhD or being competitive for an academic position when they graduate. They are laser-focused on their goal, and most of their time and energy is spent focused on this task. In some ways, this is a positive thing. Graduate school does require a lot of time and energy, and it is good to be focused. But it is also important not to neglect your social and personal life by solely attending to your intellectual development. Sometimes students forget they also need to take the initiative to develop relationships and community in a new place. It does not just happen without intention.

When Josh moved away for college his first year, he expected good friendships would just "happen." After all, for as long as he could remember, he had a good community, and he was part of a variety of different groups in high school that provided social support (e.g., church, football team, band, neighborhood). Because he expected relationships just to happen, he did not take as much initiative to meet new people and develop relationships at first. It took a while (and some lonely weekends) for Josh to realize community does not just happen—you have to take the initiative to create it.

Sometimes we have seen graduate students make this same mistake. They are so busy with their studies that they do not take the time and initiative to create the relationships and community they need for their mental health. Or they might think that their only goal during graduate school is to gain knowledge and master research. It is essential for students to find a sense of balance here. It is hard to go through graduate school on your own. You need people in your community that you can go to and rely on for support. There is a close connection between success in school and research and the quality of one's community (Rigg et al., 2013). It is tough to have one without the other.

Where are you at right now in regard to your valuing of community? How important are relationships and friendships to your experience in graduate school? How much energy and initiative are you spending on developing your community? How has your sense of community (or lack thereof) affected your ability to succeed in graduate school and research?

BUILD MULTIPLE COMMUNITIES

We rarely get all the community and support we need from one mentor or group. We have noticed that sometimes new graduate students expect all their social support and community will come from their first-year cohort. This is usually a mistake. Often there is a developmental progression that occurs with graduate cohorts. At first, they are closely connected and spend all their time together. Part of the reason is first-year students often take all their courses together, so they have a lot of common activities. Also, most beginning graduate students do not have a lot of social connections yet (they have all moved to a new place), so the first-year cohort is a common source of community and support. This is a good thing.

However, as graduate students grow and develop, a few things begin to change. First, they begin to branch off and take different courses and activities, depending on their areas of focus and expertise. There is not as much togetherness as in the first year. Also, there are natural changes that occur as students connect more closely with some people than others. Finally, there are other groups students get involved with, both within the graduate program (e.g., their research lab) and outside it (e.g., hobbies).

This is a natural process, and it is important not to put all your social eggs in one basket when it comes to community and social support. If your first-year cohort gets along well, great, enjoy those friendships. But it can also be helpful to branch out and begin to develop relationships with other students inside your program. As you make a variety of connections, your community will become stronger and more flexible. Also, it is important to develop relationships with individuals outside your program of study. Your school life does not encompass 100% of your time, and it should not take up 100% of your relationships. Research shows that people with diverse self-concepts— that is, they have complexity in how they define themselves and draw from multiple roles (e.g., child, friend, student, professional, hobby runner, amateur exotic bird documentarian)—are more resilient to struggle and failures

(Linville, 1987). When you experience hardships or difficulties at school, it can be helpful to have relationships with people outside that system with whom you can discuss your difficulties and struggles.

For example, during his training process, Donnie learned he needed a variety of relationships and communities to thrive personally and intellectually. For example, as a Christian, it was sometimes stressful to sit with the dissonance of joining groups in which many people had mistrust and sometimes even hostility toward organized religion. He had his own ambivalence, so it was helpful to hear others voice serious concerns about religion. He also wanted to find other people seeking to live as good citizens of both psychology and a religious community. So, he joined several groups interested in religion/spirituality and psychology. For example, Division 36 (Society for the Psychology of Religion and Spirituality) of the American Psychological Association (APA) includes people from a broad range of faith backgrounds, including people who are nonreligious. Division 17 (Society of Counseling Psychology) includes people who are interested in diversity and social justice as well as in engaging all aspects of someone's cultural identity in the counseling process.

It took Donnie some time to find what he needed to grow and learn. All the communities he was a part of were interesting and challenging—and none fully felt like home. For example, when he attended talks in Division 17 on religion/spirituality, typical talks often involved people struggling with organized religion and eventually finding a more private form of spirituality that avoided the trappings of oppressive systems. At least publicly, he heard fewer stories about people trying to stay connected to family and friends from one's religious community, despite experiencing dissonance. To get that, he had to find other groups or even research teams that included people explicitly seeking to relate their Christian identity to their professional roles as a psychologist. Donnie was hoping to integrate these various parts of himself, but that required maintaining a connection with different communities. He could not get all his needs met in any one group, but this took him a long time to figure out.

An even scarier experience was to realize that as part of his process and development, Donnie had changed, and what used to feel like "home" did not necessarily feel that way anymore. Donnie took his first academic job back in Atlanta, and he visited the church where he grew up. He realized that after his graduate studies and many years, not even the church he grew up going to felt like home anymore. Donnie had changed. He wanted to be part of a religious community that could support his sense of calling within the university, which included honoring diversity and being inclusive enough to welcome people who had a range of political and moral commitments.

Being a part of different communities allowed Donnie to form a broader range of relationships. He continued to form relationships with other Christians, but he also formed similarly strong relationships with other groups. One aspect of developing a friendship often involves building on shared values, so Donnie experimented with a broader set of cultural values that could forge similar social bonds. For example, he now has strong friendships with people in his department as well as collaborators on his research on multicultural orientation. The ethical code for psychologists includes a commitment to protecting and honoring human dignity (APA, 2017). This commitment provides common ground regarding values (e.g., justice, respect for autonomy) that undergird the ability to form trust across cultural differences. Thus, joining and investing in multiple communities helped Donnie learn to form trusting relationships across a range of cultural identities, which provides a foundation for professional collaboration.

Take a few minutes and reflect on your own experiences in the field of psychology so far. What groups or communities have you found for support? How has being a part of those groups and communities impacted your program of research and career? We are complex human beings with a wide range of values and cultural identities, so often, we need more than one group or community to meet our needs. Do you feel as if any part of you is lacking support? If so, how might you reach out to a different community for more help?

DEVELOPING COMMUNITY TAKES TIME

The process of finding community as you develop as a psychologist can take time—it often does not happen right away. If you have ever moved to a new place where you do not know anyone, you might have had the following experience: You start to make friends and build community, and it is great, but the friendships do not feel as deep as the friendships you had where you used to live. You might even get discouraged about this, thinking that the new friendships will never be as close as your previous friendships.

Part of the reason for this feeling is that developing relationships and community takes time. There is no way to "shortcut" the process. Relationships develop as people spend time together and share vulnerably about who they are, what they believe, and what they are going through. Community deepens as its members support each other through difficult times. For most deep relationships, you have to go through a certain amount of life together.

So, give yourself time. You are in a new place, and these are new people. It is not going to feel like a family right away. Keep taking the initiative and putting yourself out there to make connections. Be open to friendship. Over time, you may realize the friends you thought would "never be as close as your old friends" have become your new best friends. One thing to keep in mind during this process is that some people make the mistake of meeting a few friends and then closing themselves off to new relationships. It is almost as if they have "enough" community and stop being open to new opportunities. It is good to stay open—you never know when you might meet someone with whom you will form an important relationship moving forward.

How patient are you regarding new relationships and community? Do you have unrealistic expectations for how soon friendship will develop? How could you give yourself some time and let this be a process? Just as developing your skills as a researcher will take time and patience, developing your sense of community will take time as well.

COMMUNITIES FOSTER PERSONAL GROWTH

Have you ever had the experience where a relationship offered a balance of support and challenge—and allowed you to engage in a process of personal growth over time? What did that relationship look and feel like? What was true about it that gave you the space to grow and change over time? One of Donnie's most influential mentors was his training director at Clemson University, Hal Stevens (who passed away in 2016). Most supervisors did not take the time to get to know him as well as Hal did. Hal was deeply committed to racial justice, and he had a unique blend of existential and feminist/multicultural perspectives in his theoretical orientation.

One thing that was attractive about Hal was he was self-differentiated—he had a clear sense of his beliefs, values, and moral commitments, and he also exhibited a deep commitment to staying emotionally connected and engaging others with a nonjudgmental stance, even if they were different from himself. Donnie trusted Hal more than he trusted any other prior supervisors. Hal's approach was a major gift because it allowed Donnie to move toward greater integration in his professional identity. Before working with Hal, Donnie had the feeling he belonged to groups (e.g., Counseling Psychology and Christian) that did not mix well or get along with each other. Hal listened to his experience and helped Donnie move toward a greater sense of integrity. This gift allowed Donnie to become more self-differentiated and move into relationships with greater courage and vulnerability. Research in psychology is a personal process that requires honesty and integrity. We need a foundation of trusting relationships. Good relationships and communities are essential as we grow and develop as researchers and professionals.

BALANCE STABILITY AND EXPLORATION

Researcher Steve Sandage and his colleagues developed a model of spiritual growth and maturity that aligns well with the process of growing and finding support in communities (Shults & Sandage, 2006). They describe this process of growth as a back-and-forth movement between dwelling and seeking. Specifically, many people go through periods of dwelling (i.e., a sense of calmness and security that occurs when one feels grounded and safe) and seeking (i.e., a time of exploration, which can lead to greater anxiety and transformation). During periods of dwelling, we may want support from people who share similar values and can affirm our sense of purpose as we deal with the difficulties of life, including clarifying a sense of right and wrong and how to relate to injustice in the world. During periods of seeking, however, we may be more open to engaging with differences, asking ourselves tough questions, and being challenged in our beliefs, values, and worldview.

Part of the process of training in psychology is intended to destabilize our confidence about the "rightness" of our worldview—to encourage us to venture out of the comfort of our "dwelling" and engage in a process of "seeking." The strong priority in the field of psychology on diversity and being open to different perspectives pushes us to question the beliefs and values we were raised with as we work to honor and respect the views of people who are different from us. Although this is an important process, this training environment can lead to disillusionment and confusion, and it can destabilize people's existing relationships with family and friends. There is a part of this destabilization process that is necessary and good. Sometimes we need to listen, accept influence, and allow a transformation process to occur.

However, there is a balance. Destabilization can be anxiety provoking and confusing. It can feel groundless and scary, as well as empowering and freeing. You want to push and challenge yourself but not so much that you lose your sense of self and integrity. Sometimes we need to "take a stand" and differentiate from the pressures of the local system, and that often involves maintaining some connection and receiving support from one's family of origin and formative cultural communities. The problem for any trainee is a deeply personal one of figuring out how much to conform to the acculturation pressures of their training environment and how much to carve out their own way.

Take a few minutes to reflect on where you are in your training process. Where are you in the balance of dwelling and seeking? How has this process impacted your development as a researcher and professional? What has it been like for you to be challenged and pushed to question the beliefs, values, and assumptions that you grew up with? In what areas are you feeling particularly pushed or challenged right now?

GRADUATE MENTOR CORNER

We are aware that our perspective is influenced by our cultural identities, and for the profession to achieve some of its aspirational goals related to diversity, equity, and inclusion, students and mentors will need to seek a range of perspectives on the themes we raise in this book. For example, all three of us are White men seeking to form teams that can support a broad range of students who share some of our interests in positive psychology. In our development, it has helped to seek perspectives from people with a variety of perspectives and identities as we attempt to grow and learn.

As mentors, we can assist our students in developing supportive communities that can help them grow and develop during their years in graduate school. Part of the way we can assist with this is to normalize a life that is balanced and prioritizes self-care and relationships. To the extent that you feel comfortable, ask your student how they are doing with friendships and adjusting to the new environment. Encourage them to focus on their whole selves—not just the academic or work parts of their life.

As a mentor, you cannot be the only source of support for your students. You can serve as an important source of support, but they need other sources of support and community as well. They need other students in their program. They need other groups and communities outside of school. Just as "it takes a village" to raise a child, it takes a village to produce a healthy, balanced graduate student. It is okay to serve as a resource and help connect your graduate student to different sources of support within your community. This will ultimately aid in their development as a researcher because they will be more likely to have adequate levels of support when they face difficult times and challenges during their graduate school career.

The process of development in graduate school can be a challenging one. Students are exposed to many different perspectives that may be quite different from what they learned growing up. Many stage models of cultural identity development describe a similar process (e.g., Bennett, 1986; Helms, 1990). People begin with a more monocultural perspective, with little awareness of cultural differences. Then, people are exposed to a more diverse set of cultural relationships. At first, many individuals react with a defensive posture, viewing their own cultural group as superior and other cultural groups as inferior. However, over time, people broaden their cultural perspective and perhaps even their own views of self and cultural identity. This transition requires students to negotiate a sense of personal integrity, even though they may sometimes experience competing demands for loyalty from different groups.

The process of personal growth that occurs as a result of engaging in graduate training is not easy, nor should we expect it to be. As mentors, we cannot take away the pain or challenge this growth process involves, nor would we want to because this is an important impetus for personal growth. However, through our individual meetings and by connecting our students with other sources of help and support, we can be guides who help our students develop relationships and join communities that will help them navigate the training process. Because the cultural identities and experiences of our graduate students are likely different from our own, the process of building trust with different students will be unique for each relationship. Some relationships require more time and patience to allow room for trust to grow. It may be that in some relationships, students will trust us quickly, and we can serve as a primary source of support. In other relationships, it may be that students may struggle to trust us deeply, and our role may require us to connect students with other trusted sources of support. We must accept our limitations and our cultural positionality.

Our cultural background and identities often play an important role in helping students feel supported as they go through their training process. There has been strong encouragement for universities to address the racial discrepancy that exists between faculty (who are mostly White) and students (a growing percentage are students of color; Llamas et al., 2021). We are each unique in our cultural backgrounds and identities, and thus we each have a unique role to play in forming a community that treats anyone who joins with equity and fairness and subverts dynamics that allow some to flourish at the expense of others. We have more to say about such challenges throughout the book.

UNDERGRADUATE MENTOR CORNER

Undergraduates often focus squarely on the things that will help them earn admission into graduate school—such as obtaining good grades, gaining research experience, and developing professional skills useful in academia.

They are well aware of how difficult it is to earn admission and often know firsthand the pangs of rejection. And they hear stories from alums or those in their social networks about the rigors of graduate school. Many are sufficiently scared into presuming graduate school is an all-encompassing experience that demands constant time and attention. Their view narrows toward the goal of earning this prized admittance and committing to whatever it takes to succeed in the program.

Accordingly, some may diminish the importance of tending to their personal, spiritual, or relational needs. Some may think that such advice is for "other people" and that they are sufficiently strong and individualized to make it on their own. Some may even think that relying on others or thinking of their own needs is a sign of weakness. However, failing to appreciate the value of considering their whole self, including their emotional and spiritual needs, ironically leaves them more prone to burnout and less likely to succeed intellectually or professionally (Hardiman & Simmonds, 2013).

Sometimes advisors contribute to this stress. Many share with their students their tales from yesteryear, where they recount how demanding graduate school was and boast of the great lengths they went to achieve mightily in such a demanding program. We get it: Graduate school is hard. And while we understand this approach may be meant to prepare students for its rigor, it only paints a partial account of what is needed to succeed in graduate school. Supplement this half-truth with the fuller version of your life during that time, including how you sought community and the importance of emotional and social support. And if you experienced loneliness or isolation, sharing vulnerably will help prepare your students to succeed by considering the full range of resources they will need to consider when starting a program.

MOVING FORWARD

Learning to do research is a lifelong process you cannot do alone. It involves forming a broad set of relationships and joining a broad set of communities to receive the help and support you need. Often, the training process encompasses several years, and you will likely experience a process of growth and change as you engage with the university environment. Often this process involves shifts in closeness with our family or members of our formative communities as we seek to live with integrity and courage.

The implication is this: Check in with yourself regularly. No matter who you are, you will be exposed to a stressful process during your graduate training. Form strong bonds, so you have the flexibility to grow and change.

Sometimes this involves the courage to take a stand, resisting the pressures of the group. Sometimes this involves humility to accept influence and engage in a slow and gradual change process that may put one out of step with other close relationships. This process of developing and forming communities and finding the support you need will ultimately help you in your development as a researcher and professional. Do not make the mistake of going on your research journey alone. In the next chapter, we focus more specifically on the research process and talk about how we can develop skills and expertise in research.

3 BUILDING EXPERTISE IN RESEARCH

Almost every one of our students wants to improve at research. For some of them, the desire to get better is pragmatic. They want to finish their dissertation and graduate, and getting better at research will help them reach their goal in a shorter time, with less pain and suffering. For others, the desire to get better is related to their career goals. They might want a career in academia, and they know they will have to continue to do research and publish articles to get a job and get tenure; they want to become excellent so they can reach these goals. Others view research as important in light of their sense of purpose. They want to change the world or promote social justice through their research; they know their science must be impeccable if they want it to impact policy and for other people to take them seriously.

Whatever the reason, most students want to improve their research skills, which is also one of the major goals of a doctoral degree. But many graduate students struggle through their independent research projects. Why is that? If most people want to develop their research skills and are at least somewhat motivated to do so, why do most students have such a tough time? In this chapter, we draw on the psychology of expertise to offer a road map for how we can make consistent improvements in our research skills over time.

---

https://doi.org/10.1037/0000371-004
The Complete Researcher: A Practical Guide for Graduate Students and Early Career Professionals, by J. N. Hook, D. E. Davis, and D. R. Van Tongeren
Copyright © 2024 by the American Psychological Association. All rights reserved.

Take a few minutes to consider these questions. If you would like, write down your thoughts. How does someone improve and develop expertise? What are the key factors? What about in the area of research specifically? How do you think a person improves and develops expertise in research and writing?

HARD WORK IS NECESSARY–BUT NOT EVERYTHING

When we ask this question about how a person can improve and develop expertise, most people say some variant of "hard work" or "practice." At some level, this response makes sense. After all, were we not taught as kids that "practice makes perfect" (despite mountains of behavioral psychology research that suggest practice makes permanent [Rock, 1957]—meaning what you practice becomes more ingrained but may not necessarily lead to improved performance)? It is intuitive that our level of expertise in an area would be equivalent to the amount of hard work or practice we put into the task at hand.

However, look at your own life, as well as the people around you. What do you spend most of your time doing? Most of us spend the majority of our time working (or completing our education). You probably do other things as well. Maybe you have a hobby or play a sport or musical instrument. How well do you do what you do? How well do your family and friends do what they do? Usually, the answer is that we are passable. We do fine. We may do well enough not to have to worry about getting fired, but somewhere along the way, we plateau. Few of us develop expertise in an area. Most of us are, as they say in the Midwest, "fair to middling" at most things.

So, this answer is partly right: Hard work and practice do have a role in developing expertise, but it is not the complete answer. What our parents taught us was partially correct. Practice is important. But as we will see later in this chapter, just putting in the repetitions is not enough. We must engage in the "right kind" of practice.

ADOPT A GROWTH MINDSET

The other common answer people give when asked how some people develop expertise is talent. In other words, we think people who become excellent at something won the genetic lottery or have the inherent disposition to become amazing at whatever they do. Some people just have a "gift" for whatever it is, and other people don't.

Unfortunately, there is a problem with this way of thinking. As long as we succeed at everything we try, we continue to view ourselves as "talented." But developing mastery requires lots of little experiments and adjustments along the way. If you buy into the myth that "you either have it, or you do not," you have ascribed to what researchers call a *fixed mindset*, which has consistently been found to be linked to underperformance (Dweck, 2006). People give up quickly and resist hard work if they think it all boils down to inherent qualities outside their control. After all, what is the point of trying to become better if we are just "not a research person"? Luckily, scientists have not been able to find a "talent" gene, even though they have certainly tried. Instead, adopting a *growth mindset*, in which we believe our skills and proficiencies can be cultivated, is reliably related to better performance across a wide range of outcomes (Dweck, 2006).

Even for people who seem naturally gifted, you see a different picture when you dig a little deeper (Colvin, 2008). For example, Mozart's father was a famous composer and musician who started his son in intensive training in music and composition at age 3. Mozart did not have a gene for composing great music—he developed expertise through training. In a similar way, Josh remembers a conversation he had with a doctoral student who remarked that research seemed to come so "easy" to Josh. The student expressed frustration because research did not seem to come as easily for them. Now Josh is certainly not Mozart, but the misperception highlights a common thinking error. The student didn't see the many years Josh spent struggling to learn the process of research. What seemed like "talent" required a certain type of practice over a long period.

CULTIVATE DEEP PRACTICE . . . FOR A LONG TIME

So, if hard work does not result in expertise, and talent is not the answer either, how do people improve and develop expertise? And, most important, what can we learn from the science of expertise that we can apply to the research and dissertation process? The key is a certain type of practice—often called deep practice or deliberate practice—over a long period (Ericsson et al., 1993). This is how Mozart and other high achievers developed expertise, and this is how we can develop expertise in research (if we want to).

For example, Daryl got into running as a way of dealing with stress when he got his tenure-track job. When he first started, he could barely run a mile. But over time—and a lot of intentional practice and plenty of miles—he was able to increase his mileage. Now, he regularly enjoys longer runs and has completed a few marathons. But it did not happen overnight. It required deliberate practice for almost 2 years. In a similar way, Donnie did not develop expertise in a variety of advanced statistical approaches because he had a natural talent for math. In fact, Donnie fell behind during his first statistics course in graduate school. But little by little, with a specific kind of practice, Donnie was able to master several advanced statistical approaches.

Before we get too far into what deep practice involves, we share the results of a research study that we think captures the benefits of deep practice (Ericsson et al., 1993). Ericsson and his colleagues (1993) studied students at the Music Academy of West Berlin—a postsecondary school that consistently churns out great musicians. Professors were asked to nominate three groups of students: the best of the best (i.e., potential for careers as international soloists), the very good (i.e., excellent but not quite as good as the first group), and the good (i.e., students in a different department with lower admission standards, who usually became music teachers).

The three groups were similar in quite a few areas. All three groups started playing the violin at around age 8. All three groups decided to pursue careers in music at around age 15. All three groups had about 10 years of experience at the time of the study. Interestingly, all three groups spent the same amount of time per week on music-related activities (e.g., lessons, practice, classes)—about 51 hours. So, what differentiated the three groups? The main factor was the amount of time per week they spent in solo practice. The two top groups spent about 24 hours per week in solo practice, whereas the bottom group spent about 9 hours per week. The advantage of solo practice was cumulative. By age 18, the top group had spent about 7,410 hours in solo practice, the middle group spent 5,301 hours, and the bottom group spent 3,420 hours.

In addition to identifying the kind of practice experts engage in, another consistent finding is that it always takes many years to develop expertise. No matter what field of work, no one seems to achieve mastery overnight. In fact, Simon and Chase (1973) identified the "10-year rule," which posits that it takes about 10 years for people to achieve mastery in a particular field. Malcolm Gladwell (2008) popularized this idea, noting that it takes about 10,000 hours of deliberate practice to develop mastery and expertise.

But what exactly is deep practice? What does it involve? Interestingly, deep practice is not what most of us think about when we think about practice. Here is an example of shallow practice: In college, Josh liked to play basketball. (In his senior year, his coed intramural team won the championship—he still has the T-shirt to prove it.) Josh thought he practiced quite a bit, but this is how his practice went: Josh would go to the gym, do a few layups, shoot around for 10 minutes, and then look for a pickup game to join. While it is a clever strategy to make friends with people good enough to win you a T-shirt, this is not what we mean by deep or deliberate practice. In general, deep practice involves four key characteristics that are easy to remember: (a) It is Designed, (b) it occurs at the Edges, (c) it is Engaged, and (d) it is rePeatable. (Although Josh came up with this acronym [DEEP], these characteristics are based on work by Ericsson and colleagues, 1993. Variations of these principles are also nicely summarized in popular books by Colvin, 2008, and Coyle, 2009.)

Designed

First, deep practice is specifically designed to improve performance. In other words, it is not haphazard. There is a method to the practice. Usually, this means you need to find a coach who (a) is an expert in the area you want to improve and (b) has some skills in teaching or explaining the material in a systematic way. The coach needs to have enough mastery of the field to evaluate your current skill level and design practice activities that will help you take the next steps. Having a coach is important because the coach can see you and evaluate your skills in a way that is difficult to do yourself. An important part of deep practice is the ability to get feedback on your performance. A coach can see what went right and what went wrong with your performance and give you feedback so you can improve. This is often why we work in teams. Graduate programs are designed to facilitate this deep practice by pairing you with a faculty member and other doctoral students who can offer high-quality feedback.

Before we move on, we highlight a couple of important aspects of feedback that are important to consider (Ericsson et al., 1993). First, feedback needs to be close in time to the action that was completed. For example, when parenting little kids or training a puppy, you have to give them feedback on their behavior right away. You cannot come back a few hours later and give them a time-out—by that time, they will have forgotten what they did. It is the same when working to improve and develop expertise. You need feedback on your actions and behavior right away.

Second, feedback needs to be specific and balanced. You need to know exactly what you did that was good and what needs improvement. General feedback is not as helpful as specific feedback. Also, although the most important aspects of feedback are what you need to do to improve, receiving constant critical feedback can be discouraging. It is good to have feedback that is balanced—the things that are good and the areas where you need to grow.

What do you think about this first characteristic of deep practice? Think specifically about how you might apply this step to your research process. Is your mentor able to properly evaluate your skill level and provide practice tasks that are aligned with your skill level? Are they able to provide clear feedback about what you are doing well and what you need to improve? Can you clearly convey the kind of communication that would be helpful to you?

Edges

Second, deep practice occurs at the edges of the limits of one's abilities (Coyle, 2009). It is that place where you are stretched and pushed to the limit—and you do not know if you will succeed or fail. The edge of your abilities is where the magic of deliberate practice results in improvement. That is where we need to be. Psychologist Lev Vygotsky (1978) talked about a similar concept when he discussed the zone of proximal development in children. The *zone of proximal development* refers to the skills that a learner is close to mastering but has not quite mastered yet. However, with the help of a more knowledgeable and skilled teacher, they can do it.

When practicing or learning a new skill, one mistake is to try to take on a task that is too far beyond your abilities. Imagine trying to merge onto a busy interstate highway on your first day of learning to drive. Few of us would be able to navigate this successfully. When we take on something too complex or challenging, people can get frustrated, lose heart, and quit. This sometimes happens when mentors expect their students to be at a certain skill level that they are not at yet. Mentors might assign tasks that go over a student's head, which results in inadequate learning and frustration. The key is to engage in tasks that are right on the edge of your abilities—not too high and not too low—and stay there.

What do you think about this second characteristic of deep practice? Think specifically about how you might apply this step to your research process. Are you able to stay at the edges of your abilities and skills, engaging in activities that continue to challenge you—but not too much? Think about where you are at right now with your research skill. What kinds of tasks are in line with your zone of proximal development? What holds you back from taking on new challenges and trying to push yourself to the edge?

Engaged

Third, when engaging in deep practice, you have to be fully engaged. Deep practice is highly demanding mentally, and it requires an intense level of focus and concentration. It is difficult to multitask while trying to engage in deep practice. It is better to be 100% committed and focused on what you are doing. This focus enables your brain to make new connections and strengthen the existing connections that support peak performance.

This aspect of deep practice is something everyone fails at from time to time. We live in a culture that is characterized by distraction. We might be working on our research project, for example, but we also have our email open, and we see a pop-up each time we get a new email (which, for most of us, is several times an hour). We often have our phones on and receive a buzz whenever we get a text, email, or notification about one of our social media accounts. We are constantly distracted, and this is part of the reason we rarely engage in deep practice. If we want to engage in deep practice and develop expertise, we have to be ruthless about cutting out all distractions from our environment. We have to focus solely on the task at hand.

Engagement is critical and must be protected. Some people claim to be "multi-taskers," but research shows us that multitasking is a myth—"multitasking" actually involves switching between different tasks (Rosen, 2008). None of us is an efficient multitasker because that is not how our attention works. Rather, when we engage in tasks that require serial switching of our attention, it comes at a cost. For each interruption, it takes time to settle back into the previous task and devote our attention and energy (Rubinstein et al., 2001). To grow as researchers and writers, we must set aside time for deep engagement that is free from the attentional costs of switching tasks.

When thinking about staying engaged, it is important to note that we have human limits. If we give a task our best energy and focus, we cannot engage in deep practice for an entire workday. It is just too exhausting. Across areas (e.g., music, writing, sports), about half the day (4–5 hours) seems to be the upper limit—and that is after people work up to it. Each of us authors had to work up to writing several hours each workday, beginning from perhaps an hour per day for 2 to 3 days a week. In the violin study we discussed earlier (Ericsson et al., 1993), the best violinists practiced about 3.5 hours per day in two to three sessions. Their focus was so intense that many individuals reported taking naps to allow recovery and rejuvenation to help with the rigors of their training process. It is important to find out what works for you. For us, we tend to be most alert and do our best work in the morning. So, that is when we try to engage in deep practice with our writing. But we do not write all day. In the afternoon, we usually do other parts of our job, such as teaching classes, participating in meetings, or responding to email. These are still important tasks, but they are not as attentionally demanding as deep practice.

What do you think about this third characteristic of deep practice? Think specifically about how you might apply this step to your research process. How might you be able to cut out distractions and focus completely on the task at hand?

rePeatable

Finally, deep practice has to be repeated—a lot. You have to keep putting in the repetitions. To improve and develop expertise in something, you have to do it over and over again. You see this time and again in top performers. We like to have our students read about the writing routines of other writers because it helps them see that everyone develops their own approach, but all successful writers have one thing in common—they write a lot (and also read a lot). Given that putting words on a page is the key behavior, many expert writers have goals for the number of words they want to write each day. For example, Ernest Hemingway wrote between 500 and 1,000 words every day, and Stephen King tries to write 2,000 words each day. This may seem like a lot, but the only way to get there is to practice.

This principle holds true when trying to develop expertise in all aspects of research (or clinical practice, for that matter). If you want to develop proficiency in a statistical technique, for example, it is not enough to just sit through a class and learn about it. You have to practice using the analysis again and again. For example, in Donnie's first year of his doctoral program, Ev gave him a project to manage that involved developing a number of scales. He took a course on scale development, learned exploratory and confirmatory factor analyses, and probably spent 500 hours running analyses during that first year, getting feedback and support from Josh and Ev whenever he got stuck or found something interesting.

This last principle of deep practice connects to the first principle (i.e., deep practice is designed). When deep practice is working well, a feedback loop occurs. The result of the deep practice (e.g., a draft of a section of the dissertation) is given to the research mentor, who then gives feedback about what can be improved in the research and writing. This feedback, in turn, influences the design of the next round of deep practice. And so it goes. Well-designed deep practice results in feedback, which influences the design of the next round of deep practice.

What do you think about the fourth characteristic of deep practice? Think specifically about how you might apply this step to your research process. How might you set up a system where you are engaging in research and writing tasks over and over again? Are you getting enough helpful feedback from your mentor on your research and writing skills?

Putting It All Together

Let us take a few minutes to review the four core characteristics of deep practice. First, deep practice is designed. It helps to work with an expert in the field to create a plan for improvement that is specific to the field of study. Second, deep practice occurs at the edges. You want to be in that sweet spot where you are at the edge of your abilities. The practice activities need to stretch you to make gradual improvements. Third, deep practice is engaged. You have to be 100% focused on the task at hand and be ruthless about removing distractions from your environment. Fourth, deep practice is repeatable. You have to do the activity over and over again. You have to put in the repetitions and get feedback on your performance. What do you think about the four characteristics of deep practice? What is one step you could implement today to start incorporating deep practice into your research activities?

GRADUATE MENTOR CORNER

From research on expertise development, we know mentors have an essential role in helping graduate students develop their skills. Practice alone is not enough. Mentors help to pass along their way of thinking while doing certain activities. Students seek to optimize focus, energy, and motivation for training. Mentors seek to help students get the most out of their work. Deliberate practice is evaluated practice. There are many ways mentors can help their students benefit from principles of deliberate practice.

First, it is important to help students understand that the ability to successfully complete a research project requires developing a set of skills, as does anything you might want to improve. Some students get stuck in a "talent mindset" and believe they do not have the talent or aptitude to be a good researcher when the reality is they just have not developed the skills yet. As mentors, we can exacerbate this problem because research and writing can seem so easy for us. From an outside perspective, it can seem like we have a natural talent or aptitude for research when the reality is that we have been engaging in deep practice for many years. Teach your students the basics of deep practice, and do not be afraid to share your process (e.g., how difficult research and writing were for you at the beginning, how you slowly improved over time using the principles of deep practice).

Second, as research mentor, you play an important role in creating a team culture that promotes expertise development. Sometimes mentors struggle with designing appropriate practice activities because they forget how they learned the research process in the first place. They do not have the step-by-step process in mind. That is part of the reason we wrote this book—to help give some specific step-by-step guidelines for how people can improve at the research process. Think back to how you learned about research and writing. What activities were most helpful for you? Also, pay attention to your student's current level of ability (not where you think they should be). Remember the concept of the zone of proximal development. Try to design practice activities that stretch your student's abilities but are not overwhelming. Finally, feedback is essential. When students turn in a writing assignment to you, give concrete feedback right away. Give clear, specific feedback on how the student's work can be improved. Try to keep this feedback loop constant, and let it influence the practice activities you suggest for your student moving forward.

UNDERGRADUATE MENTOR CORNER

Undergraduates can begin to develop expertise in research in meaningful ways. First, students need to be connected with a research mentor or research group. Immersing students into a collaborative research environment where they can start gaining valuable experience is critical. Their opportunities should be calibrated with their skill set and year in college. Daryl's approach looks like this: He usually has sophomores work with a junior or senior on a research project in his lab. The more advanced students can offer a bit of training to the newer students to help them adjust to the lab norms and become more comfortable with the research process. The primary responsibilities of sophomores are usually (a) collecting data by running participant sessions, (b) entering data, and (c) cleaning and managing data. After students have been working with Daryl for a year—often when they are juniors or seniors—they can take the lead on a project Daryl has created by training more junior members of the lab and assigning them as the "point" person for the study. They can (a) help with the application for the institutional review board, (b) assist with data analysis, and (c) actively contribute to the presentation and writing. After successfully leading this project, students (usually seniors by this point) can take the lead on their own project, often through an independent study or senior thesis. Sometimes, a student will take the lead on a summer project. In this situation, Daryl is playing a supportive role, and they are doing the lion's share of the work. In all cases, Daryl scaffolds the experiences he offers his students (i.e., he provides support for each task and offers them increasing responsibility) to match their skill and comfort.

Second, students need consistent opportunities to practice. Schedule their research time, just like a class, and ensure they are putting in the hours. Daryl asks students to log their research hours each week. Sometimes, Daryl will ask for weekly updates where students share their progress. Accountability for their research time is key to modeling the idea that expertise comes with starting the good habits of protecting time and putting in the work early.

Finally, it is important to communicate openly with your students about your approach to research training and developing expertise. Research experiences are often quite different from other classes that undergraduates take. They can seem rather unstructured, may not meet at a regularly specified time, and can be vague about requirements. Make all the expectations explicit by naming a weekly lab meeting time, imposing the structure of a regular schedule, and setting the expectation for consistent work. This will help your students begin to develop the skills and habits necessary to thrive.

MOVING FORWARD

In this chapter, we talked about how to improve and develop expertise in research and writing. Specifically, we focused on the principles of deep practice—practice that is designed, occurs at the edges, is engaged, and is repeatable. It may seem like some people are "talented" at research and you are not, but science does not support this idea. The people we perceive as "talented" have often committed to a regimen of deep practice for a long time. You can do the same thing. In the next chapter, we get more specific and talk about the importance of setting specific goals for your research progress.

4 SETTING GOALS FOR YOUR RESEARCH

The three of us are goal oriented. We like setting big goals and working to achieve them. We get excited about challenges and like celebrating the completion of a goal and checking it off a list. For example, one time early in our careers, the three of us set out to submit 50 papers over 2 years. We called it "MI-50" (i.e., Mission Impossible-50). We even had T-shirts made. It was fun and kind of intense, almost like a game. It was a way to put something on the horizon that we could use to motivate our work on a daily basis. Although it was probably right at the edge of our capacity, it helped motivate us, and it was appropriate to our career stage (i.e., pretenure). In this case, the goal worked for us, but other times, goals stifle motivation. In this chapter, we discuss some helpful principles regarding setting goals for your research. How can we set goals that motivate us rather than overwhelm us or hold us back?

Sometimes graduate students struggle to set helpful goals regarding their research. There are a lot of ways goal setting can become problematic, but we think one of the big problems for many students is that a research project, such as a dissertation, can be such a massive, long-term project that it feels impossible to complete. The ultimate goal is obviously to complete the research

---

https://doi.org/10.1037/0000371-005
The Complete Researcher: A Practical Guide for Graduate Students and Early Career Professionals, by J. N. Hook, D. E. Davis, and D. R. Van Tongeren
Copyright © 2024 by the American Psychological Association. All rights reserved.

project, but it can take 2 years (or more) to finish it. When a goal is so far in the future, it is hard for it to feel realistic or to experience the sense of making any real progress toward it. It can get discouraging when there is such a long runway before you complete your goal. Now that you have clarified your values (as discussed in Chapter 1), the aim of this chapter is to help students set appropriate and motivating values-aligned goals regarding their research. How can we set goals for large projects that are achievable, so we can stay moving toward the ultimate destination? Before we discuss factors that contribute to effective goal setting, however, we need to clarify what goals are.

WHAT ARE GOALS?

In Chapter 1, we talked a bit about the difference between values and goals. Remember, *values* are the broad directions of committed action you can engage in throughout your life, whereas *goals* are things you can complete and check off your list. We mentioned that if you are going on a hike, for example, values are the direction you are heading (e.g., south), and goals are the specific markers along the way (e.g., getting to the top of a mountain peak).

Goals are important for a few different reasons. First, they are a consistent reminder that you are on the right track and heading in the right direction. If you know a certain mountain peak in the distance is south, for example, you can keep heading toward the mountain peak, and as long as it is in front of you, you can be confident you are heading in the right direction. In other words, goals help confirm you are staying on course.

Second, goals can help with excitement and motivation. It can be fun to set a challenging goal and work to complete it. Setting an important goal can be energizing and motivating. For example, several years ago, Josh hiked Pico de Orizaba in Mexico with some friends, which is one of the tallest mountains in North America. It was incredibly challenging, probably the most grueling physical feat he has done. But even though it was rough, he had the goal of getting to the top. The goal kept Josh going, even when he felt like quitting.

Third, goals can elicit higher levels of growth and achievement than you might have thought were possible. Sometimes we do not know how far we can go until someone or something pushes us beyond our limits. We did not know we could submit 50 papers over 2 years. And to be honest, we probably would not have done it without the shared commitment. We knew the only way we would reach the goal was if each person was responsible for their share of the goal—we were counting on each other. Sometimes the collective nature of team goals can be inspiring. There was something about the goal that helped us grow. A good goal can bring out the best in you. For example, Daryl set a goal of completing a half-Ironman triathlon. When he signed up, he did not know how to swim. It felt almost beyond the edge of his capabilities. But thinking of completing those 70.3 miles of combined swimming, biking, and running helped motivate him to get into the pool and learn how to swim. Crossing the finish line completed one of his proudest physical goals—and it showed him just what he was capable of doing. Sometimes the biggest thing holding us back is our lack of belief in what we can accomplish.

Throughout this chapter, we talk about some of the key characteristics of goals, so you can set the most effective goals for your research. Before we get into that material, it is important to reflect on where you are now. It is hard to know where you need to go without evaluating where you are currently. What are some of your key goals this year regarding your research? You might have a few, or you could have many—simply write out whatever comes to mind. If you have no research-related goals, make a note of that. Have you noticed any factors or roadblocks that hold you back from making consistent progress toward your goals? In this chapter, we will work to adjust and improve your goals so that they are more effective.

EFFECTIVE GOALS 101

For the rest of this chapter, we talk about several factors that can help you to set useful goals. In other words, how can we set goals that put us in the best position to succeed? What does effective goal setting look like, and how can we apply these principles to the research process?

Break Big Goals Into Small Chunks

As we mentioned briefly at the beginning of this chapter, one thing that is difficult about many research projects is they take so long to complete. For example, the dissertation is a huge project, and it often takes at least 2 years to complete. This can be tough for the goal-oriented person. When your goal takes this long, you do not get the consistent pleasure that comes from completing a goal and checking it off your list. It can seem like it will never be completed. This can be a disheartening experience.

When you have a long-term goal, it can be helpful to break up the big goal into smaller chunks. In other words, you take the big goal and break it up into multiple smaller goals that can be completed in a short time. You are still working toward the big goal, but you can accomplish the smaller goals along the way. This can help maintain energy and momentum.

A few summers ago, Josh and his wife, Jenn, hiked part of the Camino de Santiago, a long trail in northern Spain. They only did 3 days of the hike, but it was long—they hiked between 20 and 30 kilometers per day. They had the end goal in mind—reaching the end of the trail at the ocean, but sometimes it seemed as if they were never going to get there. But all along the way, they followed little blue signs with a yellow seashell on them, marking their progress on the trail and the number of kilometers left. Every time they saw one of those blue signs, they felt a little boost in their moods. They knew they were on the right track. They were making progress. It would not be long now before they reached their ultimate goal.

Breaking up the big goal of a research project into smaller chunks can do something similar. A research project takes so long to complete that you need little goals along the way to help keep you motivated. Completing these little goals also gives you the reassurance that you are on the right track and will eventually finish the whole thing. In a way, these smaller interim goals confirm that you are making progress and will eventually succeed in completing the entire project. In the appendix to this book, we have included sample timelines that list many of the smaller goals that make up the larger goal of an independent research project like the dissertation. Your specific timeline will be unique and negotiated with your mentor, but hopefully, this can give you a sense of what breaking up a research project into smaller chunks could look like. Take a look at the goals you wrote about your research. Are any of your goals too big? How might you work to break up your larger goal into smaller chunks?

Set SMART Goals

Consultants in the business world often talk about setting SMART goals. SMART goals are (a) specific, (b) measurable, (c) achievable, (d) relevant, and (e) time oriented (Doran, 1981; Rubin, 2002). Let us look at how these characteristics might apply to the research process.

First, SMART goals are specific. A lot of people set goals that are too broad or general. The problem with broad goals is that it is hard to know when they are accomplished. They are too vague. For example, "getting healthier" is too vague a goal. Instead, it is better to set a goal of running for 5 minutes three times per week. In the same way, goals such as "improving my research skills" or "making progress on my dissertation" are too vague. It is hard to know if (and when) these goals are completed. It is better to have research goals that are more specific, such as "complete course on structural equation modeling" or "write one page of my dissertation per weekday." Take a look at the goals you wrote about your research. Are your goals specific, or are they too vague or broad? Try taking one of your goals that is vague and rewriting it into a goal that is more specific.

Second, SMART goals are measurable. When a goal is measurable, you can track it. This is important because it is good to know how you are progressing toward your goal. It can be disheartening to have a goal and not know whether you are making any progress. A measurable goal is different—it is clearly defined, and you know whether you have completed it. For example, having a "better relationship" is hard to measure. People have different ideas of what constitutes a good relationship. If you aimed to increase your level of relationship satisfaction by 10 points on a validated measure, however, you would know whether you had reached your goal. Or if you wanted to ensure you had a weekly date night, that is something you could assess. In the same way, progress in your research should be measurable. When you set goals to obtain a skill or complete a certain part of your project, make sure the goal is measurable. Set your goals in measurable ways, such as completing a specific section or writing a certain number of pages. Take a look at the goals you wrote about your research. Are your goals measurable? Can you know for sure whether they have been completed or the extent to which you are making progress? Try taking one of your goals that is unmeasurable and rewriting it into a goal that is measurable.

Third, SMART goals are achievable. One of the big mistakes people make when setting goals is they set a goal that is unrealistic and not able to be completed. This can lead to failure and disappointment. For example, if you have not exercised in years, it is probably not realistic to set a New Year's resolution to run a marathon by Valentine's Day. It is unlikely to happen. This mistake is common when it comes to the research process. Research is developmental in nature, meaning the skills students need build on one another over time. For example, a student named Ahmed set a goal to complete his dissertation proposal in 3 months. It was an ambitious goal but probably not realistic. (The process we lead students through usually takes about 9 months to complete the proposal.) When setting goals, make sure your goals are achievable. It is okay to stretch a little bit, but make sure it is in the realm of what is possible. Take a look at the goals you wrote about your research. Are your goals achievable? Are they realistic for where you are and your skill level? Try taking one of your goals that is unrealistic and rewriting it into a goal that is achievable.

Fourth, SMART goals are relevant. People can set all sorts of goals in a bunch of different areas of their work. But you do not want to get distracted. We want to set goals that are most relevant and focused on our research progress. For example, Maria was setting research goals for her year, and one of her goals had to do with learning a new statistical technique. While this was certainly a worthwhile pursuit, it did not directly relate to her progress on her current research project. So, the goal was fine, but it was a bit unfocused. It was not directly relevant to her research progress. If your goals are broad, it can be helpful to refine and focus them. How is this particular goal moving me forward toward completing my research project? If it is not directly relevant, it might be worth thinking about whether this goal needs to be such a high priority right now. Take a look at the goals you wrote about your research. Are your goals relevant to your research project? Are they directly moving you toward the ultimate goal of completing the project? Try taking one of your goals that is less relevant and rewriting it into a goal that is more relevant.

Finally, SMART goals are time oriented. It is important to connect your goal with a specific time parameter (e.g., days, weeks, months). One reason is that the time limit gives you a guideline for when you hope to complete the goal. Goals without time limits tend to drag on indefinitely. This is not the situation you want to be in with your research project. Ideally, each of your research goals should have a clear timeline. A second reason why a time limit is important is it is natural to let our completion time for a task fill the space allotted. For example, one time, Josh overslept and only had 15 minutes to get ready to catch his train to work. It usually took him 45 minutes to get ready, so he was stressed out. But he made it with a couple of minutes to spare! What happened? Because Josh usually gave himself 45 minutes to get ready, that is how long it took, even though he could get ready faster. The same principle is true with your research goals. You will generally take as much time to complete a task as you allot to the task (within limits). Because of this, it is important to have clear and appropriate timelines for your goals. These timelines will ultimately be negotiated with your mentor, but we give some sample timelines in the appendix. Take a look at the goals you wrote about your research. Do your goals have a clear timeline? Or are they indefinite? Try rewriting one of your goals that does not have a time limit so that it includes a clear timeline.

Set Positive Goals

In addition to the guidelines to break up your big goals into smaller chunks and using the principles of SMART goals, we have found it more motivating to come up with positive goals instead of negative ones. Many people frame their goals in a negative way. For example, they make a goal not to do something or to stop doing something. Their goal is to reduce something negative rather than pursue something positive. A clear example is when someone comes up with what some call a "dead person's goal." A dead person's goal is a goal in which a dead person would be more successful than you could ever be. For example, you might come up with a goal such as "stop procrastinating on your research" or "feel less anxious about statistics." These negative goals do not give you a sense of what you should be doing instead. Rather, a goal such as "write for 30 minutes per workday" is positive and more realistic than trying to stop procrastinating.

If you find yourself having a lot of negative or dead person's goals, see if you can turn those goals into something more positive. It is more motivating to focus on something you are moving toward. An easy way to turn around negative goals is to think about what the opposite of the negative or dead person's goal would be. For example, what would you be moving toward if you were not procrastinating on your research? Maybe you would be working 1 hour per weekday on your research. What would your life be like if you were feeling less anxious about statistics? Maybe you would be meeting with a statistics consultant once per week. And so on. Take a look at the goals you wrote about your research. Are any of your goals negative? Are any of the goals you wrote down a dead person's goal? Try taking one of your negative goals and rewriting it so that it is positive.

Simplify Your Goals

Some people get into trouble because they focus on too many things at once. They might have pages and pages of goals, along with multiple steps and plans for each goal. Sometimes this kind of planning can be helpful, but other times, people get bogged down with all the things they are trying to do at once. In his book *The Power of Less*, Leo Babauta (2009) argued it is impossible to change too many things at once—we do not have the energy and attention for that. Instead, he recommended focusing on one thing at a time. Choose a goal that could make a big difference in your life and give it your best and most focused attention. When you have made progress on that one thing, move on to setting another goal. The application is clear: When trying to improve your research and writing, do not focus on too many goals at once. Pick one, and home in on that one goal. When you have made some progress on that goal, you can shift gears and focus on a new goal.

Donnie tells a story that illustrates this point. He was a college football player, which involved extensive training in the off-season. He played defensive back, and one thing players in his position practice quite a bit is changing directions. Coach P, the strength coach, was tired of seeing a particular bad habit that was popular with high school coaches: Defensive backs were taught a complicated set of steps for changing directions, such as switching from a backpedal to a sprint in the same direction. Coach P's advice, in contrast, was simple. Flip your head to where you want to go, fix your eyes on a point, and trust your body to turn on its own. Instead of a complicated set of instructions, he was focused on a more fundamental principle: The body follows the eyes.

As it turns out, a similar principle applies to research and writing—one of the most crucial steps is setting a simple goal and focusing our full attention on what we are trying to do. For example, in Donnie's second year, he needed to finish his master's thesis in one semester to stay on track in his program. He set a simple goal. Each day, he focused on doing the next thing on his thesis between when he woke up and his first appointment. So, most days, he could get in 2 to 4 hours of work, making steady progress. And over the course of a week, if he averaged 3 hours per day for 6 days per week, he would end up with around 18 to 20 hours of work. This plan worked. Little by little, the work got done. A simple rule helped structure his time and energy. When it comes to goals, complexity is often the enemy. Instead, keep it simple.

Take a look at the goals you wrote about your research. How many different goals are you trying to accomplish at once? Is there any way to simplify or pare down your research goals? What goal is most important right now? See if you can simplify your goals and focus on what is most important right now.

Create Positive Reinforcement

It is important to reward yourself when you complete a goal. Thinking back to your Introductory Psychology course, many of us learned about studies where researchers trained a rat to press a bar. How did they do it? It had to do with reinforcement. When the rat would get close to the bar, the researchers would press a button and give it a delicious treat that the rat liked. They would do this repeatedly until, eventually, the rat would press the bar all by itself because it had connected pressing the bar with getting the reward. Reinforcement is anything that strengthens or encourages our responses, such as showering children with praise when they do something that parents like.

Humans are much more complex than rats, but the principle of reinforcement still works. If an action is followed by something pleasurable, you are more likely to do the action again. The opposite is also true. If an action is followed by something painful or aversive, you are less likely to do the action again. When it comes to your research progress, reward yourself after you reach a particular goal. What would be reinforcing to you? Dinner out and a movie? A pair of shoes? A walk in nature? Set up a reinforcement schedule for yourself where you reward yourself after each accomplishment.

Think about your life and what is reinforcing for you. Come up with five rewards that you would enjoy. Make sure these rewards are realistic and doable (e.g., do not write down "a new car" unless you can afford it). Take one of the goals you have been working on in this chapter and link the reward to it. Make sure you follow through on the reward when the goal is completed.

DO NOT GET TOO FOCUSED ON GOALS

This section may seem strange in a chapter on goals, but the final point we make is to avoid getting too caught up in goal setting. Setting goals is an important practice, but it is not the final destination. Sometimes we can get so focused on setting goals and getting our goals exactly right that we forget the most important part of the process comes after we set our goals. Setting goals is the preamble to the work. It is not the work itself. Some people avoid working by setting more goals, such as writing and rewriting to-do lists when they are stressed out rather than doing the work on the list.

There are a couple of key reasons to avoid getting too bogged down in the process of setting goals. First, everyone has similar goals. This is an exaggeration, of course; everyone does not have the exact same goals. But in general, goals tend to be more similar than different across individuals. If you surveyed 100 people about their New Year's resolutions, for example, most of them would have some goal related to health, finances, or better relationships. When it comes to research, we see a similar thing. Everyone wants to make consistent progress and complete their research project in a timely manner. Most people want to improve their research and data analytic skills. Many people want to publish their research (often in the best journals) and contribute to the literature in their field. And so on.

So, if everyone has the same goals, why does everyone not achieve the same results? Why does one person finish their research project in 2 years, run multiple studies, and get multiple publications from the project, whereas a second person is all-but-dissertation (ABD) after 10 years? Often, the difference is not in their goals but in their systems and habits the people implement to make progress toward their goals. We talk about many of these habits in the subsequent chapters. But for now, remember that the goals themselves are probably not the determining factor for success.

Why is goal setting sometimes a distraction? Sometimes, people get bogged down in setting goals because goal setting has a lot to do with talking about or thinking about what you want to do or are planning to do. This all comes before the actual doing, which is where the magic happens. We want to be people known for making and keeping our commitments. This is the foundation of trust: Talk is cheap; people who make and keep their commitments are trustworthy. It is easy to say a goal out loud, such as spending an hour per day working on research and writing. It is far more difficult to do it and spend an hour per day writing over a long period. The key is in the doing. That is how you will make consistent progress on your research. Clarifying your goals is important, but it is not the main thing.

GRADUATE MENTOR CORNER

There are several ways mentors can help students set good goals for research. First, it is helpful if the goal-setting process is collaborative but primarily student driven. The student is the one who is ultimately responsible for making progress on their research project and completing the program, so the student should be the one who is ultimately responsible for setting their goals. For example, in Josh's first individual meeting with graduate students at the beginning of the semester, they discuss their research goals for the upcoming semester. Josh lets the students take the lead—after all, this is their car, and they are the driver. Josh is in the passenger seat helping with directions, but he is not in the driver's seat.

Although mentors may want to avoid getting too involved in setting goals, they have a much more important role in giving feedback along the way (remember what we learned about the science of expertise and the importance of feedback). Goals are about a strategy of investing time and energy, so mentors can give information that helps people invest their time, energy, and attention more wisely. For example, is the student proposing a vague or expansive goal? Help them break the larger goal into smaller chunks. Is the student coming up with a negative or dead person's goal? Help them turn it around into something more positive. Does the student have too many goals? Help them simplify their goals and focus on what is most important right now. Is the student proposing a goal that probably is not achievable in the coming semester? You have the benefit of experience, both completing your own research project and mentoring other students. Help the student revise their goal so the plan is realistic. Part of what is happening in this process is students are learning to make and keep commitments to themselves. Help put them in the best possible position to succeed.

UNDERGRADUATE MENTOR CORNER

Undergraduate students will have different goals based on their stage in their educational career, longer term aspirations, and current training and abilities. And many times, their goals may be bound within a single semester or academic year. Some students may want to gain more research experience by working in a research lab; for those students, learning how to run data collection sessions, entering data, or conducting a literature review may accomplish several critical research-related goals. Other students may want to play a more active role in the research process by putting together a poster, giving a conference talk, or contributing to a publication as a coauthor. Still others may desire to do an independent study or honors thesis, where they are leading the research effort. It is important to assess what seems realistic for your student, align their goals with their values and your capacity as a mentor, and establish a mutually agreed-on process to support their work. There is no one-size-fits-all approach, but setting goals with students—as well as your whole research lab—can be extremely motivating. And sometimes, our students keep us accountable and on track to do what we promised at the beginning of a term. Collectively, we often get more done.

MOVING FORWARD

In this chapter, we focused on goals. Goals stem from our values but are more specific. Ideally, goals are motivating and help us stay on track. We discussed some important principles of effective goal setting, such as breaking big goals into smaller chunks, coming up with SMART goals, turning around negative goals into positive ones, and simplifying goals. In the next chapter, we discuss how to develop good habits in your work and personal life. Habits are those things we repeatedly do. Over time, they help create our character and impact almost every aspect of our life. If we want to be successful at research, we have to develop effective research habits.

5 DEVELOPING GOOD HABITS FOR SUCCESSFUL RESEARCH

Habits, those behaviors we do on a regular basis, are perhaps the most important predictors of whether someone will succeed or fail in their research. Habits help connect many of the chapters of this book to each other. Our goals will never come to fruition unless we learn to form daily habits that align with our values. We hope this chapter will set the stage and help you develop a series of work habits that will set you up for success in your research process. In this chapter, we first define habits and talk about some of the most helpful habits to develop as a researcher. Then, we walk through a straightforward process for how to develop a new habit.

This might be the most important chapter in the entire book. When someone excels in their independent research projects, good habits are usually the cause. Alternatively, when someone fails to complete the program or is a perennial ABD (i.e., all but dissertation), bad habits are usually the culprit. For example, Kevin was an all-star student in his classes. He was bright and motivated to succeed in research. He enjoyed the research process, and he hoped to be a professor someday, so succeeding at research was intimately tied to his career goals. Yet Kevin struggled to make consistent progress on his research project. Why?

https://doi.org/10.1037/0000371-006
The Complete Researcher: A Practical Guide for Graduate Students and Early Career Professionals, by J. N. Hook, D. E. Davis, and D. R. Van Tongeren
Copyright © 2024 by the American Psychological Association. All rights reserved.

Kevin's primary problem had to do with his habits. Although he had the desire and motivation to progress on his research project, he had trouble translating this motivation into action. Kevin would get overwhelmed by the number of things he needed to get done, and he did not have a good system for organizing his time. He would move from task to task, focusing on what seemed most urgent at the time without any broader consideration of his long-term goals. Because the tasks related to his classes, teaching assistantship, or clinical work had deadlines in the short term, these tasks got most of Kevin's attention. After all, he would get in trouble if he did not complete his case notes or grade his papers on time. Research always seemed to get pushed to the back burner because it had the most distal deadline, even though he was smart and highly motivated. If Kevin was going to turn things around and start making consistent progress on his research project, he needed to change his habits.

WHAT ARE HABITS?

Habits are those actions and behaviors that we do consistently. We all have habits. Some habits might be beneficial, such as calling or texting a loved one in the morning or meditating before bed. Other habits might be harmful, such as coping with stress by consuming alcohol or anxiously and compulsively checking our phones throughout the day. Anything we do consistently can become a habit.

Habits are important to consider because once we have developed a habit, it tends to keep itself going without as much effort expended. In fact, habits become automatic—we naturally tend to act in those ways without much thought, effort, or even intention (Verplanken, 2006). Josh's wife, Jenn, grew up on a farm where when you drove a tractor, it made deep grooves in the ground because it was so heavy. After a while, if you drove the tractor over the same route, the grooves became so deep that you did not need to pay attention to where you were going. The tractor would follow the same grooves automatically. Habits are like the tractor grooves. It can be tough to develop good habits, but once a habit is formed, it happens automatically. This is good and bad news. If you develop a helpful habit, the good news is you can keep the habit going without thinking about it as much. Flossing is a lot easier when it is a habit. Unfortunately, the opposite is also true. If you develop an unhelpful habit, that habit will also keep on going automatically. If you always spend $5 on coffee each morning, it is easy to keep on doing it day after day without even realizing your goal of saving money is getting harder to reach.

RESEARCH HABITS

We know habits are important, but what habits are most important when trying to develop a thriving program of research? Which ones will give you the most return when you are trying to complete your research project? From our experience, the following are 10 suggestions for habits that will promote research progress during your training.

Habit 1. Work First, Play Second

The first habit is: "We work before we play." When Josh was young, his mother taught him to get his homework done first, and then he could play outside. Most people, unfortunately, do life the other way around. They play first, and then when they get stressed out about all they must get done, they start to work. But this often ruins our leisure time because people feel guilty about not working or are preoccupied thinking about all they need to accomplish. Rather, we like our free time to be unencumbered by work worries. Plus, if you get your work done first, you know it is done. It is a priority. If you play first, you may or may not have the time to get your work done for the day, and your free time will not be as enjoyable.

Of course, we are not saying you should never enjoy your life or that any hobby is simply an obstacle to your work goals. We all thoroughly enjoy hobbies and make it a point to protect our times of rest and relaxation. Being a workaholic is its own vice. You do want to achieve a mix of work and enjoyment, and prioritizing your work (especially during the work week) can help make your downtime more enjoyable. The most productive writers we know are not workaholics. Many of them write for 2 to 3 hours per day, but what makes them so formidable is they do it day after day, 5 days per week, and year after year. How would you rate yourself on working first, playing second? How do you order your work and free time? What do you prioritize?

Habit 2. Practice Time Management

The second habit is time management. Time management involves exercising control over the amount of time spent on particular activities. If you do not control the time spent on various activities, the time it takes to do something will fill the space you allot to it. It is important to decide ahead of time (to the best of your ability) how long you will spend on each activity throughout your day. Your life is really just time. Scheduling our time helps us take control of our lives and live autonomously. A schedule can offer freedom, not restriction. If you do not protect your time, other things will naturally capture your attention, and you will never do what you want to in life. Plan ahead—let the clock be your ally and not your enemy.

Perhaps the most important tool in our tool belt when practicing time management is scheduling. Scheduling involves planning and determining ahead of time what you will do each day. In graduate school, you have a lot of things clamoring for your time and attention. If you want to be successful, you have to be in control of your schedule. We recommend getting one of those big planners to plan each hour of your day or using the calendar feature on your computer or phone. At night before you go to bed, schedule out your next day. Remember to schedule tasks that are not urgent, such as your research. Also, make sure you schedule self-care activities such as rest, exercise, or spending time with your family. But remember the *planning fallacy*: We often underestimate how long things will take to get done. When estimating lengths of time for your most important writing tasks, a good rule of thumb is to double your initial estimate. After all, it is better to have time left over than to rush and produce suboptimal results.

Another great benefit of taking control of your schedule is that you are not at the mercy of what other people want you to do. When someone asks you to do something, instead of responding right away, check your schedule. If your schedule is planned out ahead of time, you can honestly respond and say you have another commitment, even if it is a self-care activity. Then, you can suggest another date or time that works with your schedule.

How would you rate yourself on time management and scheduling? Do you set aside specific amounts of time to perform various tasks? Or do you flow from one task to another, letting each task take however long it takes? Are you in control of your schedule? Do you plan each day ahead of time? Or is scheduling something you struggle with?

Habit 3. Complete Your Three MITs First

The third habit is to complete your three *most important tasks* (MITs) first. It can be helpful to set your three MITs each day. Ideally, your MITs are three tasks you want or need to get done today. They should be related to your most important professional goals (e.g., your research). Make your MITs short—each MIT should be able to be completed in about 1 hour. (You will need to split larger tasks into smaller tasks—more on that later.) Complete your MITs first thing in the morning before you open your email or check social media. This ensures that no matter what else happens in the day, you have dedicated time to what is most important for you.

How would you rate yourself on completing your three MITs first? Do you set your MITs each day? Do you complete them first? Or do you start your day by opening your email and responding to everyone else's priorities?

Habit 4. Single-Task

The fourth habit is to single-task. There is no such thing as multitasking; there is just attentional switching (Rosen, 2008). Humans can only truly focus on one thing at a time. When you think you are multitasking, what you are actually doing is task switching. This means you focus on one thing, then shift your focus and focus on another thing. Back and forth, back and forth. Task switching reduces your productivity. Because of this, it is a good idea to get in the habit of focusing on one thing at a time. Eliminate all distractions and focus completely on the task at hand. When you have completed the task, you can switch your focus and focus completely on the second task.

How would you rate yourself on single-tasking? Do you focus on one thing at a time? Are you ruthless about eliminating distractions from your environment? Or do you struggle with task switching?

Habit 5. Split Large Tasks Into Small Chunks

The fifth habit is to split large tasks into small chunks. When we talk about the importance of setting your three MITs for the day and making sure you can complete each MIT in about 1 hour, some people start to object. "Wait a minute," they say. "My research project is super long. There is no way any part of my research project can get completed in about an hour." This is a reality we have to deal with. When it comes to research, many of our projects are long term, taking a year or more to complete. What do we do when we are facing a massive project?

The key is to break down the large task into smaller chunks. In other words, carve out a first step you can complete in about an hour and make that an MIT for the day. For example, perhaps you need to write the Participants portion of the Method section of your paper. To do so, you might need to calculate the demographics from your data set. That could be your first MIT. The next day, carve out the second step and make that an MIT for the day, such as writing up those demographics into a paragraph. Finally, completing the rest of the description of the participants could be a third MIT. A similar approach can work for the Materials and Procedure sections, and after a while, your whole paper is coming together.

In fact, we are using this strategy to write this book. If we sat down and tried to write an entire book immediately, we would quickly become overwhelmed.

We might even get discouraged and quit. Instead of trying to write the whole thing, we break up the big task into smaller chunks. Today, for example, Josh wrote down the following as one of his MITs: "Write one page in research book." One page does not seem like a lot. It is manageable. But if we do this each weekday, we will finish the book in just over 1 year. You can use the same strategy when completing your research project.

How would you rate yourself at breaking down large tasks into smaller chunks? Are you able to carve out one step and make that one of your MITs for the day? Or do you quickly get overwhelmed by larger tasks?

Habit 6. Group Similar Tasks Together

The sixth habit is to group (or "batch") similar tasks together. Sometimes it can be helpful to group similar types of tasks together at the same time. It can waste energy to keep making major shifts in your focus throughout the day. If you group certain tasks together, you can more easily get in the zone and focus on that one type of task. The following are a few examples of what we mean. Let us say you have to complete 10 face-to-face client hours at an external practicum site. Instead of seeing two clients every day for 5 days, group your clients together and see five clients each day for 2 days. The main advantage is this strategy saves lots of time (e.g., driving, parking, getting ready to work) and reduces context switching (e.g., getting oriented). Or if you are going to respond to email, do not have your email open and respond periodically throughout the day. Instead, spend an hour responding to email in the morning and another hour responding to email in the afternoon—then shut down your email for the day. If that is not possible, given your commitments, at the very least, having your email closed while writing or working on research is key to staying focused. Or if you are going to do some research and writing, do not do it for 10 minutes here and 10 minutes there. Carve out a couple of hours so you can just focus on research. (Note that some of these examples may need to be adjusted based on your situation. The key idea is to group similar tasks together as much as possible.)

How would you rate yourself at grouping similar tasks together? Are you able to chunk the different types of tasks together at the same time or day? Or do you switch from activity to activity, struggling to stay focused and engaged?

Habit 7. Take Small Breaks

The seventh habit is to take small breaks. Working and focusing intensely is difficult, and we cannot do it for long without taking a break (Ericsson et al., 1993). We work most efficiently when we alternate between focused work and rest. Because of this, we have found it helpful to take short breaks throughout our day. Figure out the schedule that works for you, but a good rule of thumb is to take a short break every hour. Try working for 45 to 50 minutes, then take a 10- to 15-minute break. When you take your break, it is a good idea to shift gears. If you have been primarily using your mind (as we often do in research), it can be helpful to shut off your mind and engage your body. Maybe go for a quick walk outside or stand up and do some stretching. Make a cup of coffee or drink a glass of water. Move around. Get in the habit of taking small breaks throughout your day.

It can also be helpful to develop rituals or rhythms around longer periods of rest. It can be helpful, for example, to disengage from work one day per week. There is a reason many religions encourage a Sabbath rest—it helps us press the reset button. You might think you cannot afford to take a day off but experiment with it. You might find that after taking the day off, you come back to work the next day more energized and efficient than you were before. It can also be helpful to take a few days off each year for a personal retreat to reset yourself and connect with your values and the direction your life is going.

How would you rate yourself on taking small breaks throughout the day? Do you alternate focused work with short breaks? Or do you struggle to rest? If you never take a break, you might be at risk of burning out.

Habit 8. Treat Email Like a Task to Complete

The eighth habit has to do with email. Most of the habits we have discussed so far have been general—they apply to a wide range of tasks and activities. But because email is so pervasive and takes up so much time—we thought it would be helpful to talk about email on its own. Many of us are inundated with email all the time. Each of us gets several dozen emails every day. Some of these emails are important, and others are not important. If you want to be effective at research, it is important to get your email under control.

Our main recommendation is to treat email as a task to complete rather than something that spreads into all aspects of your life. Most people have their email on their phone, so they get a buzz whenever they receive an email. Or you might be working right now with your email open, and you see a pop-up whenever you receive an email. These are examples of letting your email spread into all aspects of your life and redirect your attention and energy. If you want to be effective at research, you may need to approach email differently.

Instead, try to view email as a work task to complete. Schedule a time that is convenient for you during your day to respond to email—for example, 1 to 2 p.m. During that time, work through all your emails and respond to each one. Outside your scheduled email time, do not do email. Turn off email notifications on your phone. Do not have your email up when you are working on a project. Do your email during your scheduled time—and let that be it. If working through your email once a day does not fit your job responsibilities, perhaps schedule two email times (e.g., 9–10 a.m., 4–5 p.m.). But you will likely find most people do not need an immediate response. Getting back to folks within 24 hours is usually fine.

How would you rate yourself on your email habits? Do you have set times when you work through your email, like a task to complete? Or does your email spread into all areas of your life?

Habit 9. Say No to the Tyranny of the Urgent

The ninth habit is to say no to the tyranny of the urgent. There is a model for thinking about various tasks that has been incredibly helpful for us and our students (Covey et al., 1994). The model says you can categorize every task in your life along two dimensions. The first dimension is the importance of the task. Tasks can either be important or unimportant. The second dimension is the urgency of the task. Tasks can either be urgent or nonurgent. In this model, tasks can be divided into four categories: (a) urgent and important, (b) urgent and not important, (c) not urgent and important, and (d) not urgent and not important.

Tasks in the first category (i.e., urgent and important) usually take care of themselves. These tasks are urgent and important, so they fly to the top of your to-do list. Studying for a final exam in an important class is an example of something that is urgent and important. Tasks in the last category (i.e., not urgent and not important) often do not get completed, but that is usually okay because they are not a big deal. Organizing the books in your library is an example of something that is neither urgent nor important.

The problem for most people is how to navigate the middle two categories. For most people, tasks that are urgent and not important (e.g., grading papers) take priority. Even though the task is not important, it feels urgent, so it rises to the top of the to-do list. This is the tyranny of the urgent. The problem is the tasks that are important but not urgent tend to get put on the back burner—but eventually, the lack of proactivity leads to natural and logical consequences, and more and more things become urgent.

For many students, making progress on research falls into this last category of important but not urgent. If you do not make any progress on your research project today, no big deal. If you do not work on it tomorrow, no big deal. If you do not do anything on your research project this week, it is still not that big a deal. But if you repeatedly put your research project on the back burner, you will not benefit from the steady and gradual gains of someone who gives research consistent priority for 2 to 3 hours per day over their doctoral training. Before you know it, you might have to take an extra year of graduate school or find yourself ABD.

Do you remember the children's story about the tortoise and the hare? The hare is much faster than the tortoise but eventually gets passed by the tortoise, who slowly and consistently plods along. When it comes to research, the tortoise strategy works much better than the hare strategy. People who study and build skills incrementally will be in a much better position to complete their research projects in a timely manner when the time comes. People who put off research requirements have not established a gradual base of knowledge and expertise required to complete the project. Imagine someone who reads one article per day and takes careful notes throughout their training. That person would have hundreds of hours of thinking and integration experience. So, when it comes time to write the final section of their dissertation, they will be ready to write their thoughts, get them on the page, integrate notes, and then work on revising. The person who waited until Year 4 to start thinking about research will have a much harder time—almost like someone who tries to run a marathon without training.

How do you combat the tyranny of the urgent? The key is to clearly identify the category in which to put each of your work tasks. Hone your ability to identify which tasks are urgent (vs. not urgent) and which are important (vs. not important). Then, carve out room in your schedule and prioritize those tasks that are important but not urgent. You will need to apply discipline to work on these tasks regularly.

How would you rate yourself on your ability to deal with the tyranny of the urgent? Are you able to clearly differentiate which tasks are urgent or not urgent and important or not important? Are you able to make consistent progress on those tasks that are important but not urgent? Or do you struggle with the tyranny of the urgent?

Habit 10. Write a Little Every Day

The 10th habit is to write a little every day. We hinted at this habit previously when we talked about splitting large tasks into smaller chunks. But if you want to make consistent progress on your research, you have to write every day. You have to do something consistently to get better at it. Also, writing every day allows you to pick up where you left off quickly and easily, without difficulty remembering what you were doing.

How much should you write every day? It is up to you. Stephen King tried to write 2,000 words each day (FYI: that is more than a little—do not start there). Start small with something you know you can do every day. Then work up slowly from there. For example, Josh usually tries to write at least one page each day on his primary writing project. If Josh does this regularly, he can complete even a larger writing project (e.g., a book) in about a year. He can complete a smaller writing project (e.g., a journal article or book chapter) in about a month. This habit works for him, but other people have different routines. For example, Daryl tries to write each weekday morning from 7 a.m. to 10 a.m. After this, he teaches classes and has meetings for the rest of the day, knowing he has already put in his time for writing. Donnie does not have a set time, but like Daryl and Josh, he guards his morning for writing and puts appointments or other tasks in the afternoon.

We did not start this way. We like writing, so these are the rhythms that we now enjoy. In graduate school, Daryl tried to write 1 hour per day three times a week. Then, he increased to 5 days and then up to 2 hours per session. By the time he started his first academic job, it was 3 hours every weekday, and when deadlines were looming, it may have increased to 4 or 5 hours for a time. Find out what works best for you and stick with it.

How would you rate yourself on writing every day? Have you found a routine with writing that works for you? Or are you struggling to develop a writing habit?

HOW LONG DOES IT TAKE TO FORM A HABIT?

It takes quite a while to form a habit. Phillippa Lally and colleagues (2010) examined 96 participants who were trying to adopt a healthy eating, drinking, or activity behavior over 12 weeks. Each day, participants reported whether they did the behavior, as well as how automatic the behavior felt. Then, researchers were able to statistically examine how many repetitions it took, on average, before participants felt the behavior they were trying to change became automatic. Do you have any guesses on what the researchers found? When you think about your life, what has been your experience? How long does it take when you do something regularly before it becomes a habit?

The average number of days of doing a behavior before it became habitual was 66 days. So, on average, it takes people a little over 2 months of doing something regularly before it starts to feel like it is second nature. What can we learn from this research? First, the good news is that regularly engaging in a behavior does eventually result in habitual behavior. We know this from personal experience, but it is nice to have the research confirm it. And it does not take forever. We are not talking about practicing a behavior for a year or 2. After 2 to 3 months, most people find that their consistent behaviors feel more automatic. However, it does take 2 to 3 months. You cannot perform a behavior a couple of times and expect it to feel like it is second nature. You have to do it over and over again for a long time. And it is difficult to do something over and over again when it does not feel like a habit yet. It is hard work. We need strategies to help us.

HOW TO FORM HABITS

Because forming habits is tough work and can take a fairly long time, what are some ways to help form good habits? What are some strategies to help us develop strong work habits in research? In this section, we outline five ways to help you build good habits in your life (J. P. Hook, Hook, & Davis, 2017). They are easy to remember because they all feature the letter "S."

Adjust the Surroundings

When most people try to develop a habit, they think about things like willpower or the individual changes they need to make in their life. They forget about the power of the environment and context. Your surroundings are an important determinant of whether you will develop good or bad habits. For example, what is your work environment like? Is it quiet, calm, and conducive to deep practice? What about the people around you? Are they encouraging of your work? Or do they try to distract you or complain? Some people romanticize "working in a coffee shop," but when they get there, they may be quickly distracted by all the noise and commotion and leave, failing to have put in any good hours on their project. What is one way you could adjust your surroundings to help you develop good work habits?

Be Specific

Some people, when making changes to their habits, are too general with what they are trying to do. They might say, "I want to get better at research." Statements like these are overly broad and generally not helpful. Instead, be specific. For example, say, "I want to spend 1 hour each day analyzing data or writing my dissertation." Specific habits are much more likely to be successfully adopted. That way, you can also know, beyond the shadow of a doubt, whether you have completed a task. What is one way you could be more specific when developing your work habits?

Schedule It In

Remember it takes, on average, about 66 days to build a habit. This means that when you start to develop a new habit, it will not feel natural at first. In fact, it will likely feel quite "unnatural." You may feel like doing the opposite of your desired habit. Because of this, in the beginning, it is helpful to schedule in your habit like you would an appointment. Put it on your calendar. Put an alarm on your phone to remind you about the habit. Schedule the habit until it starts to feel more automatic. What is one way you could schedule your work habits?

Start Small

Many people, when they are trying to change a habit, get excited about the change and try to do something huge. For example, you might get motivated about your research project and set a goal of writing 2 hours per day. If this is a new habit, this is probably too much too soon. Unfortunately, when you bite off more than you can chew, what usually happens is you struggle to maintain the habit, which can lead to failure and discouragement. A better idea is to start small, with something you know you can accomplish. Then, once you get some success under your belt, you can slowly improve over time (if you want). Success builds pride and other positive emotions, which helps maintain success over time. It is like getting a ball rolling downhill. But at first, any change is difficult, which is why it is helpful to start small. For example, instead of trying to work 2 hours on your research project, maybe you start with 15 minutes. This sounds small (and it is). But it is probably something you know you can accomplish. Do 15 minutes per day for a week and work up from there. What is one way you could start small when developing your work habits?

Build a Support Team

When it comes to developing habits for research and writing, we will not achieve our best results alone. We need other people supporting us, cheering for us, and helping us when we get discouraged. When you are trying to change your work habits, it can be helpful to build a support team who can help you along the way. If you are a graduate student, maybe you could identify some folks in your program who are all working toward the same goal. Perhaps you could help keep each other accountable as you work to develop strong work habits. Maybe you could develop a writing group, and you could check in with each other each week about your progress. Do whatever works for you, but do not try to change alone. What is one way you could work to develop a support team to help you develop strong work habits?

GRADUATE MENTOR CORNER

In the area of habits, we often see one of two issues come up for mentors. First, some mentors struggle with work habits themselves. Students learn more from what we do than from what we say. So, it is important to model the habits you hope your students will adopt. As you read this chapter, use the list of habits we created and consider adding your own items. We also suggest talking with your research team about the foundational habits that you want to ground your lab culture. For example, you might want to work together as a team to take responsibility for your schedule or write a little bit every day. Find creative ways to build these habits into the routines of your work together.

The second challenge mentors have is assuming these habits are something that graduate students should have mastered. They think of "study skills" as something you learn in undergrad. Because of this, they presume their students should have these things down and are surprised when students seem to drop the ball or struggle to make progress. It may seem hard to believe, but many students are able to get through college on their intellect alone, cramming for exams and earning good grades despite having poor work habits. When they get to graduate school, however, things begin to change. They are juggling multiple roles (e.g., courses, teaching assignments, clinical work, research) and have to keep a lot more plates spinning in the air. They also have to make consistent progress on long-term tasks such as the dissertation. An independent research project is not something you can "cram for." So, graduate school is often when the wheels start to fall off. We have found that it helps to create a supportive team environment in which students regularly talk about the challenges of graduate school, as well as some of the ways they have successfully formed habits that make it easier to protect time and energy for writing and research.

UNDERGRADUATE MENTOR CORNER

One of the best things you can do to help mentor undergraduate students is to model these healthy habits yourself. For example, Daryl often tells his students directly that he writes each morning, in part to set the expectation that he will be at home logging words and hours (and off email) and in part to let them know setting aside time to write is part of being a productive scholar and active academic. They set goals together as a team and then discuss how they will make a little progress on these goals each week. Daryl explains how he navigates larger projects by showing them how the smaller subprojects fit together, such as how individual studies we are conducting for a grant proposal fit into the larger idea we are testing. All these practices are designed to model healthy habits to his students. And when Daryl sees students engaging in habits that will help them flourish, he rewards that behavior. Public praise and affirmation go a long way, and a lab pizza party is always a big hit. To help students develop healthy habits as scholars, we have to start early and set an example.

MOVING FORWARD

In this chapter, we talked about some key habits that help students make consistent progress in their research. We also discussed a helpful model to begin forming good work habits—the five S's. In the next chapter, we tackle a difficult problem for many students when it comes to research—limiting beliefs that hold students back from reaching their full potential.

6 CULTIVATING POSITIVE BELIEFS TO FOSTER RESEARCH SUCCESS

As we work toward our goals in research, one challenge for many graduate students is the struggle with their beliefs about whether they can succeed. Our beliefs about our abilities and what we can accomplish (in psychology, we call these types of beliefs *self-efficacy*) can influence our actions and behaviors. To a certain extent, if we think we can, we can. In this chapter, we talk about the important role of our beliefs in helping us develop as a researcher, specifically focusing on improving self-efficacy and developing a growth mindset.

Consider the example of Maya, a graduate student struggling to make progress on her master's thesis. Part of the problem, which took a while to figure out, was that Maya did not have a lot of confidence in her research abilities. She did not have much research experience, to begin with, and she had struggled to pass the introductory statistics course in her first year. Her lack of experience, combined with her lack of early success, caused her confidence to wane. When this happened, she began to avoid getting going on her research and thesis, which caused more struggles and lowered her confidence even further. She was stuck in a negative cycle.

---

https://doi.org/10.1037/0000371-007
The Complete Researcher: A Practical Guide for Graduate Students and Early Career Professionals, by J. N. Hook, D. E. Davis, and D. R. Van Tongeren
Copyright © 2024 by the American Psychological Association. All rights reserved.

Maya's experience is common. Many students hold negative beliefs about the research process because, for most people, research is a completely new skill. Although students may have volunteered in a research lab during their undergraduate studies, such research experience (e.g., data collection or data entry) is minimal compared with the expectations of launching your own independent research program. It is rarer that an undergraduate student has been able to take full responsibility for a research project from start to finish and receive good mentoring on the process. Thus, for many graduate students, the thesis or dissertation is the first time they will have conducted their own research project, being responsible for each step from start to finish.

One of the primary ways we develop self-efficacy is to have past successes. If we grew up spending time painting as a child, for example, we are more likely to develop strong beliefs about our artistic ability when taking art class in school. But the opposite is true as well. If you have not had much success at something (and if you have not had much experience, you have not had an opportunity to achieve success), you will likely have doubts about your abilities to succeed. This is the challenge graduate students face with their independent research projects. They often come to the table with little experience and, thus, little success, leading to insecurity or doubt around their research self-efficacy.

BELIEFS AND ACTIONS

Before we talk about ways we can improve our self-efficacy about research, let us talk a bit more about beliefs and their relationship to actions and behaviors. This is key because actions and behaviors represent the bottom line. The most important thing is we want to make consistent progress on our research projects and graduate. But how do our beliefs and actions influence one another?

One of the most widely studied theories about how people change is cognitive behavior therapy (CBT; Beck, 1995). The foundation of CBT is the cognitive model. The cognitive model says that our thoughts, feelings, and behaviors are intimately connected with one another. If I am feeling depressed, for example, that feeling is likely connected with certain thoughts (e.g., "No one likes me") and behaviors (e.g., staying in bed all day). Because it is tough to change a feeling (e.g., will yourself to become less depressed), CBT tries to intervene on the other two factors by helping people change their thoughts (e.g., questioning to see whether there are exceptions or times when someone does like them) or behaviors (e.g., taking the initiative to call a friend).

Underneath thoughts are core beliefs, which are pervasive beliefs about oneself, other people, or the world. When people are struggling, their core beliefs are often more negative than positive, as well as more pervasive across time and situations. CBT tries to home in on a person's core beliefs and explore them to see if the person might be able to shift their core beliefs in a more positive direction. If a person can positively shift their thoughts and beliefs, these shifts will, in turn, positively impact their feelings and behaviors.

Acceptance and commitment therapy (ACT; Hayes et al., 1999) is another theory that takes thoughts and beliefs seriously, although it construes the relationship between thoughts, feelings, and behaviors a bit differently than CBT. Whereas CBT tries to help a person change their thoughts and beliefs, ACT theorizes that changing your thoughts is difficult. Paradoxically, sometimes if we focus on changing a negative thought or belief, that thought or belief is more likely to come to mind. For example, if we told you not to think about a pink elephant for the next 2 minutes, you would probably struggle to do this. Even though you probably have not thought about a pink elephant all day, if we tell you not to think about it, it is hard to get the pink elephant out of your mind.

Because of this, ACT does not try to get you to change your thoughts and beliefs directly. Instead, ACT encourages you to accept your thoughts and beliefs and treat them as "just thoughts." In other words, instead of trying to change your thoughts to impact your feelings and behaviors, ACT tries to weaken the relationship between our thoughts and feelings and behaviors. In other words, you might have the thought that "no one likes me," but could you accept that thought and call a friend to go to the movies anyway?

SELF-EFFICACY

Irrespective of whether you take more of a CBT approach or an ACT approach, our thoughts and beliefs are important. When it comes to the research process, it is especially important to consider a particular type of belief: self-efficacy. *Self-efficacy* refers to an individual's beliefs about their capacity to engage in behaviors necessary to produce a particular performance standard (Bandura, 1977). When it comes to research, self-efficacy has to do with our beliefs about our ability to successfully engage in research and complete the project we are working on.

Consider your own research self-efficacy. If you had to rate yourself on a scale from 1 (*very low self-efficacy*) to 7 (*very high self-efficacy*), how would you rate yourself? What factors contributed to your rating of self-efficacy?

IMPROVING SELF-EFFICACY

Research has consistently found that self-efficacy is related to higher levels of work performance (Sadri & Robertson, 1993). So, how do we improve our self-efficacy, particularly when it comes to our research skills? There are four key ways to improve your self-efficacy: (a) experience success, (b) observe successful experiences, (c) receive encouragement from others, and (d) change your state. Let us talk through each of them.

Experience Success

The first way to improve your self-efficacy is to experience some success at the task at hand. This makes sense: If you have a history of success at a task, you are more likely to believe you will be successful at the task in the future. We seem to know at a deep level that the best predictor of future behavior is past behavior. If you succeed at something one time, you are more likely to succeed at the same task a second time. So, if we want to improve our self-efficacy for research, we need to have some successful experiences.

The tough thing about this aspect of improving self-efficacy, as we talked about earlier, is most students come into graduate school with little or no real experience conducting their own research studies. This makes self-efficacy about research difficult—most people come to the table with little or no past successful experience, so there is no baseline for positive beliefs about one's research ability. And because research can be difficult and good mentoring is sometimes challenging to find, students can get off on the wrong foot with a few unsuccessful experiences, which can deplete their already fragile self-efficacy. Of course, this also highlights why creating opportunities for successful research experience in undergraduate settings is so key (and we return to this more thoroughly in the Undergraduate Mentor Corner section near the end of this chapter).

So, what can we do to counteract these challenges? We can take a lesson from good parenting. For example, what do you do if you want to teach your small child to swim for the first time? You know the power of self-efficacy, and you want to give your child a sense of early success. But your child has never swum before. What do you do?

First, you will want to avoid setting your child up for failure. Obviously, you do not just push them into the deep end without supervision or guidance. Nor would you send them away and tell them to learn on their own. Doing so is dangerous and ineffective. Rather, you guide them, provide them with flotation devices and other support, and slowly have them gain confidence in simple tasks, such as treading water, holding their breath, and making strokes while holding onto a foam board. By celebrating each small step, over time, they learn how to breathe efficiently and make it across the pool with assistance. Eventually, kids slowly learn how to swim on their own—but it is a process that requires time and small victories along the way.

In the same way, when it comes to research, it helps to set yourself up for early success. The research mentor can play a big role in this. It is important for students to have a lot of help and support early in the research process. A good mentor will understand this. They will work to give you some early success with writing and presenting so you begin to feel the natural rewards of the research process.

What do you think about this first strategy to improve self-efficacy? What successful experiences have you had with research? If you have had relatively few successful experiences, how might you work with your mentor to get more help and support, so you can put yourself in a position to gain some successful experiences?

Observe Successful Experiences

The second way to improve your self-efficacy is to observe someone else succeeding at the task you are trying to do. You can think about observation as "vicarious" success experiences. You are not experiencing the success yourself, but you are seeing someone close to you experience success. If they can do it, why can't I?

Observing the research mentor succeed at research and writing has the potential to help students improve their self-efficacy, but we argue this type of observation can have limited utility because the difference in skill and experience level between mentor and student is usually too large. For example, one time, Josh was working with a graduate student who felt discouraged after observing how Josh went about doing research because, from the student's perspective, the research process seemed so easy for Josh. The reality was, after 10 years of experience, certain aspects of research had become almost like "second nature" to Josh. Seeing the difference between the student and Josh did not help the student's self-efficacy; it made her feel more discouraged.

There are two lessons we took from this experience. First, it is essential for research mentors to lead with vulnerability. Share the tough things you are experiencing about the research process. Talk about what it was like for you when you were a graduate student, learning to do research and write your dissertation. Be open about your "resume of failure"—those experiences where you did not succeed or get it right. Demonstrate the humility necessary for any good scientist and the honesty required of a researcher. Students often put mentors on impossibly high pedestals, failing to realize their mentors have experienced their fair share of rejection—from grant applications and paper submissions to graduate programs and job openings. For example, Daryl's first paper rejection was based on a review so scathing that it included a note from the editor warning him to consider the prestige of the journal before sending another paper their way. And although it stung deeply at the time, Daryl used that as motivation to publish future research there—several times. But anyone who is going to publish a lot is also going to experience a high degree of rejection; after all, our best journals boast a rejection rate of 90% or higher. It is important to normalize such rejection as a common feature of the job, rather than a personal indictment of one's abilities or personality. Sharing these experiences can help narrow the perceived gap between mentor and student.

Second, it is essential to develop a close-knit lab where graduate students can learn from each other and see and celebrate one another's successes. Social modeling is powerful. If beginning graduate students can directly observe older graduate students conducting research and completing their independent research projects, it can be a big help in improving self-efficacy. There is not such a big gap between a first-year doctoral student and a third-year doctoral student. If the older student is succeeding and has a plan for making progress on their research, the younger student might believe they can succeed too. Find an older graduate student "mentor" whom you can follow and emulate. In addition to receiving practical help on various tasks, you might notice your self-efficacy increasing as you observe the older graduate student succeed.

Take a moment to reflect. Who have you observed in your program succeed at research? How could you work more closely with that person, so you can get a clearer and more practical view of someone who is experiencing success?

Receive Encouragement From Others

The third way to improve your self-efficacy is to have an environment where you are receiving consistent encouragement from others. Sometimes we all need a little help and encouragement from someone who is a little further down the line. Graduate students need an environment that has high levels of both challenge and encouragement.

Sometimes as faculty members, we forget about the important role encouragement plays in shaping an environment for research to flourish. For example, Josh was working with a student who was struggling because he did not feel like he was doing a good job at research. Josh was surprised to hear the student say that because Josh thought the student was doing quite well, and his research skill was in a good place for his developmental level (as a beginning student). What became clear as they talked, however, was Josh did not communicate enough encouragement. Most of their interactions came in the form of corrections—Josh correcting the student's work and telling him what he needed to do better or differently. Although this feedback was needed and is an essential part of being a mentor, Josh would have ideally balanced the corrective feedback with positive and encouraging feedback. We know that positive reinforcement is a more effective strategy for changing behavior than punishment; it is important to send clear signals about what someone is doing right rather than only providing feedback when they do something wrong.

Our sense is faculty members tend to get in this "correction mode" a lot. Faculty members are busy, and sometimes it makes sense to give straightforward feedback. But it is important to remember that learning how to conduct independent research is difficult. It was challenging for faculty members when they were learning, and it is challenging for students today. It is important to provide positive feedback and encouragement alongside corrective feedback so students can develop a healthy sense of self-efficacy based on reality.

Related to this point, as graduate students, it can be helpful to share your experience and ask for what you need. Josh now realizes it might have been uncomfortable for his student to ask for more positive feedback and affirmation. But because the student said something, Josh was able to adapt his style to meet the student's needs better. It is okay to have an honest conversation with your mentor about what you need. Another idea is to develop other relationships that provide you with support and encouragement. For example, perhaps your family, significant other, or classmates could help fill this role.

As you consider your relationship with your mentor, how encouraging is your mentor about your research? What about other close relationships? How might you have a discussion with your mentor (or others) so you can set up a context where you are receiving enough positive reinforcement and encouragement?

Change Your State

The fourth way to improve self-efficacy is to change your state. Your state involves how you are feeling emotionally and physically. A positive mood can have a positive impact on self-efficacy, whereas anxiety can undermine self-efficacy. Furthermore, how we are feeling physically can impact our self-efficacy. For example, if you are feeling well rested and energetic, your self-efficacy will be higher. If you are feeling tired or have low energy, your self-efficacy will be lower.

We take a deep dive into these issues in the next chapter. But for now, we encourage you to keep in mind the possible connection between your state and your self-efficacy. Perhaps because of the influence of CBT, we often think about our thoughts and beliefs causing our feelings and physical states, rather than the other way around. But the reverse can also be true. Our feelings and physical states can directly influence our self-efficacy beliefs (Bandura, 1997). Because graduate school can be stressful, sometimes our self-care priorities (e.g., sleep, exercise, nutrition) can take a back seat. Unfortunately, this can have a negative impact on our ability to make progress on our research and dissertation. Do not neglect the basics as you are working through your graduate program.

As just one example, many writers find walking an essential practice. There is something about getting outside and moving that helps the mind keep working in a way that can facilitate new ideas. Walking is not too rigorous, so it is possible to let the mind wander. One can look for simple pleasures. This is one of Donnie's favorite ways to take breaks and create a mental shift. Sometimes he will even bring a recorder or a small 3 × 5 notebook on his walk to jot down any ideas that come to him. Most writers do not just sit in front of a screen all the time. Sometimes we need to vary the contexts we are in to generate ideas and do work.

Our research mentor in graduate school (Ev) dictates a lot of his articles and chapters. He will start by writing out a one- or two-page outline, then go on a hike and dictate the manuscript. Often, the paper needs to be heavily edited, but the first step of getting ideas down on paper is done (although a research assistant will process his dictation). There is a classic lab story of Ev dictating a paper while hiking the Appalachian Trail. Suddenly he went quiet. The seconds passed like minutes. Then, he whispered into the recorder, "There is a bear just steps away from the trail." Even though logically, we knew Ev survived, given that he delivered the dictation to us, we still froze in terror and waited to see what happened next. Thankfully, the bear did not have an appetite for a psychology professor that afternoon, and he left Ev alone to finish the rest of his paper.

What do you think about this fourth strategy to improve self-efficacy? Have you noticed a connection between your emotional state (e.g., excitement, anxiety) and your self-efficacy beliefs? What about between your physical state (e.g., level of energy) or habits (e.g., sleep, exercise) and your self-efficacy beliefs? Are there any "basics" you have been neglecting because of the stress associated with graduate school? What is one "basic" you would like to prioritize in the next month?

MINDSET

It is important to situate our conversation within a broader understanding of mindsets, which are critical as you strive to improve your research skill and make progress on your research projects. Carol Dweck (1999, 2006), a psychologist from Stanford University, has focused her career on studying people's mindsets—or how they think about their talents and abilities.

Dweck has found there are two main types of mindsets. People with *fixed mindsets* believe their intelligence, personality traits, and abilities are fixed and cannot change. People with a fixed mindset put a lot of stock in talent—you either have it or you do not. People with a *growth mindset*, however, believe their intelligence, personality traits, and abilities are fluid. These things can grow and change, depending on the time and energy you spend working on them.

Our mindset can be an important factor in how we develop research skills and make progress on our research projects. In general, having a growth mindset is more adaptive than having a fixed mindset for a few reasons. First, having a fixed mindset can be challenging because most beginning graduate students do not have much experience conducting independent research, so they are rarely "good" at research at the beginning. For most graduate students (even very bright ones), the first independent research project is a struggle. (Josh remembers being shocked at the amount of corrective ink that covered his thesis proposal. Similarly, Daryl's master's advisor told him she used green ink rather than red to weaken the negative association and reduce the shock of seeing so much ink.) If a student has a fixed mindset, they might determine they are not good at research (and that will not change), when the reality is no one is good at research at the beginning.

Second, there are a lot of different skills that need to be learned for someone to develop a strong research acumen and make consistent progress on their research projects. Research requires a different way of thinking, and students also need to develop skills in statistics, analyzing data, and writing. Even if the student is a strong writer, research writing is a different type of writing and a new skill to learn. We can all become better writers. Students with a strong growth mindset are better able to tackle and learn the new skills needed to be successful in research.

HOW TO DEVELOP A GROWTH MINDSET

If you have a fixed mindset, you might ironically feel doomed—you have a fixed mindset, after all. But thankfully, we know people can shift their mindset to adopt a more growth-oriented stance. The process begins simply by believing change is possible, and the seed for change is experimentation: We try things, and if they do not work, we try something else. There are several ways to develop a growth mindset (check out Carol Dweck's, 2006, book for some great ideas), but we touch on three strategies that have been helpful for us and our students: (a) Be okay with imperfection, (b) view challenges as opportunities, and (c) prioritize the process.

The first strategy to develop a growth mindset is to be okay with imperfection. Graduate students often struggle with perfectionism. Many were high achievers in high school and college but then struggle in graduate school when everyone is as smart as they are and they do not pick up everything right away. It is hard to go from being at the top of your class to decidedly average among other high achievers. Many of us suffered from imposter syndrome, convinced the admissions committee had made a mistake and we do not belong in graduate school. The need to be perfect can hold people back from engaging fully in learning because you must admit what you do not know to learn the material and get help. By being okay with imperfection, students can be honest with themselves (and their mentors) about where they are and what they do not know. That is the key starting place for learning and growth, which can help students develop a growth mindset.

The second strategy to develop a growth mindset is to view challenges as opportunities. Sometimes students face a challenge and think about it as something bad, an obstacle that should not exist. They might avoid challenges or run away from them. This way of engaging difficulties can slow down progress on your research. Instead, it can help to think about challenges as opportunities for growth. If you can engage the challenge and overcome it, you could learn a new skill that will help you in your career, which makes future research easier because you have widened your repertoire of skills. Engaging the challenge, rather than running away from it, can help students develop a growth mindset.

The third strategy to develop a growth mindset is to prioritize the process. Often students can be focused solely on the end result—finishing the research project. Focusing too much on the outcome can be disheartening because the project is so long, and finishing it can seem such a long way off. Instead, it can be useful to focus on the process. What are you learning day to day? How are you improving and getting better every day? What are the daily "wins" you can take with you, even if the goal is still a long way in the future? Focusing on the process, rather than the outcome, can help develop a growth mindset.

When we talked about this principle while writing the book, Donnie shared his experience of his first year at Virginia Commonwealth University. A lot of students feel intimidated about learning statistics. No matter where one starts, there is always more to learn. New statistical approaches are always coming out. Donnie felt nervous and was not sure what to expect from the learning process. Would he need to learn a bunch of math? How hard would it be? The textbook seemed almost unreadable, as though it was written in a cryptic or forgotten language.

By his third year, something had shifted, and he enjoyed learning new statistical approaches. What happened? He focused on learning and using one statistical approach at a time. In his first year, he took a few courses related to scale development, including regression, factor analysis, and structural equation modeling. He relied on several people who knew what they were doing. Josh spent lots of time showing Donnie what he had learned. (Josh was a year ahead of Donnie in the program.) Donnie signed up for several courses and workshops. When he finished the course, he not only had new knowledge but also a new contact for troubleshooting practical problems.

This is an example of learning by focusing on practical goals, such as writing a paper that uses a new method. Our team had a few rules or mantras that helped reinforce a growth mindset. One was "By the inch it's a cinch; by the mile it's a trial," which refers to the strategy of breaking learning down into achievable small steps to avoid feeling overwhelmed by a looming task that involves many steps. Another rule is to reach out for help when you get stuck. Some people hit a barrier and stop, and progress on their dissertation grinds to a halt. We never want that to happen. And we never want people spending hours spinning their wheels. Remember, research happens in teams. As students gain confidence, they develop a broad network of helpers who are only an email away. So, when we get stuck, we ask someone to help us figure things out.

As you reflect on a growth mindset, could you pick one strategy you might want to focus on this week? What is one step you could take toward implementing this strategy in your life?

GRADUATE MENTOR CORNER

As a mentor, you can help set the stage for your advisee's thoughts and beliefs about themselves vis-à-vis the research process. One common problem is professors have often been doing research for a long time and have developed quite a lot of research expertise. When you are an expert in something, it can be easy to do things "naturally" without remembering all the specific steps it took to learn the task. When this happens, there can be a disconnect between mentor and student. The mentor makes the tasks look easy or has unrealistic expectations of the student. The student then feels as if they are not good at research, even though they might be in a reasonable place given their level of prior experience.

The key here is to focus on providing a positive and encouraging environment for students, especially at the beginning. Give a lot of positive feedback about the good things your students are doing. Provide opportunities for your students to team up with older students to observe their successes. Give your students opportunities to succeed early and often, and give ample encouragement and positive reinforcement when they do succeed. Remember the story of how to teach your kid to swim.

Related to this point is that it is important to connect the dots at the beginning of the research process. Do not assume your students know more than they do. Instead, start from the beginning and break the research process down into small, manageable steps. (Part of the reason we created this resource is to help mentors with this process.) Make it normal for students to "not know," and make sure they understand it is okay to ask questions about anything.

Finally, it can be useful to be vulnerable about your own struggles and failures as a researcher. We often talk about the importance of sharing your "resume of failure." Learning how to do research and complete an independent research project is challenging for anyone. By sharing your own struggles and failures, you can normalize the process of struggling so your students don't feel alone when they struggle. Instead of thinking they are not good at research or "do not have what it takes," they can view their struggles and challenges as a normal part of the process.

UNDERGRADUATE MENTOR CORNER

This chapter highlights one of the distinct advantages undergraduate mentors can have in shaping the research trajectories of students: accumulating early successes. Building victories around research can be critical in helping your student develop research self-efficacy. Although a gold standard may be coauthoring a paper with an undergraduate student or helping them earn a prestigious grant or fellowship, there are other ways to accrue small research wins. For example, getting a poster accepted at a regional or national conference is often a celebratory occasion for undergraduates working in our labs. We also celebrate when one of our posters or papers wins a student research award. Similarly, we are excited when our hypotheses are confirmed by the data, and the studies work out as we planned. This helps students see their hard work come to fruition.

And we are also honest when things do not go as planned. Plenty of studies do not pan out, and we process that together as a group. What can we learn? What could we have improved? What went wrong—our theorizing, our methodology, or something else? Then, we get back to work and start planning the next project. By allowing a backdrop of real difficulty and disappointment punctuated with excitatory victories, we model the tough academic reality of high rejection rates that make paper acceptances, grant agreements, award letters, and fellowship appointments that much sweeter. And we make sure we are not solely defined by our work—in that way, we are shielded from the shame and loss of disappointment and the hubris and conceit of victories. Professional success plays its appropriately sized role.

Think of ways to help your students get early wins. Are there chapters they can contribute to coauthoring? Are there poster submissions at conferences with favorable acceptance rates? Similarly, are you encouraging when the difficult times come? Can you reflect on how you have experienced disappointment and share your honest road to your academic appointment, letting them know that, for many of us, it was winding and full of turns we never foresaw—and it can still be richly rewarding? And it is important to model a growth mindset of being a lifelong learner with them. Daryl has often found undergraduate students can develop some of the most clever and effective experimental manipulations for our Introductory Psychology pool participants because they know them increasingly better than he does each year (apparently, not everyone still watches *ALF* or continues to listen to Nirvana). Modeling those healthy beliefs with vulnerability can set your students up for a career of research success.

MOVING FORWARD

In this chapter, we talked about the importance of the beliefs that students have about themselves and the research process. We discussed the importance of self-efficacy and covered ways students can improve their self-efficacy for research. We also talked about Carol Dweck's work on mindset, differentiated between fixed and growth mindsets, and talked about some practical strategies for students to develop a growth mindset. In the next chapter, we shift gears and talk about how to get our physical bodies in a peak state, so we can make consistent progress on our research.

7 NURTURING THE MIND–BODY CONNECTION TO SUPPORT PRODUCTIVITY

An often-overlooked aspect of research productivity is our physical state. This might seem like a strange topic for a book on the research process. After all, people might think that research primarily involves the mind. However, our bodies and minds are closely connected. In fact, our physical states can play a large role in our day-to-day work tasks—including progress on our research. Thus, in this chapter, we first cover some important considerations about our mind–body connection so we can be at our best in our research. Then, we talk about the concept of flow and how we can enter a flow state with our research.

The following is an example of how our physical state can impact our research process, even if we are not aware of it. A few years ago, Josh was feeling completely stuck on a writing project. He could not seem to make any progress, and the edits he was making seemed to make the paper worse. Josh was getting frustrated and upset and wanted to throw out the whole paper, which was unusual for him. (Usually, Josh is able to press pause, take a break, or get help when he is feeling frustrated.) As he looked back on what happened, Josh realized how his physical body influenced his mood

https://doi.org/10.1037/0000371-008
The Complete Researcher: A Practical Guide for Graduate Students and Early Career Professionals, by J. N. Hook, D. E. Davis, and D. R. Van Tongeren
Copyright © 2024 by the American Psychological Association. All rights reserved.

and feelings. The night before, he had not slept well, and he was feeling exhausted. Josh also had not eaten enough that day, which could have negatively affected his ability to think and work. Once he was able to recover and get a good night's sleep, his mood improved, and he was able to tackle the writing project again. It still was challenging, but he could feel a noticeable difference the next day.

We probably have all had experiences like Josh described, in which our physical state seemed to drag down our mental state. We have also experienced the other side of the coin, where we were in a positive, upbeat state: Feeling well rested, having had enough to eat, and feeling physically well can improve our cognitive abilities. The optimal level is where our skills are a good match for the task at hand—when it is challenging but not too hard. In such situations, we are still working, yet the work seems to be flowing out of us, and the pages begin to accumulate. Researchers call this a *flow state* when we achieve peak performance.

Have you experienced a similar connection between your body, your physical state, and your research performance? Take a few minutes right now and check in with your body. How is your body feeling right now? Are you tired or well rested? Are you hungry, thirsty, or full? Are you alert or sluggish? Are you anxious and uptight or relaxed?

MIND-BODY CONNECTION

There is a strong connection between mind and body. Perhaps the most impressive evidence of this close connection is the placebo effect. A *placebo* is an inert substance or treatment (e.g., a sugar pill) with no therapeutic value. However, time and again, research has found that participants who take a placebo experience a healing effect (Price et al., 2008). When the brain tells the body it is in the process of healing, something powerful happens.

The reverse is also true. The state of our physical body can impact our mood and even how we think. If we are hungry, in pain, or tired, we will not be at our best. Our work (and life in general) will suffer. However, if our nutrition is on track, we are well rested, and we are regularly moving our bodies, we give our minds the best opportunity to work at maximum capacity.

Unfortunately, graduate students often struggle in this area. It is hard to prioritize one's health amid the demands of graduate school. Graduate school can be stressful. In our programs, students often juggle several things at once, such as classes, research, clinical work, and teaching assistantships. Sometimes it seems as if students are pulled in several different directions at once and are struggling to keep their heads above water. Graduate school is often quite different from undergraduate work, where students can cram for an exam and then focus on other things for a while and rest. Some graduate students are also trying to juggle work and family, and many face financial pressures. Financial constraints while in graduate school may make it difficult to purchase healthy food. In our own experiences, taking care of our physical health during graduate school often was the first thing to go.

With all these stressors on our plates, taking care of our physical bodies can often take a back seat. Instead of taking the time to cook nutritious meals, students survive on fast food and energy drinks. Many students stay up late, trying to finish all their reading and assignments before the next day. And who has time for exercise? Even students who had a regular exercise routine in the past often struggle to work out with any regularity during graduate school.

Unfortunately, because of the close connection between mind and body, graduate students can get into a negative cycle. Not taking care of your body negatively affects your mood and thinking. But when your mood and thinking are negatively impacted, you work less efficiently, which causes even more stress. This increased stress leaves even less time to take care of your body, and the negative cycle is entrenched. How can we turn this around?

PHYSICAL HEALTH BASICS

What are some physical health basics that are important to keep in mind as we try to optimize our physical state for work on our research and dissertation? There are a few key basics to keep in mind, including (a) nutrition, (b) sleep, (c) exercise, (d) rest and relaxation, and (e) avoiding health "poisons." At the outset, we want to acknowledge that many of us are likely familiar with these physical health basics, even if we do not practice them. Still, it can be helpful to have a reminder of the key physical factors that are likely to have an effect on our minds, emotions, and work. If you want to be at your best when it comes to your research, it is important to consider and prioritize these basics.

Nutrition

Nutrition has to do with the types of foods you put in your body. To function at your best, you have to eat plenty of healthy foods and drink enough water each day. If you are not eating enough or your diet consists of fast food and energy drinks, you will not be able to think clearly and work efficiently. How are you doing with your nutrition? Are you getting enough to eat? Are you eating plenty of healthy foods and drinking enough water every day? What is one thing you could do to improve your nutrition?

Sleep

It is important to get enough sleep every day. Sometimes graduate students get in the habit of staying up late to work or pulling all-nighters to study for an exam. This does not usually work. Josh says 8 hours of sleep will sometimes do more for your exam score than cramming the night before. Most people need 7 to 8 hours of sleep per night to function at their best. The minimum is usually 6 hours. Another helpful hint is to get on a schedule where you go to bed and wake up at the same time each day—even on the weekends. The older you get, the less able you are to recover lost sleep during the week by sleeping late on the weekends. Consistent sleep is key. How are you doing with your sleep? Are you getting enough sleep each night? Are you going to bed and waking up at the same time each day? What is one thing you could do to improve your sleep?

Exercise

Our bodies were meant to move. A lot of research work involves sitting at a desk. We need to counteract that by getting active on a regular basis. It is ideal to have 30 to 60 minutes of vigorous exercise at least three times per week. It does not matter as much what activity you do as long as you get your heart rate up. Josh likes CrossFit, Donnie likes to bike, and Daryl likes to run and do triathlons. But even going for a walk or hiking a trail can make a difference. To make the most use of their time, many people enjoy catching up with a friend while on a hike or calling a loved one on the phone while going for a walk. Find an activity that works for you and stick with it. How are you doing with your exercise? Are you getting active for at least 30 to 60 minutes 3 days per week? What is one thing you could do to improve your exercise?

Rest and Relaxation

We were not meant to work all the time. There is a reason many of the ancient religious traditions encouraged people to take a "Sabbath rest." Our bodies work best when we alternate stress and rest. It is important to take some time every day to unwind. We also recommend taking at least 1 day per week when you do not work and you unplug from your email. Also, throughout your day, it can be helpful to take short work breaks. For example, Josh works most efficiently when he takes 5 to 10 minutes each hour to get up, stretch, and walk around. How are you doing with your rest and relaxation? Are you taking some time out of each day to relax and unwind? Do you take at least 1 day off work per week? What is one thing you could do to improve your rest and relaxation?

Avoid Health Poisons

Most of the physical health basics we have covered (e.g., nutrition, exercise) are things that are good for you. However, it would be remiss not to talk about some physical health "poisons" that can derail your physical state. Again, most of us are familiar with many of these health factors that negatively impact our minds, emotions, and work. But it is a good reminder to consider them. If you are struggling in your research and are regularly partaking in some of these health poisons, it might be helpful to focus on cutting these down (or out).

Physical health poisons include drugs, alcohol, caffeine, and smoking. It is normal to want to partake in some of these substances (e.g., morning coffee, happy hour with friends)—after all, graduate school is stressful. The problem is we can begin to rely on a substance as our primary coping mechanism to deal with stress or get through our day rather than doing something to solve a problem in our life or get healthy. We might also experience tolerance, where we need more of the substance to get the same effect as when we started, or withdrawal, where we experience negative symptoms (e.g., headache) when we are not using the substance. And some drugs are just plain dangerous, no matter how infrequently you might use them. In these cases, substance use can become a problem itself. If you are struggling with addiction or using drugs, please get help. Reach out to your mentor (if you feel comfortable) or a counselor you trust. Get the help you need sooner rather than later.

How are you doing with avoiding physical toxins? Are you keeping your alcohol and caffeine use in moderation? Are you using any illegal drugs? Do you feel like any of your substance use is negatively impacting your life, work, or well-being? What is one step you could take to get help with this area of your life?

In the next section, we talk about the concept of flow and how we can put ourselves in the best possible state when doing our research work.

FLOW

Have you ever been in a situation where you were "in the zone," where you got lost in your task and time seemed to fly by? Have you ever felt like this while working on your research? For many graduate students, the answer is no. Working on research can seem like a grind. It might feel like a struggle; time seems to crawl to a stop, and you have only written one sentence! Ideally, we want to be in our most focused and productive state while working on research. Psychologist Mihaly Csikszentmihalyi (2008) devoted his career to studying *flow*, which he defined as the state in which people are so involved in an activity that nothing else seems to matter.

This sounds great—ideally, we would love to be in flow all the time. Even though being in flow all the time probably is not possible, there are some things we can do to put us in the best position to experience flow in our work. In what follows, we discuss six practices to put yourself into a flow state: (a) Get your physiology right, (b) know your peak time, (c) remove distractions, (d) single-task, (e) check your level of difficulty, and (f) alternate work and rest.

Get Your Physiology Right

Some of the things we talked about in the section on physical health basics can help put your body in a flow state. In particular, it is hard to experience flow when you are hungry or tired. If you want to experience flow in your work, make sure you are eating regular, nutritious meals, so your brain has enough glucose to function properly. Also, make sure you are well-rested. You need to be in an upbeat, alert state, which requires adequate sleep.

Know Your Peak Time

Different people have different times during the day when they are at their best. For example, all three of us do our best work in the morning. As the day goes on, we get more and more tired, and by the end of the day, we are definitely not at our best. Because of this, we try to schedule our time so we complete our most important tasks first thing in the morning and move our less important tasks (e.g., email, busy work) to later in the day. We know a friend, however, who does his best work late at night. That is when he works at his peak. His schedule would not work for us, but that is okay. Everyone is different. Find the time of the day that works best for you. Experiment with different times until you find what feels right.

Remove Distractions

One of the keys to working in a flow state is to remove distractions from your environment. In today's world, we have a lot of distractions that can hamper our work. For example, many people work with their email open and get a ding every time they receive a new email. You might work with your phone on and get a buzz every time someone texts you. Each time we are distracted, it removes us from our flow state. When you work, be ruthless about eliminating distractions from your environment. Close your email. Turn off your phone. Turn off the television. If it has the potential to distract you, shut it down.

Single Task

We talked about this in Chapter 5, but some people take pride in their ability to multitask and juggle multiple tasks at the same time. The problem, however, is multitasking is a myth, and splitting your attention takes you out of a flow state. The reason is you lose momentum every time you task-switch. For example, let us say we have been working on a research project for 10 minutes. We are just getting into the flow of writing, and then we get a pop-up saying we received a new email. We switch over to our email and respond. Then, we switch back to our research, but we are out of our rhythm. We have to spend a couple of minutes reviewing where we were before starting again. Before too long, we have to task-switch again. If you want to work in a flow state, do one thing at a time.

Check Your Level of Difficulty

One of the key findings from research on flow is that you need a good match between your skill level and the difficulty of the task. Ideally, flow occurs when the task difficulty is maximally matched to your expertise. If the task is too easy, you will get bored. If the task is too difficult, you will get frustrated. Ideally, the level of difficulty will match your skill level or perhaps be a bit above your skill level—enough to be challenging but not overwhelming. If you are working on your research and it feels too difficult, you might need to reach out and get more help and support. (We have not found many students who think their research project is too easy.)

Alternate Work and Rest

Working in a flow state requires a high level of focus and energy. It's not something you can do endlessly. You need to take breaks. We have found it helpful to alternate periods of focused work and rest throughout your day. For example, you might set out to engage in focused work for about 45 to 50 minutes each hour. You could even set a timer for yourself. When you reach your time goal, take a break for 10 to 15 minutes. It can help give your mind a break and do something physical, such as going for a walk. When you are done with your break, immerse yourself in another session of focused work. Work, rest, work, rest, back and forth throughout your day.

What do you think of the six strategies to help you get into a flow state with your work? What is one strategy you could implement today to help improve the quality of your work sessions?

GRADUATE MENTOR CORNER

You can do a few key things as a mentor to help your students improve their work sessions and get into a state of flow. First, modeling is important, so it can be helpful to give your students a sense of how you combine work with an active and healthy life. Talk about the difficulties you may have had forming sustainable sleep, exercise, and nutrition habits, as well as key transitions that led to positive long-term habits. Try to take a holistic approach with your students. Encourage them in their research, but also check in about the other aspects of their life. Encourage them to live a balanced life. Remember, if their physical health basics are not in place, everything will suffer (including their research). Do not push your students too far in their work if it means their health will suffer.

Also, when trying to work in a flow state, one of the most consistent findings is the level of difficulty of the task needs to match the level of skill of the worker. One pitfall we see is that advisors assume students know more than they do when it comes to the research process. This mismatch causes students to feel overwhelmed and frustrated, which takes them out of a flow state. Try to have honest conversations with students about where they are at and how much they understand. Give them permission to ask questions, even about things they think they should know already. When instructing students about the research process, start at the beginning and go slowly, step by step. Be on the lookout for a mismatch between your students' skills and the task they are trying to complete.

Finally, it can be helpful for mentors to prioritize giving their students time for their research and writing. Sometimes, mentors can inadvertently distract graduate students by setting up a culture where the mentor and graduate students send a lot of messages back and forth about what is going on in the lab (e.g., through email, text messages, or messaging services such as Slack). There can be implicit pressure for students to respond to these messages right away. Mentors could encourage students to set up "do not disturb" hours for responding to messages, and they can also batch their communications to students so they are not sending messages throughout the day.

UNDERGRADUATE MENTOR CORNER

Students do not always prioritize their health in college. From pulling all-nighters to overusing substances, many students struggle to maintain healthy patterns, and this is often the first time in life when they are taking responsibility for making autonomous choices over this aspect of their life (and others). In addition to modeling healthy behaviors and choices, there are a few things that might help provide a structure for physical flourishing.

First, you can educate your students on the importance of caring for their physical bodies. Talk about the brain–body connection. Show them the research. Second, be aware of your own behavior: Are you sending emails late into the night and on weekends, or do your students know you take time away from work? Do you expect unreasonable turnarounds in tasks, or do you give students workday hours to complete research projects? Third, encourage your students to prioritize their well-being. If it is feasible for all lab members, think about a lab goal, such as walking in a 5K for a local charity. Making physical health a priority on par with other aspects of their development helps students see the importance of this feature in their lives.

MOVING FORWARD

In this chapter, we focused on physiology. First, we talked about some physical health basics that set the stage for effective work. Next, we talked about the idea of flow and discussed some suggestions to help you put yourself into a flow state. Unfortunately, as much as we would like things to progress in a straight line when it comes to research, not everything goes according to plan. Even strong students will likely experience adversity during graduate school. We discuss how to navigate adversity in the next chapter.

8 NAVIGATING ADVERSITY DURING THE RESEARCH PROCESS

When it comes to research, things do not always go according to plan. We might have clear expectations for how our lives will look and what our graduate school process will be, but there are a lot of things in life we do not have control over. Life happens in graduate school. Training often takes about 5 or 6 years, even without delays. This is long enough that we can almost guarantee you will face a major stressor or transition during graduate school. Sometimes graduate students can feel pushed to their limit with their workload, even when the rest of their life is going okay. So, when a major stressor or transition happens, it can be challenging to keep going. Sometimes it might feel like the wheels are about to fall off.

In some ways, the material in this chapter may seem tangential to the focus of this book—making progress on your research. Why plan for unexpected adversity in one's life outside work? Understandably, students often fall behind on their research when they encounter unexpected challenges and have not left enough margin (i.e., room to deal with the unexpected) to keep their research on track. The purpose of this chapter is to help you plan for adversity or setbacks so that, when they happen, they will not derail your

---

https://doi.org/10.1037/0000371-009
The Complete Researcher: A Practical Guide for Graduate Students and Early Career Professionals, by J. N. Hook, D. E. Davis, and D. R. Van Tongeren
Copyright © 2024 by the American Psychological Association. All rights reserved.

progress on research. Of course, we realize some events are so disrupting or life altering that research should take a backseat to prioritizing other areas of life, and our commitments will have to be renegotiated—having a clear plan can help provide structure and offer ways to navigate these difficulties. Thus, we discuss how to plan for adversity as best one can, understand and recognize our limits, and renegotiate commitments, so we maintain trust with those around us.

Like many of us, Donnie had a clear idea about how he thought his graduate school process would look. But 2 years into his graduate program, he was faced with an intense period of adversity involving a family health scare that pushed him to the limit—emotionally, relationally, and spiritually. All circumstances are different, of course. Your period of adversity will likely not be the same as Donnie's. But we walk through some of his experiences in this chapter to give an example of what it might look like to navigate graduate school and the research process when adversity hits. We hope some of these stories and lessons can help you prepare and think about what you might do if faced with adversity.

A RAINY DAY

Donnie sat in the doctor's office looking at the sonogram. He heard the words coming out of the doctor's mouth, but he could not feel anything. That was the day he and his wife were supposed to find out the sex of Catherine (now 13 years old). But something was wrong—and the sonogram technician did not have the authority to tell them what it was. Now, they were with this doctor in this strange office.

"She has what we call a diaphragmatic hernia," the doctor said. "This means that her stomach is not in the right place, and her lungs will not fully develop. She will be in very serious condition when she is born." The words sank in—sort of. A thousand questions flashed through Donnie's mind. He already knew his world would be turned upside down. But now, it had taken another sharp turn. He tried to keep listening.

"She has a 50% chance of living," the doctor continued. "We will not really know more until she is born. If she has enough lung tissue, they will stabilize her for a few weeks and then do surgery. But she may not have enough healthy lung tissue to survive, even on life support."

This doctor's visit happened during Donnie's second year of graduate school. The next few years would be quite a journey, with some harrowing lows and some awe-inspiring moments of connection and love. After around 10 surgeries, Catherine gradually developed healthy lungs, learned to eat, and grew up to become a wonderful young lady. One step at a time, Donnie's family dealt with the next challenge in front of them with the help of friends and family. At times, work was a source of connection and security. But it was not easy to navigate graduate school and the research process during this time.

WHAT CAN YOU DO TO PREPARE FOR YOUR RAINY DAY?

We hope you will not face anything so disruptive as what Donnie had to go through during graduate school. That said, we have yet to have a student who has made it through 5 years of graduate school without a major life stressor or transition. We may not like it, but dealing with some of these challenges or ups and downs is inevitable. What can you do to prepare yourself for your rainy day?

Because the future is unknown, there might not be much you can do ahead of time to prepare yourself. We deal with many of life's uncertainties this way—we "cross that bridge when we get to it." In some ways, it might be a waste of energy to worry too much about the unknown—it is hard to plan fully for an unpredictable future.

However, we suggest that you at least think about a rainy-day plan for yourself, and if you feel comfortable, discuss this plan with your research advisor. A rainy-day plan involves understanding that stressors and setbacks are a normal part of life. It involves thinking about ways you can work hard but in a way that is sustainable for the long haul—even if something unexpected happens. It is about building some margin into your life, so there can be a buffer when unexpected stress or hardship occurs. Building a margin means not always working at 100% capacity. It means working a little less than your maximum—maybe 80% to 90%—so you have extra room to accommodate unexpected difficulties or challenges. It means setting boundaries and ensuring you build in regular periods of rest and restoration. It also means having a plan for how you can cut back if you need to generate extra time and psychological energy quickly. As faculty members, we expect life to happen. In fact, we view a student's ability to handle adversity while living up to professional commitments as one of the most important parts of training.

HOW GRADUATE TRAINING AND RESEARCH STRETCHES US

Graduate school and the research process are difficult by design. The purpose of graduate school is to train you to be a leader in your field. The purpose of learning to conduct research is to be able to answer important questions using the scientific method and critically read and understand the research of others as a professional psychologist. As a psychologist, you will function in a variety of roles. Across relationships, you tend to repeat the following process:

1. Do your best work.
2. Get feedback from someone qualified to help you get better.
3. Incorporate feedback and try again, according to the new insights you received.
4. Repeat.

Part of what makes graduate training and research difficult is that working hard and getting feedback requires a lot of energy and effort. You will be engaging this process across a variety of relationships (e.g., research mentor, clinical supervision, peers in your cohort). Although what you learn while reading and doing research is important, it is not nearly as important as what you learn as you work to balance multiple roles and commitments. It is challenging to receive feedback from so many angles, but this is what supercharges your potential for growth.

Growth happens when you are operating at the edge of your competence. In weight training, the most growth happens as an athlete works on the verge of failure. The last few reps challenge the body to grow. Similarly, when you work at the edge of your abilities, with support and encouragement, you have the potential to learn and grow quickly. So, in training, we continually put ourselves at the crossroads of growth. And although this is an essential process, it also can be challenging and stressful. To thrive in this environment, we must be focused and at our best. When unexpected difficulty or adversity strikes, it can be hard to stay in this crucible of personal and professional growth.

KNOW YOUR LIMITS

Because graduate training and research are challenging endeavors, it is critical to understand your limits and notice when you are reaching them. One helpful concept to think about when we are reaching our limits is burnout (Schaufeli et al., 2009). Burnout is based on the idea of smothering a fire or extinguishing a candle. It occurs when a person experiences exhaustion and is unable to maintain involvement with their work in a way that leads to a meaningful impact. The Maslach Burnout Inventory (Maslach et al., 2008) assesses burnout using three main criteria: (a) emotional exhaustion (e.g., a feeling of being drained and fatigued), (b) depersonalization (e.g., detachment, lack of connection or empathy), and (c) loss of personal achievement (e.g., negative self-assessment, doubting one's abilities). If you are experiencing any of these symptoms regularly when you engage in your research and graduate studies, it is a good sign you may be reaching the limits of your capacity and beginning to experience burnout.

In doctoral training, we are the only ones who know our limits—and sometimes we miss the cues. Furthermore, what most doctoral students may not prepare for is knowing when to generate more margin and downshift their commitments. You are the only person who can safeguard the commitment to take care of yourself. You are the only one who can know how to give your training "a lot, but not too much" of your time and effort. If you ignore your body or try to set limits by comparing yourself with others, you may end up feeling burned out. As the saying goes from research on the effects of trauma on the brain and body, "the body keeps the score" (van der Kolk, 2014). Eventually, if you do not listen to your body, your body will slow you down—often at the worst possible time and with a much harsher result.

MAINTAIN TRUST

The goal of a rainy-day plan is simple: When you reach (or are pushed beyond) your limits, the goal is to maintain trusting relationships with your supervisors and collaborators while you do what you need to do to take care of yourself. Trust is earned through making and keeping commitments (Covey, 2006). So, when you face adversity, it is important to negotiate your commitments right away. It is important to write down all your current commitments and think about which ones you may need to change or renegotiate. Then, have a conversation with the individual with whom you made the commitment and discuss the situation. To the extent you feel comfortable, explain what is going on in your life and why you need to renegotiate the commitment. Discuss what you think would be an appropriate accommodation and see how the other person responds. Importantly, you do not have to go through this process alone. Talk to your advisor or someone you trust about how best to renegotiate your commitments.

Many things may come up in life that may affect our ability to meet our responsibilities. It is helpful to learn to think of ourselves as part of a team and a larger community. This means if something affects our ability to maintain our commitments and responsibilities, we can ask for help. If someone gets sick or needs to attend a funeral, others can cover the responsibilities, but this only works if we embed ourselves in trusting relationships. So the bottom line is that there is nothing more important than your trust with others, so guard it carefully. If you earn people's trust, they will help you when you need it.

MORE INSIGHT FROM DONNIE'S EXAMPLE

It might help to hear some of the ways Donnie navigated his time of adversity and negotiated his commitments when his family was faced with the stress of Catherine's health issues. After Catherine was born, she had to go to the University of Virginia (UVA) to see a specialist, so Donnie and his family lived over an hour from the Virginia Commonwealth University campus for much of that year.

The first thing Donnie did was talk to Ev (his mentor) about the situation. Ev helped Donnie think through a plan to move forward. One option was to slow down his progress through the program, which would have been fine. Students can sometimes be resistant to the idea of slowing down their progress or doing things like taking fewer classes or taking an extra year if a big stressor comes up. But sometimes, this is the best solution to help students maintain their mental and physical health through times of adversity. Remember, finishing graduate school is not a race. Donnie was done with most of his coursework, so he worked out a plan with Ev for when he would take his remaining courses. He decided to push most of them back to a later year to give himself more margin over the next year.

The main commitment that required Donnie to be on campus was practicum. So, he discussed his situation with his practicum supervisor, who was very supportive. The practicum site worked with Donnie and allowed him to complete his practicum for 2 days out of the week, so he could be at UVA with his family the rest of the week. His practicum site did not require him to attend staff meetings, which helped make the plan workable.

Donnie's other commitments could be completed remotely. For example, his graduate research assistantship involved being the graduate assistant to the program director. He attended faculty meetings every other week during 1 of his 2 days back in Richmond. The rest of his assistantship responsibilities could be completed remotely.

This plan worked partly because his time in the hospital involved a lot of sitting and waiting. The first 2 weeks were intense. Catherine was on a last resort form of life support that involved a machine that looked like something in a science fiction movie from the '70s. The machine took the blood from her lungs and put more oxygen in it before returning it to the heart. There was nothing much to "do," and there were times that Donnie was glad to have some of his schoolwork to do at the hospital.

As you might imagine, there were times when the emotional challenges and uncertainty were quite high. When stress was high, Donnie took things one day at a time. As the semester went on, he settled into a routine. Disruptions were disorienting and hard. But facing this adversity helped give him confidence in his ability to handle difficult circumstances in the future.

WHAT CAN WE LEARN FROM ADVERSITY?

Looking back, Donnie feels a lot of gratitude. Catherine is alive and healthy. She has the normal problems of a 13-year-old, but the health problems are resolved. His research team and program circled around him to offer support. Everyone did what they could to express care and smooth out some of the details and rough spots of his life during that season. He also was integrated into a church community. Close friends visited regularly. This kind of support is what we all need if and when the bottom drops out of life. We need to feel surrounded by a loving community.

It can be insensitive to move too quickly through the "hard" things in life. Donnie had a string of challenges and transitions between ages 22 and 35, including losing his mom to cancer, a cousin dying, Catherine's health problems, a marriage ending, and building love in a blended family. Life is difficult sometimes. We hesitate to provide a list of "lessons" that can be learned from adversity because these lessons are deeply personal and contextual. But dealing with adversity involves making some sense of the trials and ordeals of life and finding a way to move into the future.

Mostly, Donnie is glad those days are over. If the adversity did lead to any wisdom he could pass along when other people's rainy days come, it would be to be kind to yourself. Donnie is an achiever. He enjoys working hard and striving toward goals. He has the capacity to do many things through sheer willpower. He approached his research program with that same intensity and focus. Yet, in these major grief processes, Donnie was kind to himself. Looking back, Donnie is grateful he had the maturity to accept his limits instead of trying to push himself too hard. Some kinds of research work are harder when dealing with high levels of challenge, adversity, and grief. During some seasons, he let first-authored work wait, and he simply did the best he could. Instead of trying to push through his limits, he accepted the feelings he had within his body.

Another thing Donnie learned was to get out in nature and stay active during periods of stress. Connecting with yourself, understanding your limits, and knowing what you need is a basic trust worth maintaining. Under stress, Donnie worked hard to maintain his body. For example, in Richmond, he spent time biking on the James River. He still has beautiful memories of the trails that weave in and out of the riverbanks, across to Belle Isle, and then back again. Being in nature has always been a way he could seek healing and integration. During another season of grief, soon after he returned to Atlanta, he logged hours on the Silver Comet Trail. Taking care of your body and soul is a way you can make and keep a commitment to yourself.

Adversity tests us, and we learn, each in our own way, how to find a way through those times. Just like engineers examine the structural integrity of a wall, making sure it can stand up to the pressures of the building structure, doctoral students experience a variety of pressures that help them know themselves as leaders and professionals.

GRADUATE MENTOR CORNER

As mentors, it is easy to get overly focused on work and the process of training. Doctoral mentoring has the potential to be a lifelong relationship, and for those relationships to flourish, we have to remember there are many things more important than work.

For the relationship between mentor and student to work well, we need to build enough trust so our students can talk with us about some of the difficult things they face in their lives. These times of challenge and adversity affect the work we are doing together, and for us to serve as good collaborators and mentors, we have to be in a position to bear witness to the pain in our students' lives. For some difficult or existential challenges, that is perhaps the best we can do. Trying to fix or put a positive spin on things will only intensify the sense of pain and loneliness.

Students may feel different levels of comfort with letting you in on the difficult and challenging things going on in their lives. We may only see a portion of what students are going through in their personal lives. An important implication is to extend students the benefit of the doubt. If we see drops in performance that do not have a specific explanation, they may be due to circumstances we do not know about. It can be easy to make mistakes, giving feedback that is off base and not appropriately attuned to a broader range of challenges students may be facing in their daily lives.

As a mentor, it is important to familiarize yourself with your institution's guidelines and policies regarding what options are available if students experience a time of adversity and need to slow down and renegotiate their commitments. For example, what are the university, department, and program policies about how to slow down progress or apply for a leave of absence? It is a good idea to talk about these options early in graduate school to normalize the process and remove the stigma from having to slow down or shift one's initial course of research or graduate studies.

In sum, try to build the type of relationship with your student so they can come to you for support if needed. Help connect the student with different sources of help and support (e.g., counseling) that might be beneficial. Offer your students your presence, remembering life is hard sometimes for all of us. And help the student navigate the program as best they can, understanding that some things are more important than work and deadlines.

UNDERGRADUATE MENTOR CORNER

Many of the themes of this chapter apply to all levels of students, and in many ways, they apply more generally to being a human. Undergraduate students sometimes feel intense pressure to get and keep their lives in order, but life still happens. Students may experience major disruptions, and still, they have to figure out how to put one foot in front of the other. The suggestions in the graduate mentor corner apply equally well to working with undergraduates. Offer your presence and support, connect students to helpful resources (e.g., many undergraduate students do not know they likely can get free counseling from the university counseling center), dial back any pressure your lab may be putting on them, and help them navigate their commitments as best they can. Developing a sense of authentic community in the lab can offer another source of support to someone experiencing adversity.

MOVING FORWARD

In this chapter, we discussed the possibility that you may encounter major stressors that could disrupt your research program and training. This is nothing to be ashamed of; it is not only normal but also important to your training and development. Whatever your next few years hold, the important thing to remember is you are not alone. You are surrounded by people who want to help you live up to the commitments you have made to yourself, the profession, and the broader community.

As you get started, pace yourself, and build in rest and things that will sustain you over time. When you get tired, rest. When you feel strength and energy, do not be afraid to push a little harder. Training is not an easy process. It is not supposed to be. It is a process designed to expand your limits, which requires a testing process, but it is important to take time for rest and healing. If you want to keep growing, do not forget to rest and recover. The risk of burnout is real. Graduate school is more of a marathon than a sprint. Persistence conquers most things.

We have now finished the first section of the book and covered some of the key principles that are helpful to develop if you want to become an effective researcher. In the next section, we get more practical and walk through the steps of a research project from start to finish.

PART **II** PLAN: THE RESEARCH PROJECT FROM START TO FINISH

9 CHOOSING A TOPIC FOR YOUR RESEARCH PROJECT

In Part I of the book, we covered some foundational principles for becoming a good researcher. In Part II, we shift gears and cover the key steps for completing a research project from start to finish. Because many of our readers are graduate students, we also discuss steps specific to the master's thesis and doctoral dissertation, such as the proposal meeting. One of the challenges of writing this section was balancing general and specific recommendations. On the one hand, we have found that general recommendations are not often helpful for students. When you do not know how to get started, it helps to have a specific plan of action. On the other hand, there is a lot of variability in how scientists conduct their research and how mentors organize the research project for graduate students. Some of this variability is specific to one's field or subfield of study or even the requirements of the graduate school at one's university. There is not one "right" way to organize a research project, so some of the specific ways we advise our students may not work for you or your mentor. Also, best practices for various parts of the research process change over time. When in doubt, go with what your mentor recommends.

---

https://doi.org/10.1037/0000371-010
The Complete Researcher: A Practical Guide for Graduate Students and Early Career Professionals, by J. N. Hook, D. E. Davis, and D. R. Van Tongeren
Copyright © 2024 by the American Psychological Association. All rights reserved.

In this book, we decided to chart a middle path. We share some of what has worked for us and our students, but we also note typical areas where there may be differences or variability in how researchers navigate the process. As noted in the Introduction, we expect you can adapt these recommendations to find something that will work well for you and your mentor. Also, if you are a mentor and do not have a clear step-by-step approach to help your students complete their independent research projects, this framework can be adjusted to fit your needs. Throughout this section of the book, for chapters that are a bit less concrete, we also give examples from our own process.

In this first chapter of Part II, we discuss the first step of the research process: choosing a topic. It may seem like this step would be simple or easy, but for many graduate students, this is one of the more difficult steps. Deciding on a topic is not usually a one-time decision point. Rather, it is a process of narrowing and homing in on the topic you would like to study. We realize this can be complicated; in some situations and some institutions, you do not have as much latitude in choosing your topic. For example, your focus might be shaped largely by a grant your mentor has received or a recent funding opportunity on a particular topic. In other situations, you might be given a wide range of options as long as it is somehow related to your mentor's area of expertise. We discuss the various pathways of picking a topic, fully recognizing how multilayered this process often is.

If you have free choice to select a topic, you might have a general idea of a topic you find interesting. However, you may not be quite sure what specific question you would like to examine, perhaps in part because you are only beginning to orient yourself to the prior research that has been done in the area. Often, the first step is to start doing a lot of background reading on your topic (see Chapter 10 for an in-depth discussion on how to conduct a literature review). As students begin to review the research in the area they are interested in, it can be challenging to know where to start. Your mentor can ideally help you get started. In doctoral programs, graduate students often apply to work with mentors who are experts in the field they are interested in studying. Your mentor can suggest influential articles or book chapters in the area and likely has published in the area themselves. Their guidance can give you a head start in getting an introduction to the area. If you need more help getting oriented, another way to save time and energy is to read review articles and handbook chapters on the topic you are interested in. These types of papers often seek to synthesize key themes from existing research on a topic, which can orient you to some of the key debates or unanswered questions within the field. Reading a review article can help give you the "lay of the land" on a topic and also introduce you to some of the key articles in this area, which you can read next. High-quality review articles can be found in many different high-visibility outlets, such as *Psychological Bulletin, Psychological Review,* or *Current Directions in Psychological Science,* or specialty journals relevant to your research area.

As you begin to read more broadly, it is helpful to summarize the articles, so you can easily come back to them and remember what they were about. We like to summarize articles in a chart or a spreadsheet. Doing background reading not only alerts you to the existing research in this area but also gives you a sense of the unanswered questions. Often at the end of research studies, authors list their ideas for future research. These ideas can be building blocks for your project. You want to discern where the next frontier of research waiting to be completed in this area will be.

One important question when narrowing and homing in on your topic is how narrowly to focus. This is a specific question for you and your mentor, depending on your research area and how much previous research has been done on your topic. For example, a lot of people in our labs choose to do their research projects on a specific virtue, such as forgiveness. Forgiveness as a research topic is probably too broad for a dissertation. Forgiveness in married couples is still probably too broad. Forgiveness of affairs in married couples might be getting closer to the level of specificity you need when choosing a topic for an independent research project. However, narrowing it down so much that you only study forgiveness of affairs among geriatric rural Episcopalians in the Pacific Northwest during Eastertide may have gone too far. You get the idea: You want to break new ground without being so esoteric that it cannot inform the broader literature.

Another issue to consider when deciding how to narrow your research topic is how fertile versus crowded the field is. If a field is too crowded, meaning a lot of excellent work has already been done on the topic, it can be challenging to carve out a niche for yourself. If a field is in its beginning stages, however, there are more opportunities and low-hanging fruit. This was part of the reason doing research on humility was attractive to us when we were beginning our research careers. Each of us started doing work on forgiveness, but that field was crowded. We realized humility was a key part of forgiveness, and there was less existing work done on humility, so the field was more open for us to make contributions.

Often the topic for your research project is a mix of your interests and your mentor's interests. Ultimately, your topic needs to be something you are interested in because you will be devoting 2 years (or more!) of your life to this project. If all goes well, after hundreds of hours of reading and work, you will probably be among the most knowledgeable scholars in your area. Sometimes our interest in a topic fades after so much work. That just happens and is a normal part of the process. But if you start out working on something you are not interested in, it will be difficult to maintain your motivation over the long haul.

In addition to being something you are passionate about, ideally, your project will also be something your mentor is interested in and knows something about. The reason for this is your mentor will be helping and guiding you as you complete your project. Their expertise is critical. If you are doing something your mentor does not know anything about, they can help you to a point on the basic research processes, but they will not be able to guide you as well regarding the content of your project because they do not have a good knowledge base about the existing literature. They also might not be able to help you navigate barriers in the area that they would have encountered in the past. If you are passionate about doing a certain project, and it is not related to your mentor's interests, talk it over with them and see if they are open to it. If they are willing, it might be a win–win. You may even lead them into a new area of interest.

Sometimes there is a way to combine your interests with those of your research mentor and create a topic for your research that hits on both your interests. For example, one of Josh's students was interested in doing a project on dating and relationship satisfaction. Josh was not doing a lot of work in that area at the time because most of his work was focused on humility and positive psychology. However, they were able to design a research project that looked at the relationship between humility, commitment, and relationship satisfaction in dating couples, which ended up being a good mix of both their research interests.

EXAMPLE

Daryl had two different experiences with choosing a topic: one for his master's thesis and one for his dissertation. His master's advisor had a grant studying religion and coping among females in a maximum-security prison. Because Daryl was interested in religion, and there was much-needed funding in the form of a graduate fellowship, he started making weekly research trips to a maximum-security correctional facility, and his thesis focused on female offenders' adjustment to prison life. This was largely because his research mentor had so much expertise in this area, and Daryl formed his project on her experience.

For his dissertation, Daryl tried the opposite approach. He came to his PhD program excited about big questions about human nature—existential issues like human mortality and the meaning of life. The problem was that back then, few people studied such things, and even fewer were gainfully employed as social psychologists. Because of this, Daryl's advisor initially tried to persuade him to study something "safer" and easier to publish to better his chances of getting a job. That was thoughtful advice, but Daryl is both passionate and persistent, so finally, he convinced his advisor to let him study meaning in life. His advisor had just gotten a grant to run a big community-based longitudinal study on romantic couples, so Daryl included scales on meaning in life and forgiveness in several of the time points, which provided a rich data set he could use for his dissertation.

For his two graduate projects, there was a different level of mentor expertise, and each offered benefits and challenges. Daryl's master's thesis was carefully supervised and extremely structured—his advisor was an expert. But it was not Daryl's primary area of interest. For his dissertation, his passion served as the primary motivation, and both he and his mentor learned together. It had its additional challenges, but thanks to his mentor's curiosity and generous support, it yielded a fascinating project that launched one of Daryl's primary lines of research.

GRADUATE MENTOR CORNER

For the mentor, picking a topic is a crucial step because it will set the stage for the direction and nature of your relationship with your students. If you apply too little structure for directing students in choosing their research topic, within a few years, you may have a lab that involves supervising a range of projects outside your area of expertise. Especially early in your career, this strategy can be dangerous because you may be spending significant time on projects that will be difficult to publish and may not contribute to your primary line of work. Also, eventually, students will be working against deadlines, and it can take more work to help students finish projects when they are working in various directions. It may take time to adjust if you find yourself with several dissertations that fall too far outside your areas of competence.

However, going too far in the other direction can be equally problematic. For example, in Donnie's program, students must submit an empirical paper for publication before they can begin work on their dissertations. It is tempting to have students find an existing data set to meet this requirement because it has the potential to help students move quickly toward their goals. This plan can offer its own challenges, however, because sometimes students struggle to write a paper when the methodology is already settled (i.e., one has to work backward, figuring out a rationale according to what is available rather than carefully aligning the research design and measures with the purpose of the study). Writing a paper takes a lot of work, and sometimes people lack the motivation to finish projects when they were not involved in forming the research questions and developing the design.

Established mentors have a better sense of their strengths and weaknesses through trial and error. They also may have a broader range of work that falls within their areas of expertise. Also, they struggle less if they must mentor a challenging dissertation topic because they have already traversed key professional transitions such as tenure and promotion. Thus, early career mentors may want to be more cautious when helping students pick topics. We do not have easy answers for striking the right balance here. The decisions are contextual and may depend on the unique combination of interests and skills of both you and your graduate students. So, our main suggestion is to surround yourself with support from other scholars so you can benefit from feedback that will help you consider different perspectives. Perhaps you can save yourself some heartache rather than having to learn entirely from personal trial and error. We are all still tweaking our approach and trying to learn from prior experience.

UNDERGRADUATE MENTOR CORNER

Often, when working with undergraduates, we may simply "plug" them into whatever project we are working on during that semester. Largely, that is a sufficient strategy for helping students gain experience and allowing them to learn some basic skills needed for graduate school. Occasionally, students will ask to complete an independent study or an honors thesis. In nearly every case, we recommend ensuring that such a project aligns closely with your own research program. Sure, students could put their own personalized spin on a topic or take a unique approach to a research question. However, given the level of investment necessary for such a project to succeed, it is important that the project is an area in which you have both interest and expertise. These will yield the strongest projects (and most publishable papers).

MOVING FORWARD

In this first chapter of Part II of the book, we talked about the process of choosing your topic for your research project. Often, choosing a topic is an iterative process—you start with a general topic and then home in on what you are most interested in. It is also important to work with your mentor to find a topic that is acceptable to both of you. In the next chapter, we walk through how to do a literature review and find out what has already been done on your topic.

10   CONDUCTING A LITERATURE REVIEW

In this chapter, we discuss the second part of the research process—conducting a literature review. It is important to do a literature review before you decide on the specific focus of your project and start your data collection. You want to get a sense of the literature before trying to start something new. If you do not have a clear sense of what has been done previously, you might repeat something that has already been done or do something that does not make sense given the existing research. So, it is important not to skip this step.

This is one step of the research process where we must acknowledge that research mentors have different preferences for how their students conduct a literature review. We have high standards for this step. We want our students to conduct a publishable systematic literature review in which they find and critically evaluate all the empirical research on a specific topic. There are a few key benefits to this way of doing the literature review. First, learning how to do a systematic literature review is a good skill to develop. For example, when we are interested in doing research on a new topic, we will often do a systematic literature review first to gain a clear sense of what research has been done previously. Also, review papers can be strong publications that are highly cited and make a meaningful contribution to the literature.

https://doi.org/10.1037/0000371-011
The Complete Researcher: A Practical Guide for Graduate Students and Early Career Professionals, by J. N. Hook, D. E. Davis, and D. R. Van Tongeren
Copyright © 2024 by the American Psychological Association. All rights reserved.

That said, there is quite a bit of variability in advisors' expectations for this step of the research process. Specifically, many research mentors will likely require a less formal process for the literature review, such as reviewing and summarizing a certain number of articles or chapters. This could be viewed as a "good enough" method—reading enough of the literature so the graduate student has a good sense of what has been done previously and can summarize this information in a few pages. In this chapter, we walk through the steps for completing a systematic literature review because this is the most rigorous form of this step. But feel free to dial back these suggestions to match the desires and requirements of your research mentor. Specifically, we discuss clarifying the topic of your literature review, conducting the actual literature search, and writing up the literature review. Near the end of the chapter, we also discuss alternate options for those who do not want to complete a systematic literature review.

STEP 1. CLARIFY YOUR TOPIC

The first step is to clarify your topic for the literature review. This might seem a bit odd—did we not already pick our research topic in the previous chapter? We did, but that was the general topic for your overall research project. For many graduate students, the overall topic may be too broad to conduct a systematic literature review, and we need to narrow the focus for the literature review. We discuss some of these considerations next.

There are a few things to think about when clarifying the topic for your literature review. First, make sure no one has published a recent literature review on your topic (i.e., within the past 5–10 years). If someone has published a recent literature review on the same topic, it does not make sense to duplicate work, and it will be hard (but not impossible) to make a case that another literature review makes an important contribution (e.g., you could critique the findings of a previous literature review and analyze the studies differently). In such cases, your mentor can help you consider a different angle.

Second, ensure your literature review is at the correct level of specificity. If it is too broad, there will be too many studies to review. If it is too specific, there will not be enough studies. The desired level of specificity also depends on how much time and energy you have to put into this project. For example, we recently published a literature review that included over 100 studies (Hook et al., 2021). It was a good paper, but it took a long time to read and review all those articles. As tenured professors, we had the time and energy to do that. However, if your literature review is part of your dissertation project, for example, you will want to have a narrower level of specificity so your project is more manageable. A good rule of thumb for graduate students is somewhere between 15 to 30 studies. As always, guidelines have exceptions. If your topic is interesting and you can make a strong case the review is necessary, you can get away with fewer studies. You can do a review with more studies; it just will take more time and effort.

Third, getting to the correct level of specificity of your literature review is an iterative process. This process involves doing a series of preliminary searches. First, you set a wide search parameter and see how many studies meet your criteria. Then, you think about different ways to narrow the parameters so the number of studies is manageable. The important thing is you want to set criteria in a way that makes theoretical sense. You want to do a systematic literature review, which means making an honest attempt to find all the empirical articles on a specific topic. You will carefully record the steps of your search so someone can replicate it. So, if you have too many or too few studies, you need to expand or contract the parameters of your search (theoretically speaking) to have a manageable project. Your mentor can help you with this process of getting to the correct level of specificity.

STEP 2. DECIDE WHAT TYPE OF LITERATURE REVIEW TO CONDUCT

There are two main types of literature reviews—narrative reviews and meta-analyses. In a narrative review, the author reviews the findings from the included studies and makes conclusions based on those findings. The reasoning is primarily conceptual or narrative in form—not quantitative and statistical. A meta-analysis is similar, except that in a meta-analysis, the author conducts statistical analyses that combine the results of the included studies. Thus, a meta-analysis has a strong quantitative component. Studies with larger sample sizes get more weight, and you calculate an overall effect size. Meta-analyses are usually considered superior because they estimate quantitative effects across samples, but they also take more methodological skill and training. Also, meta-analyses may be less appropriate if the included studies use different measures and types of studies, so it makes less sense to aggregate across studies within the literature. Because of the complexity and learning curve necessary to learn how to do a meta-analysis, most graduate students will likely decide to conduct a narrative review of the literature unless they have direct access to mentoring from someone with appropriate expertise. In rarer cases, an ambitious graduate student may decide to take the time and effort necessary to learn how to do a meta-analysis. It is an excellent skill to develop, but it may be too big a step for students just starting to learn the research process.

STEP 3. CLARIFY YOUR INCLUSION AND EXCLUSION CRITERIA

Before you start conducting your literature search, it is important to clarify your inclusion and exclusion criteria. This provides a systematic way to decide whether a study should be included or excluded from your literature review. We set these criteria ahead of time, which makes it easy to conduct our literature search and decide whether a study should be included (or not). Your specific inclusion and exclusion criteria will depend on your topic, and it is important to work closely with your mentor to set these criteria. The following are some ideas for how to clarify your inclusion and exclusion criteria:

- **type of study:** Will you only include empirical studies, or will theoretical studies be included as well? (Empirical studies collect data from participants, whereas theoretical articles do not.) Will you include case studies? In our work with students, we generally advise them to focus on empirical studies and exclude theoretical papers and case studies.

- **type of research design:** Will you include both quantitative and qualitative studies, or will you focus on one type of research design? (Meta-analyses generally only include quantitative studies, whereas narrative reviews often use both quantitative and qualitative studies.) In our work with students, we usually recommend they include all types of research designs.

- **inclusion and exclusion criteria based on the sample:** For example, one student was only interested in studies in which the participants were clients currently in therapy. This will depend on your research question and focus.

- **inclusion and exclusion criteria based on the measures:** For example, one student only included studies that measured a particular construct similarly to how they envisioned assessing it in their own work.

STEP 4. CONDUCT AND DOCUMENT THE LITERATURE SEARCH

Now that you have determined your topic and inclusion criteria, you are ready to do the literature search. There are several smaller steps involved. First, search multiple databases for studies using specified key words. Generally (this may change somewhat depending on your topic), we like to use

PsycInfo, ProQuest Online (for theses and dissertations), and Google Scholar. With any systematic literature review, the search process is one of the most important steps, so check with your mentor as well as other reviews published in your area, so you engage in a rigorous and replicable search process.

We have a few tips for searching these databases. For psychology research projects, PsycInfo is probably the best place to start, and most of your studies will show up there. ProQuest Online is a great place to search for unpublished work such as theses and dissertations. When searching on ProQuest Online, we usually recommend using the "Anywhere except full text—NOFT" option (i.e., this searches a variety of fields such as abstract, keywords, and so forth, but does not search the entire document, which reduces the number of abstracts for review). When using Google Scholar, you will often get thousands of hits, so you need to determine how many entries you will look through. For example, the program Harzing's Publish or Perish (Harzing, 2007) will download the first 1,000 hits, and it is also possible to limit the year (e.g., 2000–2010; 2011–2021). Standards of rigor for your search can be outlet specific (e.g., *Psychological Bulletin* will require thorough search methods), but Google Scholar is currently one of the more comprehensive ways to find published or even unpublished work.

Second, review the reference sections from the identified studies to find other studies you may have missed. The introduction sections of the studies you read will also include a literature review on the topic—this can be a great place to ensure you have missed no studies in your database searches.

Third, request unpublished or file-drawer studies from scholars in the field. ("File-drawer studies" refer to studies a researcher may have conducted and not published, so they are in the researcher's file drawer.) Getting unpublished studies is important because you want to mitigate publication bias. *Publication bias* refers to the fact that published studies are often more likely to have significant findings than unpublished studies because nonsignificant findings are more difficult to get published. If you only include published studies in your literature review, it can skew your overall findings and conclusions.

What is the best way to track down unpublished and file-drawer studies? We often email all corresponding authors of the identified studies that are already on our list. We send the list of articles we have and ask if there are any others we might have missed (or studies the author has conducted that have not been published). Another way to seek file drawer studies is to send an announcement on relevant listservs in your specialty area.

It is important to keep track of how you do your literature search. Keep track of the date of the search, what databases you use, what key words you use, and how many entries come up in the search. Some of this information will go in the method section of your literature review, and it is important to stay organized in case you have to update your literature search later. Recently, scientists came up with a system for organizing and reporting the steps of a literature search called PRISMA, which stands for Preferred Reporting Items for Systematic Reviews and Meta-Analyses (Page et al., 2021). The PRISMA guidelines offer a checklist for steps to be reported in a systematic review, as well as a flow chart that can be included in your literature review paper. You can visit the PRISMA website at https://www.prisma-statement.org to download both of these resources.

STEP 5. MAKE A CHART

As you read the studies you have found, it is a good idea to summarize them in a chart. We recommend creating the chart as you read through each study so you do not have to go back and reread the studies later. We often use a table in Microsoft Word or Excel or perhaps a Google Sheet (if we have a team coding simultaneously). We recommend including the following information, although some of the specifics will vary according to your topic:

- citation
- published (yes/no)
- research design Part 1 (e.g., quantitative, qualitative, mixed)
- research design Part 2 (e.g., experimental, quasi-experimental, cross-sectional, longitudinal)
- randomized to condition (yes/no; if an experimental study)
- sample information (e.g., sample size, age, gender, race or ethnicity, sexual orientation, religious affiliation, type of sample, such as college student, community, inpatient)
- measures used
- effect size
- summary of main findings

STEP 6. START WRITING

You organize your systematic literature review paper as you would an empirical article, with sections for the introduction, method, results, and discussion. One somewhat unorthodox recommendation about writing the literature review is we usually start with the method and results sections, then write the introduction, and finally write the discussion. We have found this to be more effective because it is helpful to "know where you are going" when you write the introduction. If you do not have the main part of your paper nailed down (i.e., the method and results), it can be difficult to write a strong introduction. Before we implemented this change, we would often do some writing in the introduction that we ended up having to scrap because it no longer fit the direction of the paper. In what follows, we describe how to write each section of the literature review in detail.

Introduction

The introduction of a systematic literature review will look somewhat different from an introduction to an empirical article. (A good way to get a better sense of these differences is to read how other authors set up a systematic review). For an empirical article, a big part of the introduction is a pointed argument for why the study is needed (sometimes called a literature review but not to be confused with a systematic literature review). But for a systematic literature review paper, the whole paper is focused on the literature review. So, the introduction is a bit different (and is usually shorter). The introduction is organized like a funnel. You begin with broader themes and then logically narrow down the purpose of the review. Our introductions usually have the following steps:

- Start by introducing the topic of interest and defining the main variables you will study.

- Explain and discuss why this topic is important. Why is this question timely? Why is a review of the literature necessary at this time?

- Discuss theory that supports your hypotheses. For example, if your review is focused on the relationship between religion and forgiveness, discuss theories that might explain this link. You are not reviewing the actual studies here (e.g., you would not report that the average correlation across studies was .30 or that 15 of 20 studies found a positive correlation between religion and forgiveness). Reviewing the empirical literature happens in the results section. Here, you are discussing theory (e.g., describe a theoretical model that links religious commitment to forgiveness).

- Discuss theory that supports your mediator and moderator hypotheses (if applicable). A mediator is a third variable that helps explain the link between two other variables. A moderator is a third variable that changes the relationship between two other variables (also known as a *conditional effect*). In the example from earlier, if the relationship between religion and forgiveness is different for cisgender men and cisgender women, you would discuss theory supporting that moderator here. Again, you are not reviewing the actual studies here but rather discussing the theory for why this hypothesis might be true.

- If there have been previous reviews of the literature on your topic, it is a good idea to discuss these reviews and also discuss how your paper will be new and different and will add something unique to the literature. Emphasize the novelty of your contribution.

- End the introduction with a paragraph describing the current literature review, including your main hypotheses.

Method

There are several steps in the method section of a literature review:

- **inclusion criteria:** Write a paragraph describing the decision rules you used for including or excluding studies. In other words, what had to be true about a study for you to include it in the review? This should be decided before you conducted your literature search, so it should be easy to write.

- **literature search:** Write a paragraph or two describing your literature search. Again, this describes what you did in Step 4 (e.g., the date you conducted your search, the databases you used, the key words you used, whether you reviewed the reference sections, whether you inquired about file-drawer studies). Use the PRISMA guidelines to map out what you write in this section, and also include the PRISMA flowchart.

- **effect size (meta-analyses only):** What effect size did you use in your study—Cohen's d, the correlation r, or something else?

- **missing data (meta-analyses only):** What did you do if not all the studies had sufficient information to calculate the effect size?

- **outcome of search:** State how many articles were found in the search. (Some authors report this at the beginning of the results section.)

- **coding:** What information did you write down from each study? List the most critical columns from your chart.

- **data analysis (meta-analyses only):** Write a paragraph describing how the meta-analysis was conducted. (Your mentor can help you with this.)

Results

There are also several steps to writing the results section of a literature review:

- **description of studies:** Start the results section with a paragraph (or two or three) describing the studies as a whole.
  - **participants:** How many total participants across all studies? What were the gender, race or ethnicity, sexual orientation, and religious affiliation of the participants? What was the type of setting (e.g., college student, adult, community, inpatient)?
  - **research design:** What research designs were used (e.g., quantitative, qualitative, mixed; cross-sectional, longitudinal, experimental, quasi-experimental)? If experimental designs were used, what kinds of control or comparison conditions were used?
  - **measures:** What measures were used to assess the constructs of interest?
  - **treatments:** If this is a review of treatment studies, what treatments were used?
- **overall conclusion or effect size:** Overall, what is the conclusion regarding the primary question of interest? If you are conducting a meta-analysis, this is where you would put the overall effect size statistics.
- **publication bias (meta-analyses only):** You can run analyses to measure the extent of publication bias (i.e., do published studies have larger effect sizes than unpublished studies? Is it likely there are other unpublished studies "out there" you did not find?).
- **mediators:** Are there variables that might help explain the primary question of interest? For example, is the relationship between religion and forgiveness mediated by high levels of empathy? Is the effect of cognitive behavior therapy on depression mediated through lower levels of cognitive distortions?
- **moderators:** Are there variables (e.g., sample, measure, procedure) that might influence the primary question of interest? For example, is the relationship between religion and forgiveness greater for cisgender men than cisgender women? Do drug treatments have larger effect sizes than talk therapies for treating depression?

Discussion

There are also several steps to writing the discussion section of a literature review:

- First, have a paragraph or two summarizing the main findings of your literature review. Are the main findings consistent or inconsistent with the theory and hypotheses you presented in the introduction?
- Discuss what the findings mean. Why are the findings important?
- Discuss limitations to the review (e.g., types of participants, small sample sizes, poor research designs, poor measures).
- Discuss areas for future research.
- If applicable, discuss implications for counseling or whatever field your literature review is focused on.
- Include a conclusion paragraph.

EXAMPLE

Donnie's first literature review for his master's thesis was a difficult process. He started out doing something on attachment to God, based on a grant project his mentor had. The first problem was a rookie mistake. After gathering all the articles and starting to lay out his chart over Thanksgiving break, he ended up finding a prior review on the same topic that was published in the past few years. When Donnie went to Ev and told him about the prior review, Ev delivered the bad news that he should probably cut bait and figure out a new direction because it would be difficult to publish another review on the same topic, especially without a good rationale. In fact, Kirkpatrick (the author of the review) had not only published a strong review on the topic, but he also wrote an academic book that thoroughly synthesized the literature. (If Donnie were further along in his career, he probably could have advanced a different line of thinking, but this was his first project, so in this case, finding a new direction was the wiser path.)

Second, Donnie did not have a good sense of the overall process. He read all the articles but ended up needing to read them again because he did not know how to keep up with his notes. Donnie also got stuck when trying to figure out how to write the main sections of the review. He was able to create a summary table, but he did not understand the kind of synthesis and analysis he needed to do to write the content of the review.

Looking back, Donnie now sees the logic and mindset he was missing. For narrative reviews, part of the work is like doing an assessment report (for anyone in clinical, counseling, or school psychology). You take the data and look for points of convergence and divergence. You put the most weight on inferences that are supported by multiple studies. When there are discrepancies, you use theory and common sense to try to understand the variability in findings. So, as it turns out, Donnie was trying to write the paper before he had developed the skills to lay out the logic, which made it difficult. So, go easy on yourself for the first year or two because research training has a steep learning curve.

Donnie's literature review for his doctoral dissertation was much smoother. (In fact, we have found if mentors put in the work to help their students with their first writing project, the process of writing the dissertation is often easier because students have already been through the process once before for the thesis.) He did a literature review on humility, which focused especially on measurement approaches, given the paradox of self-reports of humility (i.e., saying I am humble could be akin to bragging about my humility, which seems potentially arrogant). He had strong training on how to think about his role as an author of a literature review—to get to know the field and help people not only get a sense of the literature but also give them a lens for viewing the field critically, including awareness of its strengths, weaknesses, and areas for potential investment. Instead of many revisions back and forth, this time, he gave the manuscript to Ev, got comments back, and addressed them, and he was done. What a difference a few years can make.

ALTERNATIVES TO THE SYSTEMATIC LITERATURE REVIEW

Although we see a lot of benefits to conducting a systematic literature review as part of the thesis or dissertation process, you and your mentor may decide to do a briefer literature review option. Much of the process is similar to what was discussed earlier. You still must clarify your topic (Step 1) and conduct the literature search (Step 4). However, instead of making it a point to find all the empirical literature on your topic, you and your mentor must decide what constitutes "enough." You and your mentor may decide on a predetermined number of empirical studies to review (e.g., 10–20), or perhaps you keep reading until you begin to feel you have a good grasp on the overall topic.

The main difference is found in the process of writing the literature review. Instead of organizing the literature review as a stand-alone publication, with different sections for the introduction, method, results, and discussion, you may organize the literature review section like the introduction of the empirical journal article. Here is one potential way to organize the section: First, start broadly by defining the topic and main constructs. For example, if your paper is about religion and forgiveness, spend some time defining both constructs. Next, if applicable, present the theory (or theories) undergirding your research study. For example, if your theory says that religious commitment will positively predict forgiveness, walk through the logic of the theory. Finally, review the past research studies that address your topic. The reader needs to know what has been done already so they know how the research project you propose fits into the existing literature.

GRADUATE MENTOR CORNER

We have a few suggestions for mentors. First, we suggest giving clear instructions on the importance of narrative reviews for a student's career. If people attempt to align all their reading and work with their research program (i.e., "never do anything for a single purpose"), the narrative review provides an opportunity to complete a theoretical synthesis that could set the foundation for their other work. Strong review papers are often highly cited because people use them to establish their conceptual arguments in the introduction of their own papers (Aksnes, 2003).

For students entering clinically oriented careers, the literature review establishes expertise and makes all other writing projects (e.g., papers in classes, the empirical project of the thesis or dissertation) easier to complete. Steady work along the way compounds over time and makes all subsequent steps of a research project easier.

Our second suggestion is to keep a folder with resources to help students with some of the key steps of the literature review. How much rigor you require may depend on your setting, as well as the professional goals of your students. In this chapter, we set potential expectations for a systematic literature review that is publishable. You may have important reasons to set lower standards for the literature review (e.g., aligning the workload with the student's career goals). Regardless, we recommend giving students clear expectations early in the research process. For example, it helps to give students clear guidance on what you expect on various aspects of the literature review, such as the search process, rigor of analysis, and so forth.

Finally, in our experience, the most difficult part of writing the literature review involves helping students write the results section, and we are still experimenting with ways of making this part easier. It is hard because a strong literature review has to go beyond just summarizing the main studies. Many beginning students will simply organize this section by summarizing studies one by one and perhaps noting the strengths and weaknesses of each. This strategy will not pass muster for most dissertation committees (or any high-quality publication outlet). What is needed is a conceptual synthesis that gives the field leverage to improve scholarship. This kind of intellectual leadership requires both the mentor and student to bring their sharpest thinking to bear on a body of work. This work is intellectually challenging, so make sure to honor the challenge and provide a strong balance of affirmation and support during this phase of the writing process—to yourself and your students.

UNDERGRADUATE MENTOR CORNER

Many faculty members find that working on a literature review (either a systematic literature review like the one we have outlined in this chapter or the literature review portion of an empirical manuscript) is one of the primary ways to get undergraduates involved in the writing process. In fact, many students report feeling more comfortable helping with the literature review part of a manuscript than contributing to other features—especially compared with writing a results section for an empirical paper. A good scaffolding technique is to build a step between the organizational chart and the literature review. For this "middle step," Daryl uses an annotated bibliography. In this, students write a paragraph summarizing the article they read. For 30 papers, writing a paragraph immediately under the citations often results in approximately 8 to 10 pages (single-spaced) of writing. The student and Daryl review this together and look for ways to distill the most important information from these paper summaries into the larger narrative of the paper. They then place the citations (and its paragraph) into the paper outline. Finally, the student revises these paragraphs once they see the broader flow of the paper and arc of the narrative. A final review for tone, voice, and consistency leads to a polished draft.

Literature reviews are a nice gateway into scholarly writing for undergraduates. They can also help you gain a better sense of a new area of research or launch a program of inquiry. Moreover, they can be undertaken by responsible and self-reliant students during periods of structured supervision (e.g., weekly check-ins) that build in time for independent work by the student.

MOVING FORWARD

In this chapter, we walked through how to organize and write a systematic literature review. The literature review is important because it sets the stage for the study you will conduct for your research project. Also, a literature review can be a nice stand-alone publication that is cited a lot and helpful for new people interested in the topic. In the next chapter, we cover the next step of the research process: designing your new research project.

11 DESIGNING YOUR RESEARCH PROJECT

Now that you have completed your literature review for your research project, it is time to design your actual study or studies. Your primary goal when conducting a research study is to answer an interesting question and discover something new to science—to make a novel contribution. You should also plan on doing something that will be published. Publishing your research is the capstone of the research process. It disseminates the new knowledge you discovered to the public. (And it is fun to see your name in print.) The following are some suggestions to think about as you design your study or studies.

SUGGESTION 1: LET YOUR LITERATURE REVIEW GUIDE YOUR PLANS

At this point in the research process, you have completed a systematic literature review on the topic you want to study. As you conduct your literature review, you will likely come up with thoughts for study ideas. Write these down. When you do your literature review, think about the following

---

https://doi.org/10.1037/0000371-012
The Complete Researcher: A Practical Guide for Graduate Students and Early Career Professionals, by J. N. Hook, D. E. Davis, and D. R. Van Tongeren
Copyright © 2024 by the American Psychological Association. All rights reserved.

questions: What are the next steps in research on this topic? What are some unanswered questions about this topic? We like to focus on the research gaps: Where are there gaps in the knowledge on this topic? As you review the literature, you will likely find that authors write about their ideas for future research in their discussion sections. These are often helpful to review when thinking about designing your own study. Take a few minutes and write down some of your ideas for your current study based on the findings from your literature review.

SUGGESTION 2: TAKE A MEDIUM-SIZED STEP FORWARD

When you are designing a new study to conduct, you want to take a step forward. This means you do not want to repeat something that has been done before. Simply repeating something is not fun or exciting, and it might be difficult to get published. So, you want to take the research forward. However, we recommend you take a medium-sized step forward. This means you ideally want your research to be related to previous research and your hypotheses to make sense, given what has been done previously in your research area. You do not need to solve all the world's problems or offer a definitive and field-shaping contribution in one research study. Science moves forward step by step over time. In the same way, for your research project, take a medium-sized step forward. Especially for projects with a lot of "red tape," such as a thesis or dissertation, done is better than perfect. Pick something you can finish on time.

SUGGESTION 3: BE CREATIVE

Think about new methods, populations, or measures. The possibilities for designing a research study are endless, so be creative. Is there a new method you could apply to a research area? For example, if most of the research in your area has been cross-sectional, could you conduct a longitudinal study? Could you design an experiment? Could you conduct an intervention? Are there new populations you could examine? For example, if most of the research in your area has been on cisgender men, could you apply it to cisgender women or gender minorities? If most of the research has been conducted on one racial or ethnic group or culture, could you sample racial or ethnic minorities or people from another culture? Are there certain types of samples that might be interesting to study, such as clients in counseling? Are there measurement issues in your research area? Could you design a new measure or adapt or change an existing measure? Be sure to balance your expertise with what you have the time and resources to learn to do.

SUGGESTION 4: DEVELOP A METHOD EXPERTISE

As you think about what type of study or studies to run, it can be helpful to consider how you might work to develop a methodological area of expertise. By diving into your thesis or dissertation project, you will develop expertise in a particular content area. But it is also worth thinking about whether you might want to gain experience in a methodological or statistical approach. For example, depending on your interests, could you develop expertise in qualitative approaches (e.g., focus groups), clinical trials, longitudinal approaches, meta-analysis, structural equation modeling, experimental designs, or something else? Mastering a particular method can help make you an attractive hire or collaborator. Because you have to pick some methodological and statistical approaches for your research project, it makes sense to focus on approaches you want to learn and develop expertise in.

SUGGESTION 5: DRAW FROM YOUR PEERS

Sometimes it can be challenging to come up with good ideas for a research study by yourself. Multiple brains are better than one. We draw from each other all the time to discuss possible ideas for future studies (and even have regular research "retreats" where we cook up research ideas together). In the same way, it can be helpful to utilize the members of your research team to help you come up with new research ideas. Lab meetings can be a great time to brainstorm and come up with new ideas.

SUGGESTION 6: MAXIMIZE DATA COLLECTION

Data collection is the most time-intensive part of the research process. Because of this, you want to maximize each data collection effort. Before you collect data, spend some time thinking about other possible papers or projects that could come from these data. Talk with your mentor or peers to come up with possible ideas. If you are interested in a different topic or think something might be related to your topic of interest, it does not hurt to throw in an extra measure. You can even put in measures that are not part of your main research project and conduct exploratory analyses. (However, you will need to be clear in your dissertation and when publishing about what parts are central to your dissertation and what constitutes another project. The same advice stands when preregistering your study and analyses: Be sure to clarify what is predicted and what is exploratory. We discuss open science and preregistration in Chapter 12, "Planning the Method Section.") Another thing to think about is including a few open-ended questions to obtain some qualitative data. Especially if you are in a new area, it can be interesting to collect qualitative data. Qualitative data can also provide you with some real-world examples of your research topic as it is experienced by your participants. Even if you do not use the qualitative data for your main research project, it could be used for another publication. For example, an undergraduate student could use the qualitative data for an independent honors project.

SUGGESTION 7: THINK ABOUT A PROGRESSION OF STUDIES

Sometimes it can be helpful to set up a progression of studies that makes theoretical sense. It is okay just to do a single study, but often it takes multiple studies to get a paper accepted into a top-tier journal. So, for your independent research project, you might think about doing a progression of two or three studies that build on each other.

EXAMPLES

Looking back, Donnie realizes this step was where his mentor, Ev, played a crucial role. Donnie had an idea for a research study and was beginning to get a sense of the field, but he did not know the standards for making a strong contribution. Ev did. So, Ev could help to push Donnie's idea forward. For example, for Donnie's dissertation, he had already run a few cross-sectional studies and had an ambitious project by any standard—to develop a measure of humility in a new and emerging field. Donnie had even gotten a grant based on an extension of his work, which was encouraging and exciting. Ev was thinking ahead to Donnie's eventual job talk, so he encouraged Donnie to add a final study that would showcase more difficult analytical skills. Donnie ran a round-robin study in which people came to the lab for a series of interactions. After each interaction, they rated themselves and each other on humility, which allowed a more complex test of the role of humility in forming groups. At the time, Donnie probably would have settled for a less difficult project, but Ev was keeping in mind the big picture of Donnie's developing career, and Ev knew it would be better if Donnie challenged himself.

As Donnie's career has advanced, he now sees there are lots of ways to get this kind of feedback at the design stage. Senior scholars tend to be generative. They got to where they are with help, so they are often willing to help others. Reading a manuscript or grant application may only take them a few hours, but they may have ideas that will save you months or even years. So, read as much as you can, but there is no alternative for strong feedback. In terms of expertise, the quality of the feedback you seek on your work will be one of the primary determinants of your growth.

GRADUATE MENTOR CORNER

We have several suggestions for mentors during the research design phase. First, never waste this opportunity to optimize the quality of feedback given to the project. When we give feedback to students, we want them to learn the key standards of our field. When you give feedback, do not just make the change or give a vague comment. Make sure you clearly explain the mindset that would allow them to improve their work.

Take advantage of teams. Part of why we write in teams is so doctoral students at all levels can see changes made by others, including experts at other institutions. We also like using grant or fellowship applications (even small awards) to motivate high-quality work. These projects bring teams together for a common purpose. For grants with larger budgets, a key factor that determines the competitiveness of the proposal is the quality of the team, so grants are an outstanding way to secure mentoring for several years.

Even though consultants (e.g., other researchers with specific areas of expertise) may only spend a few hours on the project, they do so when it matters the most—during the planning phases. They provide a way to optimize the expertise on a team (e.g., involving consultants), which is key to getting funding. We suggest a similar strategy, regardless of whether you have funding. Help your students develop an idea and then take the time to get the best feedback you can on the idea while it is in a formative stage—that is, plan carefully before you implement the plan (indeed, this is the role of a strong dissertation committee).

Focus on quality samples, measures, design, and analyses. Using a strong sample is one of the best ways to establish high value for a project. Scrutinize the measurement strategy. We are always on the lookout for ways to use multimethod approaches. Different types of measures can lead to discrepant findings, which can create conceptual tension that can energize a research program.

Finally, encourage your students to learn cutting-edge statistical methods, and involve that expertise at the design stage (see Chapter 12, "Planning the Method Section"). Your students will learn one project at a time because research is contextualized learning. Taking a class or reading a book is only part of the process. To truly possess a skill requires practical application. After your students have written several papers, they will have much more flexibility to make their own decisions and even support others. Often our teams have different people learn different skills. For example, Donnie focused on longitudinal designs, person-centered approaches, and meta-analyses. Daryl focused on experimental methods. Josh focused on multilevel modeling. We have someone else on the team with qualitative expertise. As a group, we can execute a broad range of methodologies and support students in their use.

UNDERGRADUATE MENTOR CORNER

Undergraduates often need much more guidance with study design—and they are often incredibly creative methodologists. Some of our most enjoyable collaborative moments with students have been brainstorming experimental inductions or clever ways to assess prosociality or aggression. We are often trained that the best way to be creative is to open the latest issue of our favorite journal and substitute our preferred dependent variable for the one that got published. Others have long cautioned against this approach and instead argue for building creativity in other ways (e.g., reading broadly). But perhaps an underappreciated source of methodological acumen is eager to contribute: your students. They often bring a fresh perspective to a topic that is not filtered through the latest trend in your subfield. And they are much more attuned to external validity; they know what other college students are thinking, like thinking about, and are willing to believe. They can often provide a more accurate perspective of what participants will likely experience in the study. If you involve your students in creative methodological brainstorming, it becomes much easier to teach them the rest of the research process. They develop these crucial skills, and you can learn quite a bit from them. It is a collaborative process, and it is a lot more fun for everyone.

MOVING FORWARD

In this chapter, we talked about how to design your research study. Once you have completed your literature review, it's time to think about the study you are going to run. This is an exciting step, but sometimes it can be tough to know what direction to go in. The importance of feedback from your mentor and others in your lab is critical at this point as you work to sketch out the study you will conduct. In the next chapter, we get more detailed and discuss how to write the method section of your study, which maps out the finer details of what you will do.

12 PLANNING THE METHOD SECTION

Normally, when conducting a research project, you would wait to write the method section until after you have collected your data. However, when you are completing a thesis or dissertation, you are usually required to plan and draft your method section before you propose your research project. Because of this, we wanted to discuss how to plan and draft the method section here. The method section describes how the study will be conducted. There are three main parts to the method section: (a) participants, (b) procedure, and (c) measures. We also discuss two additional sections that are often included in theses and dissertations: research design and planned analyses, as well as the growing trend in our field of emphasizing open science and preregistration.

PARTICIPANTS

The participants section gives a description of the participants in the study. (If you complete this section before collecting data, you will not have the exact numbers for your participants yet, but you may be able to make some

---

https://doi.org/10.1037/0000371-013
The Complete Researcher: A Practical Guide for Graduate Students and Early Career Professionals, by J. N. Hook, D. E. Davis, and D. R. Van Tongeren
Copyright © 2024 by the American Psychological Association. All rights reserved.

educated guesses about who you anticipate the participants will be according to prior studies completed by your mentor or other graduate students. You will put this information in your participants section before your proposal.) In other words, who are the people that completed the study, and what were their demographic characteristics? How does a researcher go about deciding who their participants will be? In general, you want to think about the general population of individuals you would like to make an inference about and target your sample toward this goal. For example, if you are studying the effects of cognitive behavior therapy on depression, you may want to recruit a sample of participants who have depressive symptoms. For many graduate students, convenience samples are used (e.g., college students). There are some limitations to these types of samples (e.g., lack of generalizability to other groups), but they are often used because they are easy to access.

If any participants' data were removed, you would need to explain this clearly and offer a justification. Data exclusion rules should be determined a priori (i.e., ahead of time) and made explicit. Many preregister their hypotheses and include a data exclusion rule in that preregistration, including their rationale for these decisions. Depending on your research project, there may be different kinds of demographic information that you will put in the participants section. But in general, most participant sections include the following information:

- number of participants
- gender identity breakdown (numbers or percentages)
- type of sample (e.g., undergraduate students, clients in therapy)
- age (range, mean, and standard deviation)
- race or ethnicity breakdown (numbers or percentages)
- religious identification breakdown (numbers or percentages)
- sexual orientation breakdown (numbers or percentages)

Most independent research projects such as theses or dissertations also require you to complete a power analysis. A power analysis is a way to determine how many participants you need to recruit for your study to find a significant effect, given the effect size you think you will find. It is important to conduct a power analysis before starting data collection, so you know how many participants you must recruit to ensure your study is sufficiently powered. You can use a computer program such as G*Power to conduct your power analysis. There are several different parameters you need to include:

- **analysis:** Pick the statistical analysis you plan to conduct. You will likely work with your mentor during the study design process to decide on your statistical analysis plan, so you should know this ahead of time.

- **power:** Select your desired level of power. Power is the likelihood that your sample will produce a statistically significant result if there is an effect in your population. The common standard is 80% or greater.
- **effect size:** Select the effect size you anticipate your study will find. The effect size refers to how large you anticipate the relationship between your variables or the treatment effect (i.e., the difference between groups) will be (e.g., small, medium, large). This is an educated guess because you have not run the study yet. Thus, you do not know what the effect size will be. One way to make an educated guess is to look at prior research and use the same effect size previous studies found. If there is not any prior research, one option is to select a small to medium effect size.
- **alpha level:** Select the *p* value you will use in your statistical analysis. The *p* value is the probability you will find a significant result if there is no effect in the population. The common standard is .05, and some researchers prefer more stringent *p* values (e.g., .01, .001).
- **one-tailed versus two-tailed test:** Select whether you will employ a one-tailed or two-tailed significance test. A one-tailed test only looks for a relationship or difference in one direction (e.g., positive or negative), whereas a two-tailed test looks for a relationship or difference in both directions. Unless you have a compelling and justifiable reason to do otherwise, we recommend using a two-tailed significance test.

In what follows, we present two examples of participants' sections. One is from a paper in which the data have already been collected, and the second is from a thesis or dissertation in which the data have not yet been collected.

Participant Section Example: Regular Research Study (From Hook et al., 2013)

Participants were 134 adults (40 men, 92 women, 2 other) recruited from a university counseling center and department clinic, all of whom were currently in therapy. Participants ranged in age from 18 to 71 years ($M = 26.40$, $SD = 8.90$). Participants were predominantly White (70.1% White, 6.7% Black, 8.2% Asian, 6.7% Latino, 8.2% multiracial) and heterosexual (76.1% heterosexual, 9.7% gay/lesbian, 10.4% bisexual, 3.7% other).

Participant Section Example: Thesis or Dissertation

> A power analysis using a small to medium effect size ($d = .35$), alpha = .05, and estimated power of .80 revealed the need for 204 participants. The sample for this study will consist of undergraduate students from a large mid-Atlantic urban university. On the basis of previous experience with this population,

participants will likely report a variety of racial or ethnic backgrounds and socioeconomic backgrounds, which will be summarized after data are collected. (Adapted from Hook, 2006, p. 109)

PROCEDURE

The procedure section describes how the study will be conducted. Like the other parts of the study, the procedure will be planned with the help of your mentor. The procedure section walks the reader through the steps the participants will take to complete the study. After reading the procedure section, the reader should be able to replicate your study. There will probably be some steps of the procedure that are unique to the study you are doing for your research project. But in general, most procedure sections include the following information:

- how the participants will be recruited for the study,
- the compensation (e.g., money, extra credit) that will be given in exchange for participation,
- how the participants will be given informed consent for the study,
- how the participants will complete the study (e.g., participate online, come to the lab),
- what the participants will do (e.g., complete questionnaires, complete a discussion), and
- how participants will be debriefed.

Next, we present an example from a procedure section (from Hook et al., 2013). Although this example is from a study in which the data have been collected, the procedure section for a thesis or dissertation will look similar—but in future tense instead of past tense.

> We recruited participants from a university counseling center and department clinic using flyers. Participants were eligible for the study if they were currently attending therapy (median number of sessions was seven). Participants completed the study in exchange for a gift card. Participants completed the study online. Participants read a consent form that explained the procedures of the study and their rights as a participant. Participants then indicated consent and completed the questionnaires. After completing the questionnaires, we debriefed participants and gave them a gift card for their participation. (p. 359)

MEASURES

The measures section describes each measure used in the study. Like the other parts of the method section, the measures will be planned with the help of your mentor. You will have a paragraph for each measure. Depending on your research project, there may be some variation in this section. In general, the description of each measure will include the following information:

- name of the measure
- name of the construct (i.e., what is the "thing" that the measure is measuring?)
- number of items
- if the measure has subscales, a list of the subscales and the number of items in each subscale
- at least one example item (if the measure has subscales, it is a good idea to include one example item for each subscale)
- description of the rating scale—how many response options and the endpoints of the scale
- past evidence for reliability and validity. *Reliability* assesses the extent to which a measure is consistent. Types of reliability include *internal consistency* (i.e., do all the items on the measure get at the same construct?), *test–retest reliability* (i.e., if you give the measure to the same person at two different times, how consistent would the scores be?), and *interrater reliability* (i.e., for observational measures, if two people make ratings of the same thing, how consistent are their scores?). *Construct validity* assesses the extent to which a measure measures what it is supposed to measure. *Convergent validity* means the measure is related to other measures it is supposed to be related to. *Discriminant validity* means the measure is not related to other measures it is not supposed to be related to. Usually, the original scale development paper for a measure will report evidence for reliability and validity.
- the score you are using in this paper. For example, are you using the mean of all items or analyzing the subscales individually?
- whether higher scores indicate higher or lower levels of the construct
- Cronbach's alphas for the present study. Cronbach's alpha is a common measure of reliability for a measure. (If you are completing this section before collecting data for a thesis or dissertation project, this will not be part of the section because you will not be able to calculate it yet.)

There are two primary strategies for gathering the information to write the measures section of the paper. First, look at the scale itself. You can find most of the information you need by looking at the measure (e.g., number of items, subscale information, description of rating scale). Second, find the original scale development article that presents the scale. By reading through this article, you will most likely be able to find all the information you need (e.g., a description of the scale as well as evidence for reliability or validity).

Next, we present an example description of a measure (from Hook et al., 2013). Although this example is from a study in which the data have already been collected, the description for a measure in a thesis or dissertation will look similar, except Cronbach's alpha for the current study will not be included.

> Working alliance. Participants completed the short form of the *Working Alliance Inventory* (WAI-SF; Tracey & Kokotovic, 1989). The WAI-SF consists of 12 items that measure three aspects of a strong working alliance with the therapist: task (e.g., "What I was doing in counseling gave me new ways of looking at my problem"), goal (e.g., "My counselor and I were working towards mutually agreed upon goals"), and bond (e.g., "My counselor and I trusted one another"). Participants rated the degree to which they agree or disagree with each statement on a 7-point rating scale from 1 = *strongly disagree* to 7 = *strongly agree*. High scores indicate a strong perceived working alliance with the therapist. Tracey and Kokotovic (1989) found evidence supporting the estimated internal consistency and the factor structure of this subscale. For the present sample, we used the total working alliance score. The Cronbach's alpha coefficient was .96 (95% CI [.95, .96]). (p. 356)

RESEARCH DESIGN

The research design section is simple and describes the research design for your study (e.g., cross-sectional, longitudinal, experimental; quantitative, qualitative, mixed). It can often be just a couple of sentences. It is often not included in the method section of a journal article (it can be viewed as unnecessary), but some mentors may prefer to have the section included in a thesis or dissertation project.

The following is a brief example of how the description of the research design section might look: This study utilized a quantitative, cross-sectional research design.

PLANNED ANALYSIS

The planned analysis section describes the statistical analyses that will be used to test the individual hypotheses. It is sometimes not included in the method section of a journal article unless the study is using a complicated statistical analysis. However, when graduate students are planning their independent research project, they will work with their mentors to outline their hypotheses, as well as the statistical analysis that will be used to analyze each hypothesis. Thus, mentors sometimes want this section included in a thesis or dissertation project.

Here is a brief example of how the description of a planned analysis section might look (adapted from Hook, 2010):

> Descriptive statistics for the appropriateness of using religious techniques in couple counseling will be examined. A one-way analysis of variance (ANOVA) will be conducted with appropriateness as the dependent variable and type of couple counseling conducted (professional, pastoral, and lay) as the independent variable. If the ANOVA is significant, I will follow up this test with a post-hoc Tukey HSD to examine specific differences between groups. A regression analysis will be conducted with appropriateness as the dependent variable and religious commitment as the independent variable. (p. 46)

OPEN SCIENCE AND PREREGISTRATION

The idea of open science has been increasing in popularity over the past several years. Open science encourages researchers to be up-front and public about their research methods and research hypotheses before they collect their data and to report and share their data, analyses, and conclusions (irrespective of whether the findings support the original hypotheses). The open science framework is a great step forward to increase the trustworthiness of findings within psychology, and we encourage students to get involved with this process.

There are different ways to preregister your study, but one of the most common is the Open Science Framework. (There are some other places to preregister studies that are more specific to the type of study conducted, such as ClinicalTrials.gov if you are conducting a clinical trial.) You can sign up for the Open Science Framework at osf.io. After you create an account, you can preregister your research study. You fill out several online forms that describe your study, including your hypotheses and analyses. Then, when you submit your paper for publication, you can provide a link to your preregistered study on the Open Science Framework website. By allowing readers to view your preregistered hypotheses and analyses, it gives more weight to your findings. Also, in some journals, you can apply for badges that indicate your study was preregistered.

In addition to preregistering your studies, some journals also have a process in which you can submit a registered report, which is a copy of your research study, hypotheses, and proposed analyses. If the registered report is accepted, the journal will guarantee you a publication, even if the findings do not support your hypotheses. The field of psychology, in general, is moving more in the direction of open science and preregistration. Thus, it is important to understand, and it is a good practice to get into the habit of preregistering your studies before collecting data.

GRADUATE MENTOR CORNER

As a mentor, you play an important role in helping students plan and write the method section for their research project. For example, it is important to think critically about the participants, procedure, and measures for the proposed study. Often, when you work with students, you are trying to strike a balance between conducting the best possible study and being realistic about conducting a study that is doable and practical, given your student's time constraints. Sometimes it is necessary to encourage a student to dial back an ambitious plan if you believe it may be difficult for the student to complete the study in a reasonable amount of time.

In helping students write the method section, it is helpful to give them clear examples and guides for how you would like the method section to be constructed. This chapter could be used as a potential guide, and you could also refer students to papers you have written or thesis or dissertation projects of older students you have mentored. For beginning students, it is helpful to have examples to work from. When students have clear examples and clear guidance for planning and writing their method section, it will help them learn the basics of scientific writing quicker, allowing you to focus your feedback on more complex research skills that require greater expertise and challenge.

UNDERGRADUATE MENTOR CORNER

We have covered most of the key aspects of methodology in other sections, so we focus this section on introducing students to open science. Depending on when you received your training and how strongly open science was prioritized in your program, you might range from complete novice to well-versed in its methods, values, and commitments. Each subsequent graduating class is learning that open science is now in the fabric of doing research. It is not an "add-on" but is as important as measure selection and sampling strategies. Many funding agencies require a commitment to and plan for open science practices as part of their grant process. To the extent that we introduce our students early to these processes and explain why we are doing it, we can increase the use and accessibility of open science practices for future scholars. Introduce them early, make it part of all your work, and embrace its benefits.

MOVING FORWARD

In this chapter, we drilled down into the details and talked about the steps of planning and writing your method section. Most graduate students will write this section before proposing the thesis or dissertation. Writing the method section can be exciting because it details what exactly you will do for your study and what you expect to find. In the next chapter, we talk about one of the most important milestones of the research process for graduate students: the proposal meeting.

13 PREPARING FOR THE PROPOSAL MEETING

Before we get into the nuts and bolts of this chapter, we note that it is specifically designed to help graduate students who must propose their thesis or dissertation in front of a faculty committee before progressing in their research. If this does not describe your situation, you can feel free to skip this chapter. Most graduate students, however, after finishing writing a literature review and method section, must propose their research project in front of a faculty committee before proceeding (e.g., collecting data). Thus, in this chapter, we first discuss the proposal meeting generally, including its purpose. Then, we get more specific and talk about some helpful steps for preparing for the proposal meeting.[1]

---

[1]After graduate students complete their independent research project, they generally must present the results of their research at a defense meeting. However, we did not include a separate chapter on the defense meeting in this book because many of the principles of preparing for the proposal meeting are similar to preparing for the defense meeting.

https://doi.org/10.1037/0000371-014
The Complete Researcher: A Practical Guide for Graduate Students and Early Career Professionals, by J. N. Hook, D. E. Davis, and D. R. Van Tongeren
Copyright © 2024 by the American Psychological Association. All rights reserved.

THE PROPOSAL MEETING

Before we get into the specifics of how to prepare for the proposal meeting, let us talk briefly about what the proposal meeting involves and why we do it. At its core, the proposal meeting is an opportunity for you to present your research proposal in front of a committee of faculty members. Although norms vary by department, you will often prepare a short presentation (i.e., 30–45 minutes) about your research project, including the background literature, hypotheses, and methods. Then, your faculty committee will have an opportunity to ask you questions about your proposed research project and give feedback and critiques.

There are several purposes of the proposal meeting. First, it is an opportunity for you to present your research. Presenting research is a common practice in the scientific community, and the proposal meeting gives you an opportunity to practice that skill in a formal way. Also, the proposal meeting allows you to showcase your research competence—both regarding your content area and methodology. Thus, for the graduate student, it is an important assessment of your level of competence. Finally, the proposal meeting is a chance for you to work collaboratively with your committee to design the best possible research project. Your committee will likely have questions or feedback that will allow you to sharpen your research project and avoid pitfalls you may not have been aware of. Keep in mind that their goal is to help you conduct the best research study feasible, and you will be evaluated on how well you carry out what you commit to doing in the proposal.

PREPARING FOR THE PROPOSAL MEETING

Now that we have discussed the proposal meeting in general, including its purposes, let us get more specific and talk about how to prepare for the proposal meeting. Before we get into this material, it is important to recognize that the norms for how proposal meetings are conducted vary by university and department. Thus, although we offer some general suggestions and thoughts here, it is critical to follow the norms and guidelines of your specific university and department. There are several steps to prepare for the proposal.

- **Learn the norms.** It is essential to have a good sense of the proposal meeting norms for your university and department. The details of the requirements of the proposal meeting should be outlined in the department handbook. Although many students do not read the handbook, it is useful to review the sections that describe the requirements for the proposal meeting. Also, your advisor and older graduate students will likely be helpful in educating you about the norms for how the proposal meeting should be run. The proposal meeting is not something to go into underprepared. It requires significant advanced planning and preparation. Understand what is required and adhere to the norms for your setting.

- **Choose your committee.** Your committee will often include your mentor (who usually chairs the committee), along with other faculty members. (The number of faculty members required varies by department, but it is usually about three to five.) Often the committee will mostly consist of faculty members in your department, although many departments allow (or even require) you to include a faculty member from outside your department. Choosing your committee is an important decision because they have quite a bit of power over your research progress. There are several things to consider when selecting your committee.
  - Does the potential committee member do research related to your topic? If so, they might be a valuable asset to help you design a stronger overall project.
  - Does the potential committee member have expertise in an area that will be helpful in your completion of the project (e.g., expertise in a certain statistical analysis you need to learn or methodological expertise in an approach you must learn and implement)?
  - Do you get along with the potential committee member? Do you feel as if they have your best interests in mind? Is the potential committee member supportive? This does not mean they will not give you constructive feedback or challenge you—rather, it means they value quality science and conveying feedback in a way that respects you as a person rather than being obstinate or antagonistic.
  - Does your mentor get along with the potential committee member? In a perfect world, politics should not matter, and although it is exceedingly rare, we have seen students find themselves in a difficult situation when committee members do not get along with each other. It is best to avoid that, so make sure to run your committee by your mentor and get their feedback.

- **Ask your committee members if they are willing to serve.** There is no one "right" way to ask potential committee members if they are willing to serve, but the following is one strategy that has worked well for us. First, email each committee member and ask if they would be willing to meet with you to discuss your project. Then, when you meet, briefly explain your research project and why you would like them to be on your committee. Finally, listen and respect their decision. If they say no, do not press. Sometimes faculty members are too busy and do not have the time to commit to your project. It is usually not a good idea to pressure someone into joining your committee.

- **Prepare your presentation.** The presentation is an important part of the proposal meeting, so it is good to spend time and prepare. We hesitate to get too detailed about the specifics of the presentation because norms vary according to the requirements of the department and the preferences of the advisor. For example, Josh has his students prepare a PowerPoint presentation of around 30 to 45 minutes, but other advisors have different preferences. When preparing the presentation, it is a good idea to introduce your topic and any terms the committee needs to know to understand your study and briefly review the background literature. Then, explain the methodology of your studies, your hypotheses, and your planned analyses. It is essential to practice your presentation. We recommend students practice their presentation several times and practice speaking out loud. (Speaking out loud is more helpful than simply running through the presentation in your head.) It can also be helpful to schedule a practice run in front of your mentor and other students in your lab. Ask your mentor if a lab meeting can be dedicated to this practice.

- **Schedule your presentation.** Again, norms vary by department, so check with the department handbook and your mentor to determine how long a block of time to schedule. Plan ahead; it can be difficult to get multiple faculty members to coordinate their schedules. You likely will need to work with your departmental administration to officially schedule a time and prepare any necessary forms. For example, many departments have an official form committee members must sign to indicate you passed the proposal.

- **Circulate your proposal document to the committee members in advance of your presentation.** The specific format of the proposal document varies according to your department requirements and mentor preferences, but the core parts of the document were covered in Chapter 10 ("Conducting a Literature Review") and Chapter 12 ("Planning the Method Section"). The time you need to give your committee to read the document also varies by department (often around 10 business days). Make sure to check on this and give your committee the required time to read and review your document. It can be nice to ask committee members how they would like the proposal document delivered—some may prefer email, whereas others may prefer a hard copy. Your department may also have guidelines for how the proposal document is circulated. When in doubt, follow the norms and guidelines of your department.

- **Present your proposal.** The presentation itself is often anxiety provoking for students. It is often difficult to completely ease this anxiety, but the following are some tips for helping the process to go smoothly.
  - Dress professionally.
  - Relax. You are an expert on this topic. You have been working on this project for a long time. This is your time to shine and explain to your committee what you have prepared. If you have tools and strategies to moderate anxiety (e.g., deep breathing, visualization, meditation), now is the time to use them. For some individuals, it is easier to shift their anxiety to excitement than to try to relax because anxiety and excitement are both high-arousal emotions (Brooks, 2014).
  - Be gracious when answering questions and discussing the project. Try to limit your defensiveness and embrace humility. Remember, the purpose of having committee members is so you can work together as a team to design the best project possible. For example, committee members may come up with ideas or problems you and your mentor have not considered. This is good. It is better to identify and fix problems now than to wait until after data have been collected and it is too late. Most suggestions will be relatively minor and easy to incorporate. Some committee members may have suggestions that will alter the nature of the project or add quite a bit to your workload. In this case, it is okay to discuss why you chose to design your study the way you did.

- **What happens next?** After you complete your presentation and answer questions from your committee, you will usually leave the room, and your committee will discuss your project. The main decision is whether to pass the research proposal. If you pass, the committee will often give you a list of changes they would like you to make before proceeding. Try not to get discouraged about needing to make changes to your project—this is a normal part of the process. It is like getting a "revise-and-resubmit" decision on a manuscript, and it is good news: The changes are part of the process of strengthening the project. Once you make the necessary changes, you can proceed with the next step of your research project. It is rare for students to fail outright, and policies vary by program, but some projects may require serious revisions, whereas others may only need minor tweaks.

PROPOSAL MEETING EXAMPLE

When Josh was getting ready to propose his thesis, he was nervous! It was his first time presenting his original ideas and research to someone other than his mentor, and he did not know how they would react. Josh checked in with his research mentor to discuss choosing his committee and selected two other faculty members with whom they both felt comfortable. Then Josh sent them his completed proposal draft and prepared his presentation. He was anxious on the day of the proposal meeting, but overall, it went mostly well. The committee had a few tough questions about his hypotheses and his plan for data analysis, and Josh realized he would need to brush up on his statistics knowledge before he was ready to defend his thesis. But at the end of the meeting, they approved his project, and Josh was on to the next step.

GRADUATE MENTOR CORNER

We have a few thoughts for mentors, especially if you are early in your career or entering a new department. First, norms for proposals can differ widely, so be sure to check the requirements in the department manual and ask others about norms and expectations. For example, how does the program tend to view the role of the mentor during the proposal meeting (e.g., how involved is the mentor, how much is it permissible for the mentor to help the student if they get stuck answering a question)? Are committee members willing to give heavy feedback on analyses at the proposal, or do they expect mainly to offer feedback at the defense?

Second, in working with the student to prepare for the proposal meeting, one of your roles is quality control. If you do a good job, then at the proposal, committee members will collaborate with the student to help create the best possible project. For example, we knew that if Ev (Josh and Donnie's mentor) or Jeff (Daryl's mentor) thought the proposal document was ready, we likely had already cleared the most rigorous review. Other committee members might have ideas that would help refine the manuscript, but we had high confidence we were ready if our mentor said we were ready. This helped reduce the stress of the process. We knew it was a collaborative process.

Third, set clear boundaries. Some students work to deadlines. Many programs have a hard deadline (e.g., to apply for an internship, the dissertation proposal must be completed by October 1). Still, students may work to the last minute, so you may have to set your own boundaries to avoid a last-minute fire drill. For example, some colleagues never plan proposal meetings over the summer. Some mentors will not allow students to schedule a proposal meeting unless a full draft of the proposal document is submitted within 2 months of the program deadlines. These kinds of clear expectations help students plan their writing process more effectively, rather than running into unknown limitations (e.g., it often takes several days to read a proposal document, and if a document requires multiple revisions, even a highly responsive mentor may have difficulty giving sufficient feedback with a short timeline).

UNDERGRADUATE MENTOR CORNER

Undergraduates can enjoy the fact that their graduation is not tied to completing a dissertation (although some may complete an undergraduate thesis). That said, we do suggest involving undergraduates right away in watching dissertation defenses or job talks. The more students hear professional talks during undergrad, the more comfortable they will be transitioning into the speaker role. In fact, in our labs, we often give students opportunities to present to the team or at national conferences. Although presentations are not incentivized as strongly as publications, they can play a powerful role in helping students feel integrated into the field, given the concrete and public opportunity to exchange ideas.

MOVING FORWARD

In this chapter, we discussed planning the proposal meeting. Although this is a relatively brief part of the research process, it can be one of the more anxiety-provoking steps because it is the first time you put your research ideas out there to some folks outside your mentor and lab. Ideally, it is a growth-inducing process that allows you to work as a team to design the best project possible. In the next chapter, we talk about what can be one of the more fun parts of the research process—collecting your data.

14 PLANNING FOR AND CONDUCTING DATA COLLECTION

After you pass your research proposal, it is time to collect your data. This is one of the more exciting parts of the research process. Unfortunately, it is also sometimes one of the more difficult and time-consuming parts. In your timeline, it is one of the hardest parts to accurately forecast. Part of the reason is that there are certain aspects of the data collection process that are not fully under your control (e.g., waiting for approval from the institutional review board [IRB], waiting for participants to sign up for your study). In this chapter, we discuss the data collection process in general and then walk through the main steps for collecting data.

THE DATA COLLECTION PROCESS

The data collection process is often an exciting time for researchers because the planning part of the study is mostly complete—you are now doing the work that will answer your research questions. The data collection process

---

https://doi.org/10.1037/0000371-015
The Complete Researcher: A Practical Guide for Graduate Students and Early Career Professionals, by J. N. Hook, D. E. Davis, and D. R. Van Tongeren
Copyright © 2024 by the American Psychological Association. All rights reserved.

often takes a different skill set than graduate students may be used to—completing a data collection effort usually requires a high degree of organizational and problem-solving skills. Several steps are necessary to complete the data collection process, including submitting your study proposal to the IRB at your university, preparing for data collection, and collecting your data.

SUBMITTING YOUR STUDY PROPOSAL TO THE IRB

Before you begin data collection, you must submit your study proposal to the IRB at your university. The IRB is an administrative body tasked with protecting human subjects involved in research and ensuring you conduct ethical research. The IRB at a university is usually composed mostly of faculty researchers as well as members who are not scientists and individuals from the community. The process for submitting your proposal to the IRB differs at different institutions, but it generally involves filling out an application that asks you to describe your research study in detail, including your plans to ensure confidentiality and protect your participants from harm. You also generally must submit copies of your questionnaire, experimental protocol, informed consent sheets, and plans for advertising your study. Because the processes for the IRB submission vary, ideally, your mentor or older graduate students should be able to help you through this process. Start early. Some IRBs can take several weeks to respond, and when they do, they often require revisions—which may take several weeks to be approved.

Some researchers express frustration with the IRB process because it can feel like an arduous process to get your study approved. However, the IRB is an important part of the research process because it is an independent assessor that ensures the researcher is protecting human participants. The field of psychology has a history of not always protecting human participants from harm (e.g., the Stanford prison experiment, the Milgram obedience studies), so it is important we take appropriate precautions when conducting research. Also, because we may not always recognize ethical problems in our own research studies, it is important to have an independent board evaluate our research plan.

Although a detailed discussion of how to conduct ethically responsible research is beyond the scope of this book, we encourage researchers to read the ethical principles for their profession (e.g., American Psychological Association, 2017). For example, the ethical principle of beneficence and nonmaleficence requires we do our best to provide benefit to and not harm the participants that engage in our research studies. Also, the principle of justice requires that the opportunity to participate in research and receive the benefits of research are available to all persons, irrespective of their backgrounds or identities. Finally, the principle of respect requires that research safeguards participants' rights to privacy, confidentiality, and self-determination (e.g., informed consent).

After you submit your study proposal, the IRB will either approve your project (which means you can get started) or come back with a list of changes they would like you to make. For example, they might ask you to alter a particular procedure for recruiting participants or change your informed consent document or process. When you respond to the requirements and submit your study proposal again, they will review it again and make a decision on your revised proposal. Do your best to respond to the changes requested by the IRB thoughtfully and respectfully. Eventually, when the study is approved, you can move on to the next step.

PREPARING FOR DATA COLLECTION

While your study is under review, we encourage you to start preparing for collecting data. The steps for preparing for data collection vary depending on your specific study, but the following covers some of the common things you may need to prepare for.

- With the creation of online data collection platforms such as Qualtrics and Survey Monkey in recent years, many researchers are collecting data online. There are some advantages to online data collection, such as higher levels of convenience for participants when completing your study. If your data will be collected online, you must type the surveys into your online survey platform.

- However, the data collection for many studies cannot be done online. For example, if your study involves an experimental protocol, or more intensive forms of data collection (e.g., drawing blood), you may need to collect your data in person (e.g., have participants come into the lab to complete your study). If your data will be collected in person, you must print copies of your questionnaires and consent forms and/or prepare the experimental materials or equipment.

- For many in-person data collection efforts, you will not be able to collect all of the data by yourself. You may need a team of people to help you. Many researchers work with undergraduate or graduate research assistants to help with collecting data. If this describes your situation, you must organize and meet with your research assistants to make sure your team is trained. It is a good idea to host several "run-throughs" to iron out the details of the data collection. It is also important to create a document that details the study procedures and protocols to ensure the study is run the same way for each participant. (The procedure and protocol of your study are planned ahead of time and approved by the IRB.)

COLLECTING YOUR DATA

Once you are ready to get started, the data collection process entails several steps. Again, the specifics will vary according to your study. But we discuss some aspects of data collection that are mostly consistent across studies. For example, you must schedule your participants. Depending on your study, this may happen automatically (e.g., a participant clicks on a link to complete your study online), or you may have to do it manually (e.g., schedule a participant by email or phone to come into the lab at a specific date and time to complete your study). Some universities use experiment management websites (e.g., Sona Systems) to help organize data collection scheduling. Also, you must oversee the data collection and compensation process for participants. Depending on the requirements of your university, you may need to follow certain protocols for compensation (e.g., track compensation, collect identifying information of participants).

Depending on your study and the type of sample, the data collection process could take a substantial amount of time. If you are collecting data from college students and have a convenient way to recruit participants, data collection could be done in a month. However, if your sample is more complex (e.g., recruiting community adults currently in therapy), data collection may take longer. It is important to consider the time data collection will take, given the timeline you are working with. Your mentor should help you come up with a reasonable plan for data collection, given your situation and timeline. One guideline is to plan for at least 150% of the time you originally anticipated. Data collection often goes slower (and sometimes much slower) than you thought it would. You do not want to find yourself rushing to meet a deadline.

EXAMPLE

When Donnie started at Virginia Commonwealth University, Ev put him in charge of data collection for a transition to parenthood study. Donnie planned on using these data for his dissertation. However, at a conference, another professor warned him that the data collection could take longer than expected. He was doubtful of the feedback, however, because he had a "perfect plan." He had a connection to get flyers into every doctor's office in the greater Richmond area. They had $350 to pay couples, so the plan seemed great.

Donnie was wrong. Eventually, he realized the only thing that worked to help with recruitment was visiting parenting classes at hospitals in person. The team got about one couple for every two classes. So, the data collection ended up taking several years. The lesson is clear. In research, things often take longer than expected. The data collection, in particular, can be the slowest part of the research project. The entire timeline depends on how long it takes to finish this step.

GRADUATE MENTOR CORNER

Most students have prior organizational skills that help them with the data collection phase (unless they are using an advanced data collection method, such as gathering biomarker data). Because of this, you can encourage students to draw on these skills to help organize a streamlined data collection process. Also, when collecting data, it can be helpful to remind students to "never do anything for a single purpose." Before our students spend a lot of time collecting data, we encourage them to think about how to make the best use of the data for more than one purpose. For example, they could add extra measures to give them another potential paper to write.

If a student is collecting data from a unique sample or using a method of data collection you are not familiar with, it can be helpful for the student to involve collaborators who have experience with the sample or approach they are planning to use so they do not have to recreate the wheel. Some samples or types of data collection (e.g., unique populations such as children or married couples, collecting physiological data) can be tricky unless one has expertise and experience in effectively collecting these types of data.

A final warning when advising students is to pay attention to data quality. Shirking, in which participants do not complete a research study honestly (e.g., answering each question with the same response or responding haphazardly), is often a major problem, especially in online studies. It is a good idea to have students include attention-check questions to catch people who are not completing the study honestly. For example, you may include certain questions that ensure participants are not completing the study haphazardly (e.g., "Please select 'strongly disagree' for this question"). Also, to help our student collect quality data, it can be helpful to include steps that may help reduce attrition (e.g., for a daily diary study or workbook study, we might have people come in person for instructions).

UNDERGRADUATE MENTOR CORNER

In terms of sheer hours, undergraduates often spend most of their research time collecting data (or entering it). In many ways, they are the hands, eyes, and ears of the data collection process. Because of this, Daryl usually spends several hours, spread over several days, training undergraduate students to run studies (e.g., how to meet with participants, the informed consent process, how to hand out questionnaires or lead the participant through an experiment, how to debrief participants and give compensation). Because data collection is so important, it is good to overprepare. For example, Daryl likes to discuss contingency plans, how to handle different situations that might arise, where to find the original documents to make copies, how to get a hold of him in case of an emergency, and how to cover unexpected absences or illness, so no participant is left waiting. Students have a lab manual with all the lab's procedures, and Daryl pairs more advanced students with newer students when launching a study to help with the training process. By the end of the process, students can usually write the method section without much effort because they lived it during the past semester.

MOVING FORWARD

In this chapter, we covered one of the more exciting parts of the research process—collecting data. We talked about submitting your proposal to the IRB and preparing and organizing your data collection process. Although the data collection process can be time-consuming, it can also be fun because you are getting the data that can answer your research question. You are one step closer to finishing your project. In the next chapter, we walk through the process of analyzing your data and writing the results section.

15 ANALYZING DATA AND WRITING YOUR RESULTS

After you finish collecting your data, it is time to analyze the data and write up your results section. This part of the process can be anxiety provoking, but it is not as intimidating as many of us make it out to be. In fact, it is often quite enjoyable to see if our predictions were right; did the data support our hypotheses? Analyzing your data involves three main steps: (a) data cleaning, (b) exploring descriptive information, and (c) analyzing your hypotheses. These steps correspond to the three main sections of your results section. We walk through each step in this chapter. The purpose of this chapter is to acculturate you to the general process of analyzing data and writing your results section, but there is no way we can cover the range of analytical skills needed for all areas of study. This is one of the steps where you will want to draw on the expertise available to you in your team and broader training environment. The cutting-edge approaches for data analysis advance quickly, so keeping up with publication norms in your area is essential for your project to have a strong chance at publication. In addition, although this is one way to structure the results section, your mentor may have different norms or suggestions for how they like it to be organized. Also, it is important to become familiar with the journal reporting standards

---

https://doi.org/10.1037/0000371-016
The Complete Researcher: A Practical Guide for Graduate Students and Early Career Professionals, by J. N. Hook, D. E. Davis, and D. R. Van Tongeren
Copyright © 2024 by the American Psychological Association. All rights reserved.

for your field to ensure your paper aligns with current best practices (e.g., Appelbaum et al., 2018; Levitt et al., 2018).

DATA CLEANING AND CHECKING ASSUMPTIONS

You can think of data cleaning as preparing your data or getting the data ready for analysis. You want to take a look at your data and make sure there are no mistakes. Also, there are certain assumptions your data should meet for your analyses to work correctly. You will check your data for these assumptions and fix any problems. During data cleaning, check for (a) data entry errors, (b) missing data, (c) outliers, and (d) normality.

First, check for data entry errors. Sometimes mistakes happen when entering data. We want to know if there are any big mistakes before we get started. It is important to check your descriptive statistics for all your main variables. Check your minimum and maximum values for each variable, and make sure they are within the correct range of your scale. For example, if your scale goes from 1 to 5, and someone has a score of 50, there was a data entry error. Make sure to fix any data entry errors before going on to the next step.

Second, check for missing data. Ideally, you will not have much missing data. But sometimes mistakes happen or participants do not fill out all the questionnaires. To check for missing data, first look at the total number of participants in your data set. Then, look at the descriptive statistics for each variable you plan to use in your analysis. See if you have any missing data. If you have missing data, talk to your mentor and decide on a plan to address it. One issue is whether the missing data are minimal (e.g., an item missing here or there) or widespread (e.g., missing data on many measures). If the missing data are minimal, you may want to work with the data you have (follow the publication norms in your area). If the missing data are widespread, sometimes it is necessary to drop cases from your data set.

Third, check for outliers. *Outliers* are extreme values (e.g., very high or very low). Outliers are problematic because they can have a large effect on your analyses—a stronger effect than one participant's score should have. One issue to consider with outliers is whether the score is a valid response. If you determine the response is not valid, you may want to remove the case from the analysis. If you determine that the response is valid (but just extreme), you could leave the outlier in or do something to reduce its impact on the analysis (e.g., winsorizing is a method that sets extreme outliers to a specific percentile of the data). If you are unfamiliar with best practices in your field for how to handle outliers, it is important to discuss these issues with your mentor or a statistics consultant.

Finally, check for normality. *Normality* refers to the distribution of your variables. When your variables are normally distributed, it means most participants have scores around the mean, and fewer participants have scores higher or lower than the mean. In terms of a picture, your distribution will look like a nice bell-shaped curve. There are two main ways you could have problems with normality. *Skewness* means most of the participants have scores bunched up on either the low or high end of the scale, and there is a "tail" of scores to the left or right. *Kurtosis* means the distribution is either flatter or more peaked than it should be. In regression, violations of the assumption of normality can cause problems for your analysis. One option for correcting normality is to transform the nonnormal variables (e.g., taking the square root of all scores on a variable and analyzing that transformed variable). However, there might be situations when we would not expect data to be normally distributed. For example, if a treatment effect is present, we might anticipate a bimodal distribution. Thus, conversations around normality are context dependent and require knowledge regarding the nuance of the phenomenon under investigation and the methodology employed. As you develop more sophisticated statistical skills, there are more options for using analyses that are more flexible at handling nonnormal data. Thus, if you run into problems with normality, it is a good idea to consult with your mentor and research team to decide the best way to proceed.

EXPLORING DESCRIPTIVE INFORMATION

In your research project, after you clean your data and check your assumptions, it is often a good idea to explore the descriptive information for your variables and include a table that presents the descriptive information for your study. There are three main types of descriptive information that you will explore and report:

- **mean for each variable:** This is the average score across all participants.

- **standard deviation for each variable:** This refers to how spread out the scores are. In other words, are scores bunched up tightly around the mean (low standard deviation), or are they more spread out across the possible range of scores (high standard deviation)?

- **correlations between all variables:** This refers to the relationships between variables. In other words, are higher scores on one variable

TABLE 15.1. Intercorrelations of the Cultural Humility Scale With Therapy Variables

	M	SD	1	2	3	4	5
1. CHS Total	42.99	8.34	—				
2. CHS Positive	27.58	5.36	.84*	—			
3. CHS Negative	15.42	4.83	.80*	.34*	—		
4. PEI	92.30	18.66	.57*	.73*	.17	—	
5. WAI-SF	60.47	13.17	.73*	.76*	.41*	.77*	—

Note. CHS = Cultural Humility Scale; PEI = Patient's Estimate of Improvement; WAI-SF = Working Alliance Inventory, short form. The CHS Negative subscale is reverse coded such that higher scores indicate higher cultural humility. From "Cultural Humility: Measuring Openness to Culturally Diverse Clients," by J. N. Hook, D. E. Davis, J. Owen, E. L. Worthington Jr., and S. O. Utsey, 2013, *Journal of Counseling Psychology, 60*(3), p. 360 (https://doi.org/10.1037/a0032595). Copyright 2013 by the American Psychological Association.
*p < .001.

associated with higher or lower scores on another variable? The following are a few important points about correlations:

- Correlations can range from –1 to 1.
- A positive correlation between two variables (i.e., above 0) means that high scores on one variable are associated with high scores on the second variable. A negative correlation between two variables (i.e., below 0) means that high scores on one variable are associated with low scores on the second variable. A correlation of 0 means there is no relationship between the two variables.
- The magnitude of the correlation represents the strength of the relationship. Correlations closer to 0 represent weaker relationships. Correlations closer to –1 or 1 represent stronger relationships. One guideline is that correlations of around .10 (or –.10) are considered small, correlations of around .30 (or –.30) are considered medium, and correlations of around .50 (or –.50) or above are considered strong (Cohen, 1988).

A descriptive information example is presented in Table 15.1.

ANALYZING YOUR HYPOTHESES

This section is the main part of your results section. In this step, you will analyze each of your hypotheses and present the results of your analyses. It is beyond the scope of this book to describe how to conduct specific statistical analyses; ideally, your mentor will be able to help you with your analyses. (If you are looking for an easy-to-understand resource to help run some of the most common statistical analyses, we recommend the series of statistics books by Andy Field, 2018). When you describe each hypothesis in your results section, you will have a few main parts:

- Restate the hypothesis (e.g., "We hypothesized that client perceptions of a therapist's cultural humility would be positively associated with perceived improvement in therapy, and this relationship would be mediated by working alliance").
- Describe the analysis you used to test the hypothesis (e.g., "To test whether the mediated effect of cultural humility on improvement through working alliance was significant, we used the bootstrapping procedure outlined by Preacher and Hayes [2008]").
- Say in words whether the hypothesis was supported (e.g., "This hypothesis was supported").
- Provide the statistics (e.g., "Using a bias-corrected bootstrapping procedure based on 5,000 resamples, controlling for beginning severity and gender, we found that the indirect effect of cultural humility on improvement through working alliance was significant (est. = 1.17, SE = .21, 95% CI [.79, 1.64])").

GRADUATE MENTOR CORNER

We have a few suggestions for helping students learn to analyze their data and write up their results. First, we keep articles, guides, and examples handy for how to run and write up various statistical analyses that students can use as a model. Ideally, when a student is working on learning a particular analysis, we send them a write-up using the same or a similar analysis so that they can borrow from the organization or the model write-up. Also, make sure your students understand parallel structure for how to organize a results section. For example, for each hypothesis, restate the hypothesis, describe the analysis used, give the statistics, and then explain to a layperson what the results mean.

Consistent with the deliberate practice theme in this book, your most important role when assisting students with analyzing data and writing up results is to give high-quality feedback. Perhaps in some fields, "those who cannot do, teach," but this does not work for psychology professors. Our expertise is a limiting factor in our ability to help others grow. If we do not know what we are doing, we will not be able to give feedback to sharpen our students' work. Our skill (or those we can tap into for help) is a limiting factor for how much we can help our students.

Similarly, to help students progress in their abilities to analyze data and write up their results, encourage them to invest heavily in improving their methodological skills. Building an area of methodological expertise is a great way to contribute to a larger team. For example, it may take decades to rise to the top of a field in terms of conceptual innovation, but within a year or two, students may teach themselves a new statistical approach that is in high demand. Then, they can partner with other conceptual experts, which will accelerate their learning and the quality of the teams they join. The benefits compound quickly (e.g., stronger teams, quicker learning, better projects).

UNDERGRADUATE MENTOR CORNER

Undergraduates often feel anxious or unprepared to tackle data analysis and results sections. In fact, many will seek guidance from their mentors when analyzing their data and writing this part of the manuscript. Daryl often finds that most students require collaborative data analysis—working together with the statistical software to conduct the statistical tests, interpret them, and write the results. First, Daryl usually sets aside large blocks of time with his students to work through analyses (e.g., a minimum of an hour in a computer lab). Second, they go over the results and output several times and revisit them often. Daryl encourages his students to mark up the output in ways that help them understand what the results mean and which numbers are necessary to report in the results section. Third, Daryl often provides his students with templates for reporting different results (e.g., correlations, t tests, ANOVAs) so they can see how it looks in print. He provides plenty of structure and encourages them to ask for help if they do not understand; this is never a place to guess or assume what something means. And whenever possible, he tries to make this part fun. After all, given what we know about associative learning, we want to build positive associations with data analysis. Pizza can help.

MOVING FORWARD

In this chapter, we walked through analyzing data and writing up the results section of your paper, including data cleaning, exploring descriptive information, and analyzing your hypotheses. At this point, we are almost done with writing up our research project. In the next chapter, we walk through the final main part of the write-up—the discussion section.

16 CRAFTING THE DISCUSSION

After you finish the results section of your research project, it is time to think about and write the discussion section. The discussion section is the end of your research project. This is where you summarize your findings, integrate your work with broader research, and offer final thoughts about what you found in your study. You also give the implications of your findings—in other words, what do your findings mean? You also can link what you found to past theory or research and describe how your study fits in with the existing literature on your topic. Finally, you give the limitations of your study, as well as areas for future research. There are five main parts of the discussion section, which we discuss in detail next. As with the other chapters in this book, this is one framework for organizing your discussion section, and the style and content of your discussion will depend on your method, the results, and the purpose of your paper. Your mentor may have different preferences. When in doubt, as we have mentioned before, follow the preferences of your mentor.

---

https://doi.org/10.1037/0000371-017
The Complete Researcher: A Practical Guide for Graduate Students and Early Career Professionals, by J. N. Hook, D. E. Davis, and D. R. Van Tongeren
Copyright © 2024 by the American Psychological Association. All rights reserved.

PART 1: REVIEW YOUR MAIN FINDINGS

In the first section of the discussion, review the main findings of your research study. In other words, what were your most important findings? What is the take-home message for your study? Importantly, in this section, you should not just repeat what you said in the results section. Instead, summarize your most important findings plainly and clearly, and then link what you found to past theory or research. *Past theory* refers to the things scientists have thought about or discussed regarding your topic of study, whereas *past research* refers to previous empirical findings about your topic. Remember in the literature review how you discussed the theory that led to your study? Now that you are finished with the study and have presented your results, think about whether your findings are consistent with the theory or whether there are differences. Also, think about whether your findings are consistent with what has been found in previous research or whether there are differences. Finally, you can begin to talk about the implications of your findings. What do your findings mean? Why are they important?

Sometimes it can be challenging to figure out the most important findings of your study or think about its key implications. As you develop as a researcher and become more familiar with your topic area, you will likely have an easier time determining the most important findings from your study. As a beginning researcher, however, the critical findings are often (a) your hypotheses (whether supported or not), (b) consistent effects or associations, (c) key moderators or mediators, and (d) anything surprising or unexpected. It can also be helpful to talk over your findings with your mentor or fellow graduate students. They may have feedback or ideas about possible implications for your study. This is a great time to use your mentor and lab team members to help come up with additional foci for this section.

PART 2: LIMITATIONS OF YOUR STUDY

In the second section of the discussion, talk about the limitations of your study. Every study has strengths and weaknesses. It is important to be straightforward and honest about the limitations of your study. How do you figure out what its limitations are? Think about the methodology (e.g., research design, participants, measures, procedure, analyses):

- What was the research design of your study? If it was cross-sectional, for example, meaning all your measures were given at one time, this is a limitation because you cannot make causal inferences about the relationships between your variables. Also, if your study was cross-sectional, you cannot explore how the variables in your study changed over time.

- Who were the participants in your study? Every sample has limitations. If you used a sample of college students, for example, your findings might not generalize to children or older adults. If you used a sample of mostly White participants, your findings might not generalize to racial or ethnic minority participants. If you sampled from only one country or culture, your findings may not generalize to other cultural settings.
- What measures did you use? For example, did you use all self-report measures? If so, that might be a limitation because self-report measures are prone to certain response biases, such as socially desirable responding. Did the measures you use have prior evidence for reliability and validity in your type of sample? If not, discuss that as a limitation.
- Were there any limitations with the procedures? For example, think about the process of recruiting participants or the activities participants completed once they were enrolled in your study. Did any issues or problems come up that should be acknowledged? For example, did several participants drop out of the study or guess the hypothesis?

In this part of the discussion section, in addition to discussing the limitations, some researchers like to discuss the strengths of the study as well. (Most researchers discuss the strengths before they discuss the limitations.) It is not essential to discuss the study's strengths. Many researchers prefer to let the strengths of the study speak for themselves and do not feel a need to highlight them here in the discussion section.

PART 3: AREAS FOR FUTURE RESEARCH

In the third section of the discussion, it can be helpful to discuss areas for future research. Your study represents one piece of the puzzle on your topic. Research progresses step by step as more studies accumulate. There is probably much more research that could be done on your topic, and in this section of the discussion, you get to think about what some of these next steps might be. In other words, what new areas would be interesting to explore? What future study could address the limitations of your study to advance research substantively? One way to jump-start your thinking about areas for future research is to look at the limitations you noted for your study. You might be able to think about a direction for future research that could shore up some of the limitations you mentioned. For example, if your study was cross-sectional, one direction for future research might be to explore your topic using a longitudinal study, or you may want to conduct an experiment. If you used a sample of college students, it might be important to examine your variables using a sample of older adults. If you used only self-report measures, it might be important to use behavioral measures in future research. And so on.

In addition to thinking about how to shore up the methodological limitations of your study, this is your time to brainstorm and think about what might be interesting to explore in the future. If you could map out the next 5 years of research on your topic, what might you want to know? What important research questions would you like to explore? What lingering questions do you still have about your topic? This is another great place to tap into the expertise of your mentor or students in your lab to help brainstorm potential next steps.

PART 4: IMPLICATIONS

In the fourth section of your discussion, discuss the implications or practical applications of your research study. In other words, how might your research be helpful or make a difference for individuals and groups? For example, if your research project was related to counseling, you might want to have a section that discusses the implications of your study for counseling. In other words, how might your findings help counselors do a better job with their clients? There may be other things you could write about in this section, depending on your topic. For example, if your research project was focused on religion and spirituality, you might have a section discussing the implications of your study for pastors or clergy. Or if your research was related to education or classroom instruction, you might have a section discussing the implications of your study for instructors. Like other sections of the discussion, this is a good place to brainstorm ideas with your mentor or other graduate students.

PART 5: CONCLUSION

We generally include a final paragraph that wraps up the entire paper. In this final paragraph, you can briefly summarize the main topic or problem your study was designed to address, the main findings, and why your study was important or makes a difference.

GRADUATE MENTOR CORNER

If mentors put in strong work on earlier parts of a paper, the discussion section becomes a natural extension of all the prior hard work. If your student wrote a strong literature review, writing this section of their paper will be much easier. They have already done much of the reading and thinking. Now, they are contextualizing their perspective in a particular study. They will not have to spend a lot of time synthesizing or getting familiar with the state of the field because they already did that with the literature review. The discussion section is one of those parts of the paper that gets easier to write as students gain expertise.

This is part of the reason it is difficult to write a dissertation under a tight deadline. Often students have not benefited from the more gradual process of sharpening their skills, both statistically and conceptually. We try to give lots of warnings to students hoping to streamline the time they spend on research. We encourage students to invest early and often in their research training because everything takes longer than expected. The best way to streamline work on a dissertation is to prioritize the project and make consistent progress over time. Working with a tight deadline will likely mean unpredictable setbacks.

We also suggest keeping a personal file of discussion sections organized according to your style, so you can give students a model to work from. (Also, make sure students consider an example from the target outlet. This can save a lot of revision time because some outlets have unique preferences for their sections.) Sometimes the easiest way to teach something is to give someone a strong example they can use as a template. We also involve other doctoral students in the revision process. Students will teach each other, learning from each other's strengths and experience.

UNDERGRADUATE MENTOR CORNER

We have found that undergraduate students often find more freedom in the discussion section than other parts of the paper. They see it as a place to plainly state the main findings from the results, discuss whether the hypotheses were supported, and make suggestions for future work. And they can usually readily identify limitations and ideas for improvement. However, they frequently have difficulty understanding how the current work relates to other theories or what the findings might mean for the larger field. This typically requires more mentorship and is a useful way to teach effective ways to weave a study into the larger conceptual and theoretical tapestry of the research corpus. Having a clear outline and probably taking the lead on writing that dimension of the paper will likely lead to greater success.

MOVING FORWARD

In this chapter, we talked about how to write your discussion section—the final main section of your paper. The discussion is where you can expand on your study, its place in the relevant literature, what the findings mean, and why they are important. In the next chapter, we briefly cover one last piece of the paper you need to complete—writing the abstract.

17
WRITING THE ABSTRACT

After you have completed and written all the main sections of your research project, you need to write your abstract. The abstract is a brief paragraph that describes the main parts of your study. It is usually around 150 words, although it is important to check the requirements of your institution (when submitting your thesis or dissertation document) or the journal (if you are submitting your research project as a journal article) because different outlets have different requirements.

The process of writing the abstract is sometimes overlooked by researchers because it does not seem difficult and can often be drafted quickly. However, it is an important part of your research project, so it is a good idea to spend some time and energy on this step. The abstract is important because it is accessible to everyone (even before a person decides to download and read your paper). Because of this, many people will read the abstract to decide whether to read the entire article. The abstract is like a movie preview designed to encourage you to see the full-length feature. If you want people to take the time and energy to read your research paper, it is important to make sure the abstract is well written and covers the most important points of your paper in a succinct manner.

---

https://doi.org/10.1037/0000371-018
The Complete Researcher: A Practical Guide for Graduate Students and Early Career Professionals, by J. N. Hook, D. E. Davis, and D. R. Van Tongeren
Copyright © 2024 by the American Psychological Association. All rights reserved.

What type of information is included in the abstract? Again, the specific requirements vary by journal, but the following are some guidelines for the key kinds of information that are generally included in the abstract:

- First, list the overall goal or topic of the study. We find it helpful to "grab" the reader by giving a general description of the study and why it is important at the beginning of the abstract. A statement of the relevance or importance of this topic is a great place to begin. Similarly, if your findings are counterintuitive, immediately setting up that logic can be helpful.
- Second, give a brief overview of the method. Briefly describe the participants, procedure, and measures of the study. In other words, who completed the study, and what did they do?
- Third, give a brief overview of the results. What were the most important findings from your study?
- Fourth, give a brief overview of the discussion. What was the main conclusion of your paper? What are some of the key implications of your study?
- Finally, note how many words the abstract has. Journals have different word limits for abstracts, so it is important to check with the journal for their specific requirements.

For most journals, all the information in the abstract is written in one paragraph. However, some journals require structured abstracts, in which the parts are divided into sections (e.g., introduction, method, results, discussion). Again, make sure you follow the abstract-formatting requirements for the journal you are submitting to.

How can we write a strong abstract that communicates the main points of our research study in a straightforward yet engaging manner? We have a few recommendations for writing strong abstracts. First, review the requirements for abstracts for the specific outlet you are preparing your manuscript for. If a journal has specific requirements for the content and formatting of the abstract (and many do), you want to follow these guidelines exactly. Second, keep the focus of your abstract on the method and results of your study. This is the part of your paper readers are often most interested in. In other words, what did your participants do, and what were your main findings? You have limited space when writing the abstract, so focus on the main findings. Finally, although there is not a lot of room to be creative when writing the abstract, the first couple sentences can be one place where you can grab the reader by introducing the main topic of your study in an interesting way. As with the other parts of your manuscript, get feedback from your mentor and fellow graduate students in your lab when writing your abstract.

In addition to writing the abstract, some journals require a public significance statement or clinical impact statement. This is a brief statement (one to two sentences) that describes the key finding or implication of your study. Writing this statement can be challenging because you are being asked to boil down an entire paper to a brief statement. It can be helpful to brainstorm how the findings from your study could have an impact on the general population or clinicians. In the following section, we present two examples of abstracts and one example of a clinical impact statement from previously published papers.

ABSTRACT EXAMPLE 1 (HOOK ET AL., 2013)

> Building on recent theory stressing multicultural orientation, as well as the development of virtues and dispositions associated with multicultural values, we introduce the construct of cultural humility, defined as having an interpersonal stance that is other-oriented rather than self-focused, characterized by respect and lack of superiority toward an individual's cultural background and experience. In 4 studies, we provide evidence for the estimated reliability and construct validity of a client-rated measure of a therapist's cultural humility, and we demonstrate that client perceptions of their therapist's cultural humility are positively associated with developing a strong working alliance. Furthermore, client perceptions of their therapist's cultural humility were positively associated with improvement in therapy, and this relationship was mediated by a strong working alliance. We consider implications for research, practice, and training. (128 words)

ABSTRACT EXAMPLE 2 (HOOK ET AL., 2022)

> It is important for psychologists to engage cultural differences in an effective manner. Thus, it is critical to examine personal characteristics that might help psychologists develop cultural competence. The current article reviewed empirical studies that examined the relationship between differentiation of self and cultural competence. Differentiation of self refers to the ability to self-define (i.e., identify and articulate one's beliefs, values, and goals) while remaining emotionally connected to others who may be different. Interpersonally, individuals with high differentiation of self are able to balance autonomy and connectedness. Eight studies were reviewed; most studies reported a positive relationship between differentiation of self and cultural competence. Effect sizes ranged from small to medium. Potential moderators included (a) different components of differentiation of self, (b) different ways that cultural

competence is assessed, and (c) demographic characteristics of participants. We conclude by discussing limitations, areas for future research, and implications for clinical practice. (150 words)

CLINICAL IMPACT STATEMENT EXAMPLE (HOOK ET AL., 2022)

This literature review found that differentiation of self (i.e., being able to identify and articulate one's own beliefs, values, and goals while remaining emotionally connected to those who may be different) may be an important characteristic for psychologists who want to develop multicultural competence. (p. 1)

GRADUATE MENTOR CORNER

We often encourage students to complete the abstract last, along with other details about the paper, such as the title page and references. Compared with the other sections of the research project, students do not find writing the abstract too difficult, and they can usually write a first draft without too much trouble. That said, it can sometimes be challenging for students to decide how to narrow down the main points of their study (which might be quite extensive) into a single paragraph (in the case of the abstract) or a sentence or two (in the case of the public significance statement). It can be helpful to brainstorm with students and try to home in on the most important findings of the study. Like the other sections of the paper, it can be helpful to give students examples of abstracts you have written, so they have a clear model and example to work from.

UNDERGRADUATE MENTOR CORNER

Our institutional policies often reward verbosity and repetition. We often set minimum page requirements for assignments, leading students to elongate their narratives and find ways to bloat their writing. They assume writing well means being long-winded. However, in scientific writing, brevity is preferable. It is challenging to write concisely, so many students struggle to summarize an entire paper in less than 200 words for the abstract. Here is where some of the best pedagogy regarding writing occurs—helping students identify the critical elements of a paper and communicate them clearly and directly. Often the abstract and introductory paragraph of a paper are revised and rewritten numerous times to achieve the desired effect. From what we know about the primacy effect, it is important to make that first impression memorable.

MOVING FORWARD

In this chapter, we covered how to write the abstract of your paper. The abstract is a succinct, paragraph-length description of all the main parts of your study. It is important to capture all the important elements of your paper because readers will often briefly look over the abstract before deciding whether to read an entire paper. Once you finish writing your abstract, you are pretty much done with all the sections of your research project—congratulations! In the next chapter, we walk through the process of presenting your research at a conference. This is a great opportunity to get your research out there to others who might be interested in it, as well as practice your public speaking skills.

18 MAKING A CONFERENCE PRESENTATION

In this chapter, we talk about the process of presenting your research project at a conference. An academic conference is a professional meeting for researchers. (We share some examples of different types of conferences in the next section.) Everyone gets together—usually at a convention center or big hotel—and there is a schedule for when various researchers give talks about their latest research (usually lasting an hour but sometimes more and sometimes less). When you attend a conference, you can listen to talks on topics that interest you presented by the leading researchers in your field. You also have the opportunity to network and meet people who are doing work that interests you. Finally, you can present your own research, which is the focus of this chapter.

Before we get into the specifics of making a conference presentation, let us discuss why it is important to present your research at conferences. One reason is that it enables you to disseminate your work more broadly to other researchers. Usually, conference presentations focus on recent work that is not yet published. So, a conference will include cutting-edge research in your field. By presenting your research, you get the word out about your work early. You might be able to make connections and meet people interested in

---

https://doi.org/10.1037/0000371-019
The Complete Researcher: A Practical Guide for Graduate Students and Early Career Professionals, by J. N. Hook, D. E. Davis, and D. R. Van Tongeren
Copyright © 2024 by the American Psychological Association. All rights reserved.

your work. The second reason is more practical. Presenting your research at conferences is an expected part of the profession. Being active in presenting your research at conferences looks good on your curriculum vitae (CV) and can help you get a job. If you do not have any conference presentations on your CV, search committees will take notice because it is an important part of the profession. Let us explore some of the steps for presenting your research at a conference. Specifically, we walk through choosing a conference, submitting a proposal, preparing for the presentation, and networking.

CHOOSING A CONFERENCE

The first step is to choose a conference at which you would like to present. Conference announcements are common across listservs. With so many possibilities, how do you choose the conference that is right for you? Let us talk about the different types of conferences. First, there are large disciplinary conferences. A good example is the American Psychological Association (APA) annual convention. These are large meetings that draw lots of people from all subfields of psychology. The benefit of a big, general conference like APA is that most people in the field attend a conference like this, so there are plenty of networking opportunities. The drawback of this type of conference is that it is so huge it can be easy to get lost in the crowd. It can also be a bit overwhelming to navigate as a graduate student. And it can be expensive if the location is far away.

There are also several smaller conferences. Some of these smaller conferences are general in topic but regional. For example, Josh's students sometimes attend the Texas Psychological Association conference or the Southwest Psychological Association conference. These conferences are smaller. There are not as many programming sessions as at the APA conference, for example, but the meetings are often cheaper to get to and easier to navigate. There are also smaller conferences based on topic area. For example, every few years, APA Division 17 (Society of Counseling Psychology) organizes a conference focused on counseling psychology. APA Division 36 (Society for the Psychology of Religion and Spirituality) also organizes a conference focused on religion and spirituality. These conferences can be good to attend because they are more focused on your area of interest and are smaller and easier to navigate.

We recommend attending a mix of big and small conferences. If you are able to go, the APA annual convention is great for getting your research more broadly disseminated and networking because many people attend this conference. We are also aware that financial resources may play a role in your decision. If money is a limitation, attending a smaller regional conference is a good option. Your department or college may have travel funds available or travel grants for which you can apply. Your mentor may have some grant funds or other sources of support available. It is helpful to be honest with your mentor about this and look for possible sources of funding. And, if you are able, it is a good idea to attend conferences focused on your specific topic area because you will likely be more interested in the presentations, and it will provide a great chance to network with folks doing similar work to you. It is impossible to attend every conference, but many academics average between two and three per year (if it is financially viable).

SUBMITTING A PRESENTATION PROPOSAL

Submitting a proposal to present your research at a conference is relatively simple, but it can be confusing if it is your first time. The main thing you need to prepare is an abstract—a brief (usually 150–300 words) description of the presentation you want to make. In Chapter 17, we talked about how to write the abstract for your research project. The abstract for your conference presentation will be similar, although you may need to adjust it somewhat because your conference presentation may be more specific than your research project. We talk about this in more detail in the following chapter, but the thesis or dissertation research project is often expansive, with many different research questions and hypotheses. Because you have limited time when presenting at a conference, you may want to focus on one or two main research questions and hypotheses. The decision about what to focus on is up to you, but your mentor will be able to help you with this process. That said, the process for writing the abstract for a conference presentation proposal is similar to writing the abstract for your research project. The following are the main parts of the abstract:

- First, list the overall goal or topic of the study.
- Second, give a brief overview of the method. Briefly describe the participants, procedure, and measures of the study.
- Third, give a brief overview of the results. What were the most important findings from your study?
- Fourth, give a brief overview of the discussion. What was the main conclusion of your study?

Depending on the conference, there may be other smaller parts of the submission you need to prepare. Most of these sections are relatively simple and probably do not need a lot of explanation. For example, you need to have a title for your presentation. You may need to select a general category under which your presentation will fall. For example, when submitting a conference proposal to APA, you need to select a division for your conference presentation. You may need to write a few learning objectives for your conference presentation—in other words, what will your attendees learn from your presentation? You may also need to decide whether to present your research project as a paper or poster. A paper involves presenting your research project in front of an audience. A poster involves creating a poster (like the science fair you did in elementary school but more sophisticated), standing by your poster, and discussing the research project with people who walk by.

PRESENTATION PROPOSAL EXAMPLE

To give you an idea of what an abstract for a conference presentation might look like, the following is an example of a proposal abstract that Josh submitted to the APA conference a few years ago:

> In recent years, promoting multicultural competence has been an important goal in the field of counseling psychology. Although the multicultural competence movement has historically focused on issues related to race and ethnicity, the scope has broadened in recent years to include other important aspects of identity, including one's religious affiliation. Recently, cultural humility was introduced as an important aspect of multicultural competence. Cultural humility involves overcoming the natural tendency to view one's own beliefs, values, and worldview as superior, and instead being open to the beliefs, values, and worldview of the client. Research has shown that cultural humility is an important factor in developing a strong working alliance with clients, which in turn is related to better outcomes in therapy. In the present study, we present data from 45 clients who identified their religion/spirituality as the most salient aspect to their cultural identity. Cultural humility was positively associated with therapy outcomes; however, this effect was moderated by the client's religious commitment. The relationship between cultural humility and outcomes was positive for clients with high levels of religious commitment but was not significant for clients with low levels of religious commitment. We conclude by providing implications for research, training, and practice with religious/spiritual clients. (Hook et al., 2014)

PREPARING FOR THE PAPER PRESENTATION

After you submit your conference presentation proposal, you have to wait to see if it gets accepted. If it does not, do not despair; it is notoriously difficult to get paper presentations and symposia (i.e., when multiple presenters share a time slot and present papers on a similar topic) accepted, and rejection rates can be high. Paper presentations and symposia are more challenging to get accepted than poster presentations. If your proposal is rejected, you will need to talk with your mentor about whether it is still a good idea to attend the conference. Ideally, you will present research at conferences you attend, but there are other reasons to attend, such as networking or learning about new research in your area. If your proposal is accepted, the next step is to prepare for your paper presentation. You will often prepare a PowerPoint presentation that covers the main parts of your research study (i.e., introduction, method, results, discussion). The following are a few tips that have been helpful for us when preparing for a conference paper presentation. As with many of the chapters in this section of the book, these are some helpful tips that have worked well for us and our students, but they are not rigid rules. Your mentor may have different preferences, and you may develop preferences yourself as you develop and grow as a researcher.

- Do not make your slides too busy. Putting too much information on your slides can distract your audience because they are more focused on reading the slides than listening to your talk. It is better to make your slides briefer and use them as jumping-off points for your talk.
- It can be helpful to start your presentation with a "hook" to get your audience invested in your topic. Telling a story or inviting your audience to think about a personal experience related to your topic are great ways of doing this. Why is your topic important? Why should the audience care? Get their attention before diving into the specifics of your study.
- Practice your conference presentation several times before the real thing. We recommend going through the entire talk out loud. (This is a better way to prepare than simply talking through the presentation in your head.) Practice giving the talk to family, friends, or your research lab. This is also important because you want to time the talk well. If you have too much information and feel like you are rushing, cut down on the number of slides and material you are planning to present.
- Scout out your room ahead of time to make sure you know where to go. Make sure all your technology is in working order. If you have to provide a projector, make sure you have one. If you have to bring connections and adapters for your computer, make sure you have those. It is best to get all those details out of the way ahead of time (e.g., at least the day before your presentation).
- Bring handouts of your slides to give the audience. This is helpful so they can listen to your talk rather than furiously scribbling down the information on your slides.
- Dress professionally. It is better to overdress than underdress.
- It is normal to be nervous about giving a presentation, especially if you have not done much public speaking before. The more you do it, the more

comfortable you will feel. But at first, you just have to do the presentation anyway, even if you feel nervous. One tip based on the research from psychologist Alison Brooks (2014) is to tap into your excitement rather than trying to calm down. Excitement is a high-energy emotion like anxiety, so it is easier to shift between these two emotional experiences. You are ready and prepared to give this talk; try to have fun with it.

PREPARING FOR THE POSTER PRESENTATION

Many beginning graduate students and undergraduate students will start their presentation experience by presenting a poster. There are a couple of reasons for this. There is usually room for more posters in a conference schedule, so posters are generally easier to get accepted than paper presentations. Also, posters are often less anxiety provoking for students than getting in front of an audience to give a talk, so posters can be a helpful stepping-stone when getting experience presenting your research.

There are two main parts to preparing for a poster presentation: (a) creating the poster and (b) presenting the poster at the conference. The following are some helpful tips and guidelines for creating the poster:

- The poster will generally include the main parts of the paper: (a) abstract, (b) introduction, (c) method, (d) results, and (e) discussion.
- It can be helpful to work from a model when creating a poster for the first time. See if your mentor can share a few examples of posters they have created.
- Less is more. As in preparing slides for a PowerPoint presentation, try not to make your poster too busy. Think of the poster as a jumping-off point for talking about the details of the study. We usually recommend students think of bullet points rather than paragraphs.
- Print your poster ahead of time. Make sure you know how long it takes to print your poster so you do not run into problems near the deadline when you have to leave for the conference.

The following are some helpful tips and guidelines for presenting the poster at the conference:

- Print out copies of the poster, so conference attendees have something to take with them that summarizes the main points of information about the poster.

- As when you are giving a paper presentation, scout out the room, and make sure you know where you are going ahead of time.
- Prepare a 2- to 3-minute summary presentation of the poster and the study you completed. Practice this summary presentation ahead of time so it is smooth. When someone walks by and starts to look at your poster, engage with them. Ask them, "Would you like to hear what we did?" If they say yes, give your 2- to 3-minute summary presentation. This is a good way to begin a dialogue about your project.
- Presenting a poster is a good way to connect with other researchers interested in the same topics as you. This can be a great way to network and find future collaborators.

NETWORKING

Conferences are one of the best ways to connect with other researchers in your area. When you give a conference presentation, people will likely want to meet you and ask questions. Often these individuals are interested in your research area or may even be doing research connected to your topic. Similarly, when you attend a conference, there may be people you hear speak whom you would like to connect with.

Networking is one of the biggest benefits of attending conferences. Take advantage of this opportunity and reach out to other researchers whose work you find interesting. Introduce yourself, hand out your business card (which means you might need to make a business card before attending a conference) or exchange contact information, and try to make connections. You never know when you might meet someone who will be a great collaborator or even offer you a job at some point. One of Josh's students got his first academic position partly because of a connection he made at a conference.

Another strategy is to contact someone you would like to meet before the conference and schedule a time. This could be more informal, such as asking if they will be at a certain talk or poster session or inviting them to your talk or poster session. It could also be more formal and direct, such as asking if they would be willing to meet for a coffee or a chat between sessions. Your mentor might well introduce you to other colleagues in the field. Academics are usually friendly people, and many remember those who helped them along the way—it does not hurt to reach out and ask to meet them.

CONFERENCE EXPERIENCE EXAMPLE

In graduate school, Josh's advisor encouraged him to get started right away on presenting his research at conferences. Josh started with poster presentations, which was a great way to get his feet wet presenting. Presenting a poster was not as nerve wracking as presenting a paper—he stood in front of his poster, and if someone was interested in his project, he gave a short summary of the project and asked if they had any questions. Most of the time, it led to a conversation about the project, and it was encouraging to see that people were interested in the research study he had completed. The conversations also gave him some interesting ideas for future studies. Attending conferences also enabled Josh to make connections with other researchers whom he would work with down the road. For the most part, everyone was kind and wanted to help. Josh still remembers conversations he had early in his career with researchers he looked up to—people like Mark McMinn and Dave Myers—who were willing to take a few minutes out of their busy conference schedules and have coffee with a young graduate student. They probably do not even remember the conversations, but it was meaningful for Josh to make those connections and learn about their experiences.

GRADUATE MENTOR CORNER

As mentors, we want to create a climate that encourages people to join a broader professional community. Many of our students hold different cultural identities. Frequently, to meet all their relational needs, they may need to join several professional groups. We can promote a positive and encouraging environment that helps our students disseminate their work in various ways. For many students, the community element is what shifts the work from not just important but also fun.

Another strategy we use (with ourselves as well) is to encourage students to use conference presentations to set a clear deadline to help us make consistent progress on a research project. For example, if we have a paper we want to submit to a journal, a good strategy is to submit a poster presentation. Presentations are easier to prepare if the manuscript is already written, so we often use the presentation deadline to reinforce other writing goals. This approach can be helpful for students too. They often have several roles and various instructors, supervisors, or mentors vying for the priority of their attention and time. So, concrete deadlines for a conference are a way to lock in certain commitments.

UNDERGRADUATE MENTOR CORNER

It is valuable to bring undergraduates to conferences, if possible. Daryl's psychology department makes this a regular part of the academic year and consistently takes groups of students to the Midwestern Psychological Association annual convention in Chicago, which is within driving distance (i.e., 2.5 hours) from Hope College. It is valuable to have students go in groups to make it more enjoyable and less isolating. Be sure to communicate your expectations for the conference—what talks and how many do you want them to attend? What sessions do you want them to make a point of seeing? How much freedom do you want to grant them to navigate the program (or city) on their own? A few students might see this as a sightseeing trip, and while we encourage cultural appreciation in a new city, those experiences should be ancillary to the primary goal of making the most of attending the conference.

MOVING FORWARD

In this chapter, we covered the basics of presenting your research at a conference. Presenting your research at conferences is a great way to disseminate your work and connect with others interested in it. In the next chapter, we walk through the process of preparing your research project for publication. Ideally, our research would be widely distributed and impact the world in a positive way. The best way to get your research out there is to publish it.

19 PREPARING YOUR RESEARCH PROJECT FOR PUBLICATION

At this point, you have successfully completed your research project and perhaps presented your work at a conference—congratulations! This is a big deal—you are one step closer to finishing your program. However, from a research standpoint, there is still one more step to go—it is time to prepare your project for publication. Sometimes graduate students feel exhausted at this point and may feel tempted to skip the publication process. However, this is a mistake. For most researchers, the ultimate point of doing research is to discover things that are new to science and help make the world a better place. Your research will not have the impact it could if it does not get published. Plus, it is fun and rewarding to see your hard work in print. There are several steps for turning your research project into a publication, which we cover in this chapter.

NARROW THE FOCUS OF YOUR PROJECT

For graduate students completing a thesis or dissertation, it often takes some work to narrow down the research project into a form that is ready to submit to a journal. One reason is that graduate student research projects (e.g., the

https://doi.org/10.1037/0000371-020
The Complete Researcher: A Practical Guide for Graduate Students and Early Career Professionals, by J. N. Hook, D. E. Davis, and D. R. Van Tongeren
Copyright © 2024 by the American Psychological Association. All rights reserved.

thesis or dissertation) are often broad in scope. Graduate students writing up their thesis or dissertation often write up all the steps of the research process and write up each of the hypotheses in detail, irrespective of whether they worked out or fit together into a coherent narrative. But for a journal article, your paper needs to be lean and mean. Every part of the paper—the introduction, literature review, method, results, and discussion—needs to fit together and flow well. So, you may find yourself cutting parts of your thesis or dissertation or running additional analyses to craft a story that flows well. Your mentor should be able to help you with this step.

What stage are you at in narrowing down your research project so it is ready for publication? When you think about your project, are there aspects you might need to cut down? Or are there additional analyses you think might be helpful to run? Many journals have page limitations (e.g., 25–35 pages) or word limits (e.g., 5,000 words) on manuscript submissions. Some theses and dissertations can be hundreds of pages, so you may need to trim considerably (or consider multiple publications from your overall project, if applicable).

REVISE SECTIONS OF YOUR PAPER (IF NEEDED)

This section applies mostly to graduate students working to transform a longer thesis or dissertation document into a publication. Many graduate programs require a thesis or dissertation with several chapters, including the introduction and literature review, method, results, and discussion. If you conducted a systematic literature review (as discussed in Chapter 10), it is often possible to publish at least two papers from your thesis or dissertation: the systematic literature review and an empirical paper that focuses on your method, results, and discussion.

In Chapter 10, we walked through how to write the various sections of the systematic literature review. If you follow this model, the literature review of your thesis or dissertation document can often be transformed into a journal article submission without much editing or rewriting. However, for the empirical paper, you will likely need to edit the manuscript to fit the format of the target journal. For example, it will need to be adapted to include all the required sections for the journal you are submitting to (i.e., introduction, method, results, and discussion). Thus, you will need to craft an introduction section that includes a more pointed literature review for the empirical study. (If you elected to do a briefer literature review option for your thesis or dissertation, this section of your paper can often be adopted as the introduction to your empirical publication with less editing and rewriting.)

Because we have not yet discussed how to write the introduction section to a journal article, we thought it would be helpful to share our process for writing this section. It can be helpful to liken the introduction to the empirical journal article to a funnel. At the beginning, it starts broad (e.g., introducing your topic and talking about why it is important). Then in the middle, it gets a little more specific (e.g., defining the main constructs, reviewing theory and research that presents the important background information for your study). At the end, it gets very specific (e.g., discussing your specific study and your hypotheses). The following are the main parts of the introduction:

- **opening paragraph:** In the opening paragraph, introduce the overall topic. This is often a good place to make an argument for why this topic is important or why your study is needed. We will often end the opening paragraph with a sentence that encompasses the main goal of our paper.

- **literature review:** The literature review is the main part of your introduction section. In this section, you introduce the main constructs, theories, and relevant research to your study. The exact way this will look will vary across studies. But in general, you will cover three main things:
  - **define main constructs:** You need to give the definitions for your main constructs. (A *construct* is a fancy name for a "thing" you study.) So, if your paper is about forgiveness, for example, you will need to define forgiveness in the introduction.
  - **present the theory (or theories) that undergird(s) your research study:** Sometimes your study will be based on a particular theory. A theory is a fancy way to talk about someone's thinking about how something works or how variables might relate to one another. For example, we have a theory that says humility is related to developing and maintaining social bonds. If your paper is about humility and forgiveness, you might discuss that theory in the introduction.
  - **review relevant research:** You need to review past research studies that address your topic. The reader needs to know what has been done previously, so they can understand how your study fits in with the existing literature on this topic.

- **present study:** After you finish the literature review, you will move on to talk about your study. First, give an overview of what you plan to do in your study. Then, list your research questions and hypotheses. Research questions get at why you are doing the study in the first place. What do you want to find out? Hypotheses are linked to the research questions and are statements of what you expect to find in your study. Your research questions and hypotheses should line up with the analyses you do in your results section.

In addition to writing or revising the introduction, you may need to revise the other sections of your empirical paper as well (e.g., method, results, discussion). In general, however, the process for writing these sections for a publication is similar to the information we presented in the individual chapters on these topics (e.g., Chapter 12, "Planning the Method Section"; Chapter 15, "Analyzing Data and Writing Your Results"; Chapter 16, "Crafting the Discussion"). Thus, the main revisions to these sections will include cutting down material from your thesis or dissertation to fit the narrower focus of the project you are preparing for publication. The content of the material and the process of writing will be similar.

CHOOSE YOUR TARGET JOURNAL

After you have finished revising the sections of your paper (if needed), the next step is to choose your target journal for submission. Think of all the articles you read while doing your research. Where were many of those papers published? Journals vary on a range of factors, but seeing where other papers relevant to your work have been published can be a good place to start. Again, this is another area where your mentor should be able to help you because they probably have a better sense of where your research study would be a good fit. Ideally, they will have published in that journal before and understand what kinds of papers will likely be received well by that journal. The following are some things to think about as you try to select your target journal.

- **topic area:** This might seem self-explanatory, but each academic journal has a particular focus regarding the types of papers they tend to publish. For example, the *Journal of Counseling Psychology* (*JCP*) publishes papers in the following areas: counseling activities (including assessment, interventions, consultation, supervision, training, prevention, psychological education, and advocacy), career and educational development and vocational psychology, diversity and underrepresented populations in relation to counseling activities, the development of new measures to be used in counseling activities, and professional issues in counseling psychology (https://www.apa.org/pubs/journals/cou). Does your paper fall into one of these categories? If so, it might be a good fit for *JCP*. But if not, you are probably better off finding a journal that is a better fit for the topic of your research project. You can find the focus of each journal on their website.

- **prestige:** Some journals are more highly regarded than others. One of the most common metrics of journal quality is called the impact factor. A journal's *impact factor* is a measure of the frequency an average journal article is cited in a particular year. In general, the higher the journal's impact factor, the more influential it is and the more difficult it is to publish a paper in that journal. Many top-notch journals have a rejection rate of 90% or greater. American Psychological Association (APA) journals tend to be more prestigious than non-APA journals. We usually recommend starting with the most prestigious journal in your topic area, and if it gets rejected, moving down from there. Create a list of four to five journals, so you have a clear plan, given the selectivity of the best journals. Your list can include increasingly less selective journals that would still be a good fit for your paper and provide a nice platform for your work.

- **journal requirements:** When choosing a particular journal, it is important to consider its requirements. For example, some journals require preregistration of research studies, which we talked about in Chapter 13. Other journals may have other requirements, such as data sharing, that you may or may not be willing to meet. Before you submit, make sure your research study is consistent with the requirements of the journal.

- **predatory journals:** Perhaps you have had the following experience: You receive an email from a journal that seems to be related to your field of study. The email might even have listed one of your previous articles and talked about how great it is. They ask you to submit another paper and almost guarantee it will be accepted for publication. Too good to be true? Yes, most likely. There is a group of predatory journals that are driven by self-interest (usually financial) and not scholarship. They are characterized by false or misleading information, deviation from best editorial and publication practices, lack of transparency, and aggressive, indiscriminate solicitation (Grudniewicz et al., 2019). Sometimes it can be difficult to determine whether a journal is predatory. If you have a question about a particular journal or think it may be a predatory journal, check with your mentor before submitting. A potential resource is Beall's List (https://beallslist.net/), a website that lists potentially predatory journals and publishers.

We should note that even with these considerations, it is not always clear what the best journal for your paper will be. For example, you might have a few journals you think could be a good fit. It is okay to pick one to try first and see what feedback you get from the reviewers. Sometimes there is not one "perfect" journal to submit to.

SUBMIT YOUR MANUSCRIPT

After you select a journal, the next step is to submit your manuscript. Make sure you check the journal website for all the details about what is required to submit to the journal. For example, you will often need to write a cover letter and submit a title page with all author information, as well as a masked version of your manuscript without any author information. Make sure you follow the instructions carefully (e.g., do not exceed the page limit). After you submit the manuscript, the paper is either rejected by the editor without review (i.e., desk rejection) or it goes out for review. Some journals are faster with reviews than others, but do not be surprised if you have to wait 3 to 6 months for the journal editor to render a decision.

RESPOND TO REVIEWER CRITIQUES

When you submit a manuscript, you will receive one of three decisions. Rejection is the most common response. This is a disappointing outcome, and it means the journal does not want to publish your manuscript. It is easy to feel hurt, angry, or even humiliated when your work is rejected, but it is a common experience, even for strong researchers. Remember, rejection rates often hover around 90% at top journals. When a paper is rejected, try to remember this sort of thing is "part of the deal," try not to take it personally, and move on. When your work is rejected, you will often get feedback from the editor and reviewers about your work. It can be helpful to read this feedback and think about whether there is anything in it that might improve the manuscript when you submit it to another journal.

Remember, however, that the new journal you submit to will have its own editor and reviewers with opinions on the manuscript (which may differ from the first set of reviewers). Because of this, we recommend getting your manuscript under review at a different journal quickly. For people who publish a lot, this is a key behavior. Successful researchers do not worry much about their ego or waste a lot of time. They respond methodically and quickly to feedback, trusting that, despite some unpredictability in the peer review process, persistence will produce positive results. If you believe a reviewer recommendation would improve your manuscript, incorporate it. But if you are not sure, get it under review again, and then you can see whether the new reviewers have a similar opinion.

In rare instances, your manuscript may be accepted right off the bat. When this happens, the editor usually will ask you to complete some small changes but let you know that the manuscript is accepted pending those changes. This is rare and hardly ever happens, so you should not expect it. Celebrate this rare event when it occurs, but do not expect to see it regularly.

The main result you are hoping for is a revise and resubmit. This means the editor does not accept the manuscript but sees enough promise in the paper that they invite you to submit a revised version. Often there will be a long list of requested changes from the editor and two to three reviewers. Although it may not seem like it at the time (because sometimes the list of requested changes can feel onerous), this is a great outcome. Usually (but not always), if you do a good job responding to the reviewer critiques, you will eventually get the manuscript accepted for publication.

Our strategy for responding to the reviewer critiques involves several steps:

- We copy the reviewer critiques verbatim and paste them into a new Word document. This is the framework for our letter to the editor, detailing how we responded to each reviewer critique.

- We work through each critique. We make the requested changes in the paper and explain in the letter how we responded to each critique.

- We try to address each reviewer critique when possible. We try to take an agreeable and friendly tone. When a reviewer makes a suggestion that is impossible to incorporate, we try to figure out a way to at least respond partially to the critique. For example, if a reviewer wants us to include a measure in the study that was not a part of the data collection, it is not possible to fully accommodate the reviewer's request. However, we might respond by including the reviewer's suggestion as a limitation or area for future research in the discussion section.

- In rare circumstances, we might disagree with a reviewer or believe the paper would be worse if the reviewer's suggestions were followed. In these cases, we make an argument and explain our position in a carefully reasoned and matter-of-fact way. Regardless of the reviewer's tone, we maintain a professional, cordial, and agreeable stance even though we disagree with the reviewer. We try to do this only when necessary and when we have a strong conviction about the issue.

After you respond to the reviewer critiques and resubmit your manuscript, there is another period of waiting. In some cases, the editor will review your revised manuscript (as well as your responses to the reviewer critiques) and decide whether to publish the manuscript. In other cases, the editor will send the revised manuscript out for another round of reviews (sometimes the manuscript is sent to the same reviewers and sometimes to different reviewers). Eventually, you will again receive one of three decisions: acceptance, rejection, or another revise and resubmit. Sometimes this can be an arduous and lengthy process. Do not give up—remember, once you are given a revise and resubmit, the editor likely sees some promise in the manuscript. If you stick with it and diligently respond to the critiques of the editor and reviewers, your manuscript will likely eventually be published.

GRADUATE MENTOR CORNER

As mentors, we have an important role in preparing our students to engage effectively in the publication process. Some students get discouraged by how random the peer-review process seems to be. Sometimes strong papers get rejected, and weaker ones get a revise and resubmit. At one point, we asked Ev if his acceptance rate increased over time (we hoped this would happen to us after a few papers). He said it had not changed much throughout his career. Reviewers are reviewers. The process involves a heavy dose of chance for any one outlet. We try to do strong work, and we have found we can find an appropriate home for most of our papers. When you talk with students about the publication process, try to set appropriate expectations and norms. Encourage students to deal with what is within their control, do their best, and leave the rest to chance.

If you have set up your research team to be a supportive structure that prepares people for peer review, when they encounter negative feedback from reviewers, it will not be as jarring as it could be. The culture of your team can help students develop a mindset that takes the ego out of the process. In some cases, even if your student receives a revise and resubmit (which is a great outcome), the comments may be so critical that students feel like giving up on the paper. In our group, we have a saying: "Never leave a revise and resubmit behind." In fact, we have some epic examples, mostly from Josh, when a paper seemed doomed for the file drawer, yet he persisted, and somehow, we found a strong home for the project.

Because there is a strong dose of chance in the publication process, it is helpful to encourage students not to connect their self-worth to any single outcome. Try to model this by sharing your stories of rejection and failure in publishing. Encourage students to see rejection as a transient "part of the process" of research rather than something that reflects permanently and negatively on their skills or abilities.

Even if a paper does not get accepted, we encourage students to view the reviewer feedback as part of their development as researchers and writers. Even if the paper does not get a revise and resubmit from the first outlet, we learn something and get valuable feedback on our work. Before submitting to a second journal, we can address any comments that will likely come up with subsequent reviewers.

UNDERGRADUATE MENTOR CORNER

Although the mentor is likely the one who submits the paper and navigates the editorial process when working with undergraduate students, some undergraduate students may have been involved in helping with the writing process and will be coauthors. So, it can still be useful to teach students about the publication process, and keeping them up to date on the correspondence from the editor is helpful in their development. Often, the advisor serves as the corresponding author—the person with the contact information on the project should someone have a question—because the undergraduate student is likely moving on and changing their email address. Of course, the undergraduate student can still serve as the first author (if earned), and at times, it might make sense to list both the student and mentor as corresponding authors. Being involved in a publication as an undergraduate student can help increase the likelihood of the student being accepted for graduate school, and it also can help the student understand the research process more deeply.

MOVING FORWARD

In this final chapter of Part II of the book, we walked through the final step of the research process—publishing your findings. Publication is the capstone of the research process and enables you to get your research out into the world where it can be read by other scientists and laypersons. Publishing can be arduous, but it is worthwhile because science progresses one step at a time. In Part III, we take a step back and think more broadly about developing your leadership skills in your research career. We start by exploring the concept of leadership and giving back.

PART III: PROGRAM: DEVELOPING LEADERSHIP SKILLS AND JUMP-STARTING YOUR RESEARCH CAREER

20 STEPPING INTO LEADERSHIP IN YOUR RESEARCH CAREER

Graduate students focus mostly on building their skills and competencies when they start their research journey. For example, how can I learn and develop the skills I need to move forward on my independent research projects? How can I jump through the necessary hoops of my program to defend my dissertation and graduate? How can I grow my curriculum vitae (CV) to make me competitive for a job after I graduate?

In a certain way, this self-focus is developmentally normative and necessary. As a beginning researcher, you do need to focus on yourself. There are a lot of things to learn, and at the beginning of your research career, you must focus on building your skills. Collaboration can be a wonderful gift, but if you do not develop the necessary research skills and abilities, it will be difficult to move forward and reach your professional goals.

However, at some point in your research career, you may find that your focus begins to shift. You might get to the point where you feel more comfortable with your skill set as a researcher. When you are making consistent progress on your research and feel well within a zone of comfort, your vision might begin to broaden. Instead of focusing solely on your own development and accomplishments, you might look around and notice other people are

---

https://doi.org/10.1037/0000371-021
The Complete Researcher: A Practical Guide for Graduate Students and Early Career Professionals, by J. N. Hook, D. E. Davis, and D. R. Van Tongeren
Copyright © 2024 by the American Psychological Association. All rights reserved.

moving toward a similar goal as you, but they are a few steps behind where you are. You might feel the pull to take what you have learned as a researcher and help someone else, to give back. At this point in your development as a researcher, you can begin to step into leadership. In this chapter, we discuss what leadership can look like at different stages of your career and explore some potential contexts for leadership. Then, we discuss some of the most important qualities of a good leader.

All three of us noticed this shift beginning to occur near the end of graduate school. We had each completed our first independent research project (i.e., the master's thesis) and had run some research studies in addition to our theses, and we were feeling more comfortable with the research process. We were getting going on our dissertations, and the research process did not seem quite so daunting the second time around. Our research team (the Positive Psychology Research Group) met regularly, and we had several undergraduate students working with us. We started to think about how we might help involve the undergraduates working in our lab more in the research process (beyond simple tasks, such as data collection and entry). We tried to set up each undergraduate student with their own extra research project, with us serving as mentors or helpers. We were hoping to pass along some of the lessons we had learned over the first few years of graduate school.

Our first steps into leadership were a mix of success and failure. We remember one undergraduate student who took the lead on a research project and ran with it. The study worked out, and eventually, we got the paper published in a good journal, with the undergraduate student as the first author. Other attempts were not as successful. Sometimes we tried to get an undergraduate student to take the lead on a project, but they were not motivated, so the project stalled out. Other times, the student was motivated, but they did not have the necessary skills to take the lead on a research project, so it did not work. It was not the fault of the student—the task we gave them was too far outside their level of ability.

When we graduated and began our faculty positions, the leadership opportunities expanded. We each had research labs, which were made up of graduate students and undergraduate students. Before, we were mostly working on our own projects; now, we also had to manage the projects of each of our students and guide them as they moved toward their career goals. There were also leadership opportunities available in our programs and departments, as well as in the professional organizations we were a part of. However, it was sometimes a struggle to figure out what kinds of leadership responsibilities were appropriate to take on. How much time should we spend working on our own research projects, and how much time should we spend giving back and serving the university and organizations we were a part of? These are the types of questions we tackle in this chapter.

Where are you at right now regarding leadership? What leadership positions (if any) have you taken in your research lab? Your program or department? The broader profession? What have those experiences been like for you?

THE TRANSITION

We noted at the beginning of the chapter that as your career progresses, most people shift from focusing only on their own work and development to taking on a broader perspective and giving back. But how and when does this transition happen? What are the main stages of career development, and how should you think about leadership at each stage?

Stage 1: Beginning Graduate Student

The first stage of career development is as the beginning graduate student. This is when you are just starting out and learning the basics of research. The beginning graduate student stage usually lasts 2 to 3 years until the student completes their first independent research project (usually the master's thesis). Our recommendation at this stage is not to worry too much about leadership and service. There is a lot to learn about research, and the focus should be on developing your skills and abilities. The biggest threat to graduating on time is the risk of not completing your research requirements, which can be a costly mistake (e.g., giving up a year or more of salary if you have to spend extra time in graduate school). These are huge opportunity costs in terms of money and the loss of potential expertise. For example, even if you plan on being a clinician, failing to complete your dissertation on time may cost you the ability to focus on your clinical training when it is most important for you to refine your skills. If there is a leadership position you want (e.g., being a student representative to the faculty in your department or an American Psychological Association [APA] division), that is fine, but it is a good idea to limit the time commitment at this stage. For example, if you are going to take on a leadership role, perhaps choose only one and set good boundaries for your time investment in this capacity.

Stage 2: Advanced Graduate Student

The second stage of career development is the advanced graduate student. Advanced graduate students have finished their first independent research project, so they understand the basics of the research process. They are likely working on their second independent research project (usually the dissertation).

The dissertation is a lot of work, to be sure, but our experience has been that students usually find it easier than the master's thesis because they have gone through all the steps of research before.

At this stage of one's career, the graduate student can begin to think about taking on some leadership opportunities. For example, there might be an opportunity in one's research lab to mentor an undergraduate student on their research. Perhaps some service positions in the department would be good leadership learning experiences. There might even be some leadership positions in a professional organization that could be interesting to pursue, such as being the graduate student representative on a board or committee. Depending on whether you have begun to publish your research, journals may reach out to you to ask you to review articles.

Our main recommendation is to be cautious about taking on leadership or service opportunities because the priority still needs to be finishing your program requirements, graduating, and building one's CV so you can be competitive for a job. We have sometimes seen students get so heavily involved in leadership and service opportunities that their timeline to graduation gets delayed. Some have even failed to graduate altogether. However, if the time commitment is not too large, it can be beneficial to take on some moderate leadership opportunities as you move into this stage of your career development, in part because as you build your professional networks, more people will become familiar with you and your work—which can help when you are applying for positions.

Stage 3: Early Career

The third stage of career development is the early career professional (the first 10 years postgraduation). Early career professionals have gotten their first job, which is a terrific accomplishment. Like advanced graduate students, early career professionals usually need to be focused on building their research program and CV. If you are currently in a postdoctoral position, you might be aiming for your first tenure-track faculty position. If you have a tenure-track faculty position, you are likely focused on doing what you need to do to gain tenure and promotion.

Our advice for early career professionals is like that of advanced graduate students. It is fine to take on some leadership and service opportunities but be cautious about the time commitment. Protect your time. Because you have not yet received tenure (if you are in a tenure-track position), most of your time and energy should still be focused on your research—conducting high-quality studies, preparing manuscripts for publication at top-tier outlets, and writing research grants. Be sure to gain clarity from the department, college, and university about what is required for tenure, and then be focused on those benchmarks. Feel free to take a leadership position or two as long as it aligns with your goals and required benchmarks, but do not get so caught up in service responsibilities that you struggle to progress toward your primary research goals necessary for tenure and promotion.

Stage 4: Tenured (Associate) Professor

The fourth stage of career development is the tenured (associate) professor. At this point in one's career trajectory, there is less pressure on your research productivity. Because of that, there is more flexibility and freedom to take on additional leadership and service opportunities. (And in most colleges and universities, the service expectations begin to increase as well.) If you have a goal to make full professor, you cannot let your research fall too much onto the back burner—you still need to be making consistent progress. But you have more choices—you can dial back your research and take on more leadership positions.

Stage 5: Full Professor

The fifth stage of career development is full professor. At this point in one's career trajectory, there is a lot of freedom. Some full professors remain strongly focused on their research productivity, whereas others shift their focus to other endeavors. Many will choose to take on large leadership or service opportunities to give back and help the next generation of psychologists. Because there is less pressure to produce at a high level, there is flexibility to decide how you would like to spend your time and energy.

You can see a natural progression during one's career regarding leadership and service opportunities. At the beginning stages of one's career, it is probably wise to say no to most leadership and service opportunities and only take on those responsibilities that are (a) not time-consuming and (b) central to one's interests and mission. As you progress in your career, however, there is less pressure on your personal research productivity and more time and space available to engage in leadership. As people progress in their careers, there is usually a natural shift toward wanting to be more generative and give back to the broader community. Where are you in your career trajectory? What level of leadership and service engagement (e.g., low, medium, high) do you think is wise for your career stage? What has been your experience so far with taking advantage of leadership opportunities?

TYPES OF LEADERSHIP OPPORTUNITIES

Now that you have a sense of the right level of leadership opportunities to take advantage of according to where you are in your career trajectory, what are the main types of leadership opportunities available? How can you get involved and give back? We discuss three main categories of leadership and service opportunities: (a) leadership in your research lab, (b) leadership in your program or department, and (c) leadership in the broader profession.

Leadership in Your Research Lab

One great opportunity to practice your leadership skills is in your research lab. Strong leaders involve others in their work and leverage their skills and opportunities to benefit others on their team. In most research labs, there are graduate students at varying levels of development. For example, Josh usually takes one new graduate student each year, so, at any given time, he usually has a 1st-year, 2nd-year, 3rd-year, 4th-year, and 5th-year student. Josh also generally has a few undergraduate students working in his lab. If you are an advanced graduate student, there might be ways you could help the younger graduate students in your lab with research. Or even if you are a beginning graduate student, you could involve an undergraduate student in your research project, and they could help and observe you go through each step of the research process.

One strategy we have found to work well is to pair up an advanced graduate student with either a beginning graduate student or an undergraduate student on a particular project, such as a paper or conference presentation. In many cases, this can be a win–win. The advanced graduate student can provide the expertise and knowledge necessary to complete the project. The beginning graduate student or undergrad can help as much as they can, given their level of skill and expertise. The newer student gets the experience of being involved in the project without the pressure that comes from having to take the lead and be fully responsible for its execution. And the more advanced student gets some help in getting the work for the project completed.

One of the benefits of taking a leadership role in your research lab is that because the focus of the group is on research, these kinds of leadership experiences do not take away time and energy from completing your independent research and building your CV—they can contribute to your research efforts. Take a few minutes and reflect on your research lab. What opportunities might be available for you to take leadership and give back?

Leadership in Your Program or Department

As you progress through graduate school, there are often opportunities to get involved with leadership in your program and department. For example, when Josh was in graduate school, he served as the student representative to the program faculty. In this role, Josh was a liaison between the graduate students and faculty. He gathered student concerns and communicated them to the faculty, and he also attended the faculty meetings and communicated important information back to the students. It was helpful to get an inside look at what it was like to be a faculty member and run a program. In any program and department, various committees often include a student representative. In most cases, not many students want to be involved, so if you volunteer, the position can often be yours.

When getting into leadership and service positions in your program and department, it is important to be vigilant about guarding your time. As a graduate student, your primary responsibility should be focused on making progress on your independent research and program requirements. Leadership and service opportunities in your program or department may not directly contribute to that goal, so they should be considered "extra." It is a good idea to be cognizant of the time commitment these tasks will take. One guideline might be to take on one leadership or service opportunity at a time and see how it goes. There is no need to "load up" on leadership opportunities—you will have plenty of time later in your career to do that. Take a few minutes and reflect on your program and department. What opportunities might be available for you to take leadership and give back?

Leadership in the Broader Profession

The final area of leadership we would like to talk about is leadership in the broader profession. There are two primary areas of opportunity. First, there are usually plenty of opportunities to get involved in the professional organizations you are a part of. There are larger, general organizations such as the APA and divisions within APA that correspond to different topic areas. For example, the three of us are members of Division 36 (Society for the Psychology of Religion and Spirituality). There also may be specialty organizations on a particular topic (e.g., cognitive behavior therapy, different areas of diversity) that you may want to get involved with. For example, Daryl was a program chair for Division 36 for 3 years, and he organized the Psychology of Religion and Spirituality Preconference for the Society for Personality and Social Psychology for several years. These were also opportunities to network and meet new colleagues and collaborators (and friends).

The second big opportunity for leadership in the field involves helping with the editorial process for various professional journals. Once you start publishing papers, journals will contact you and ask if you are willing to review new articles for their journal. As you advance in your career, you could also serve on the editorial board for a journal (perhaps as consulting editor) or as an associate editor or lead editor of a journal.

It may seem like we are risking redundancy, but for graduate students, we would again advise some caution when taking on leadership and service commitments for the broader profession. Your research builds your reputation, so you need to develop a strong reputation before premium leadership opportunities become available. It is good to get involved in some leadership opportunities because it shows your dedication to the field and your desire to get involved and give back. However, like taking on leadership opportunities in your program or department, taking on too much too soon could derail you from making progress on your own research, which is most important when you are trying to graduate and get a job. So, the main recommendation is to have some balance. It is good to take on some leadership positions, but do not go overboard and load up. When in doubt, wait until later in your career when things are more stable and secure. There are always more ways to serve in the future. Take a few minutes and reflect on your involvement in the broader profession. What opportunities might be available for you to take leadership and give back?

QUALITIES OF A GOOD LEADER

Now that we have discussed some of the different types of leadership opportunities that are available, you want to ensure you are engaging the role with your very best. But what makes a good leader? When you take the initiative to step into a leadership opportunity (big or small), what qualities should you try to develop to be effective as a leader? In this next section, we cover three key aspects of leadership: (a) integrity, (b) balancing drive and humility, and (c) balancing support and honesty.

Integrity

The first key quality of a good leader is integrity. Integrity means your words and actions are consistent. In other words, you walk your talk. You make and keep your commitments. Authenticity is key. It can be disorienting if a leader tells you to do something, but you observe their behavior and realize they are not doing the thing they are telling you to do. It is hard to follow a leader like that. So, when you take on a leadership position, make sure you are paying attention to your own behavior. For example, if you are working with a younger graduate student and you recommend that they develop a particular habit for work (e.g., prioritizing your writing schedule or most important tasks [MITs]), are you prioritizing your writing schedule and MITs? If you preach self-care, are you practicing self-care yourself? If not, get your own house in order before instructing someone else on what they should do. Make sure your words and actions line up.

Think back on the leadership experiences you have engaged in recently. How are you doing with integrity? How well do your words and actions line up with one another?

Balancing Drive and Humility

A second key quality of a good leader is to have a combination of both drive and humility. In his book *Good to Great*, Jim Collins (2001) analyzed the CEOs of companies who achieved incredible success for their companies and maintained it for the long haul. He found these leaders had an uncanny combination of drive and humility. The drive aspect made sense and was expected. Many leaders are selected on the basis of their ability, knowledge, and expertise. Most successful leaders are incredibly driven and work hard to get to the top of their field.

But the humility aspect was surprising and unexpected. When we think of leadership, humility usually is not the first word that comes to mind. On the contrary, we often think of a leader who is strong and has a vision that is clear and unwavering. But exceptional leaders can complement their competitive drive with a strong dose of humility. Humility enables us to acknowledge and own our limitations. Humility allows us to be other-oriented and focus on the needs of the people we serve rather than just focusing on our own needs and wants. When stepping into leadership, it is important to be strong and move forward in the direction you want to go. But also lead with humility. Do not be so rigidly stubborn that you fail to consider the needs of those you serve or different ways of achieving your goals. Let other people speak into your life and point out the possible drawbacks or downsides to the direction you want to go. Be open to change and doing things a different way.

Think back on the leadership experiences you have engaged in recently. How are you doing with leading with both drive and humility? Are you balanced as a leader? When you struggle, do you tend to struggle more with drive or humility?

Balancing Support and Honesty

The third key quality of a good leader is to balance support and honesty. In her book *Radical Candor*, Kim Scott (2017) talked about an important consideration when working with others. Most leaders err in one of two ways. Either they are kind when giving feedback (but do not give clear feedback about a person's performance or how they need to improve), or they are clear when giving feedback (but are mean or harsh about it). Scott argued that you do not have to choose. Great leaders who develop trusting, effective relationships with people who work for them (a) are clear about expectations, performance, and what needs to be improved; and (b) are kind and supportive and communicate feedback (even negative feedback) in a caring manner.

Both qualities are important when working in a leadership capacity. If you are not crystal clear with your feedback (positive and negative), the people working with you will not know how to improve, leading to all parties getting frustrated. For example, early in his career as a professor, Josh sometimes felt bad giving negative feedback to students. Because of Josh's struggles to give clear feedback, sometimes his students would get stuck in the same struggle for a long time. Clear feedback was necessary for students to improve. But it is also essential to be kind, caring, and supportive. The people working for you will not follow your lead unless they know you care about them and have their best interests in mind. Make sure you have both—be clear and caring.

Think back on the leadership experiences you have engaged in recently. How are you doing with leading with both support and honesty? Are you balanced as a leader? When you struggle, do you tend to struggle more with support or honesty?

GRADUATE MENTOR CORNER

As a mentor, you have a great opportunity to both (a) model good leadership in your relationship with your graduate students and (b) encourage and provide opportunities for your graduate students to get involved in leadership roles themselves. When engaging with your graduate students, it is essential to model good leadership because this will implicitly help them develop good leadership skills when working with others, as in the twist on the Golden Rule "Do unto others as you would have them do unto others." Check in with yourself first.

When helping students develop leadership skills, we try to help them earn trust across a broad range of relationships. Leadership involves developing motivations beyond personal goals and aspirations to prioritize forming strong and mutually beneficial relationships with others. In this case, leadership taps into our core need to belong and contribute to a community. Promoting leadership opportunities helps students experience the joy of taking on new challenges and doing things that cannot be done alone but require teams. As we develop skills and expertise, we enjoy sharing our gifts with others—equipping them to help build a vision and develop high-performing teams that balance support and challenge.

Like any skill, learning to lead requires certain abilities. Often skills are easier "caught than taught"; the best way to help a group grow in leadership skills is to form a team that invites people to share their gifts with others and constantly look for ways to grow and improve how they do their work. Your role is to work with other leaders on your team to create a strong culture that encourages everyone to work hard, help others, and develop trustworthiness. The social environment can extend across research, teaching, and service, and as the group gains greater capacity, it will have people with a range of gifts, personalities, and interests.

A second thing we can do is organize opportunities in your research lab to help graduate students develop leadership skills. We try to set our research labs up with a developmental approach. Likewise, as people gain experience, they share their skills and experience to help others learn more quickly. In other words, we are collaborative, and the graduate students take on more leadership responsibilities on the research team as they advance in the program. We often pair up advanced graduate students with beginning graduate students or undergrads to work together on projects, which provides a structure for mentoring and leadership to happen naturally.

For example, on Donnie's team, there is a clear progression of roles. In Year 1, students' primary goal is to finish their predissertation. If they achieve this goal, in Year 2, they are asked to invest in more complex forms of data collection. In Year 3, students lead a leadership seminar, a course in which students can seek support for developing their project management skills as leaders. We have a stable structure, but as co-instructors of the course, students have a chance to invite speakers that align with an area of focus for the semester. In Year 4, students aspire to the "Nikki" role. Nikki was Donnie's former graduate student who served as a postdoc for 2 years and came to play an integral role in the life of their team. She was kind and supportive of new students and generously helped others who wanted support with analyses. So, early in training, students on the team learn they are aiming for a generative stance (as opposed to the common dynamic where senior students become increasingly absorbed in their own requirements for graduation). This is just one example of organizing a leadership structure within your leadership team. If you do not have a structure in place, think about implementing something that fits with how you run your research lab.

A third thing we do is promote initiative among our students. We want to take on projects that align with students' sense of purpose and allow them to test their skills in a new way that requires them to learn and grow. If we can understand a student's primary motivation, we can help design leadership opportunities to fit their goals. For example, Jayden, one of Donnie's students, was interested in careers integrating science in practice, so he has regularly helped with outreach and teaching opportunities. For example, he helped structure a prepracticum course in which students conducted psychoeducational workshops within the university as well as other community organizations. He also helped design an online positive psychology course, a seminar focused on applying positive psychology to prevent burnout in clinicians, as well as an outreach program in partnership with the university counseling center. As he clarified areas where he was willing to invest a lot of time, it helped us make better decisions about how to direct his research. He ended up taking on a much more ambitious project for his dissertation—such as designing and evaluating intervention studies—because he had already invested so much work into developing his interests.

UNDERGRADUATE MENTOR CORNER

Our main thought related to mentoring undergraduates (or students not currently enrolled in a doctoral program) is to develop a culture that rewards initiative. We just described the benefits of having a clear progression of responsibility, but this progression is not fixed or rigid. Sometimes we have students join our lab and immediately demonstrate high levels of initiative and responsibility. We trust them quickly and keep giving them more opportunities.

However, we do have a warning. In the first year or two, it sometimes helps to give people concrete roles and responsibilities. In Donnie's first 2 or 3 years at Georgia State University, he wanted a more egalitarian structure for his team, so he tried to have students in a clinically oriented master's program do the same things as his doctoral students. The plan did not work well. Most students were not ready for some of the more abstract tasks of trying to design independent work, and they needed more scaffolding. Once he realized the error, he started experimenting with different training structures that would incentivize initiative while still giving students ample structure and support. Undergraduate students often need more structure and support than doctoral students.

MOVING FORWARD

In this chapter, we talked about the importance of leadership and giving back. As you develop your skills and abilities in research, there is a natural progression where you broaden your focus from working only on your own projects to collaborating and helping others who are not as experienced as you are. This can be an incredibly generative and rewarding experience, but remember it is important to match your leadership and service responsibilities to your level of career development. In the next chapter, we offer some specific suggestions and ideas for developing your overall research program. As you grow as a researcher, it is important to not only complete a particular research project but also develop an overall narrative for a program of research.

21 DEVELOPING A RESEARCH PROGRAM

As you begin to make the shift from graduate student to professional, one of the things you need to start thinking about is developing your program of research. This is a somewhat different process from choosing a topic for your thesis or dissertation, which we talked about in Chapter 9, although the two processes are related. When you choose a topic for an individual research project, the process is more circumspect—you have a specific project with a specific deadline, and you need to choose a direction for that one thing.

But when you start to think about developing a research program, the process is broader. When this first takes place varies. Some students are eager to dive into a line of research early on but may not know where to start. Others are still getting acculturated to conducting research and may be focused on the first project. Others jump on many projects when opportunities arise, but they lack a coherent thread. In our estimation, many doctoral students begin to think about their program of research—a line of consistent research on a central theme or topic—near the end of graduate school, when they must talk about their program of research as part of their job applications. But as you will see from reading this chapter, it can be helpful to start thinking of your

---

https://doi.org/10.1037/0000371-022
The Complete Researcher: A Practical Guide for Graduate Students and Early Career Professionals, by J. N. Hook, D. E. Davis, and D. R. Van Tongeren
Copyright © 2024 by the American Psychological Association. All rights reserved.

program of research earlier than that, even right from the beginning. When you develop a program of research, you are thinking about a theme for all your research projects and how they fit together. You are also thinking not only about what you have done in the past but also where you are going in the future. In short, you are considering what topic(s) you would like to focus on understanding for the next 5 to 10 years. Once you have taken the time to select a theme for your research program, it will help shape your decision to take on new projects or join collaborations—they should fit under the broader umbrella of your overall direction of research. In this chapter, we discuss some ideas for how to transition from conducting individual, one-off research projects to developing a coherent program of research.

The process of coming up with a program of research can be a bit vague, so it is sometimes helpful, as Stephen Covey (1989) would say, to begin with the end in mind. If you are going into a research career (e.g., academia), you will generally be required to give a job talk in which you present a series of studies detailing your research program. (Even if you are not focused on academia, if you want to develop a career where research is an integral part of what you do—such as working in a research hospital, writing books, doing community-based research, or consulting—it is helpful to think about your program of research.)

If you do have to give a job talk about your research, ideally, you will not just talk about a single study (e.g., your dissertation) but rather a program of research that encompasses multiple studies you have completed over the course of graduate school. It is critical to show how these studies are related and fit together in a way that makes sense—a bit like telling a story or narrative of your collective work so far. You want to make the case that you are pushing forward the research in a particular area in a systematic and thoughtful way, in which each study builds on or extends your previous work. You want to communicate (a) your overall area of interest, (b) the studies you have completed and the contributions you have made so far, and (c) the broader direction of your research program in the future. It takes work to ensure it fits together in an easy-to-understand way.

However, reality is usually messier than that. If you are the type of person who came into graduate school knowing exactly what you wanted to research and all your research projects built neatly on one another, you are the exception, and talking about your research program will not be too difficult. But for most of us, the development of our research program did not happen on a linear trajectory. A few of your early research projects might have been a mix of your interests and your advisor's interests. You may have been an opportunist: There were projects you could contribute to, so you collaborated a bit more broadly to get research experience and publications on your curriculum vitae (CV). Or your research interests may have shifted over time, and the various projects you have completed showcase some of your shifting interests. Other times, projects just did not work, and you abandoned them. There might have been some valuable opportunities to work on a grant in an area that was outside your main research area. These are all common things that happen as a person is developing their research program—the key is figuring out how to connect the dots and come up with a narrative that describes your research program.

AN EVOLVING RESEARCH PROGRAM

Research programs often evolve over time. One of the perks of a job in research is the freedom to choose what to study. If you get interested in a particular topic, you can shift your program of research toward that new area, which keeps your scholarship new, interesting, and fresh.

Still, it is a good idea to balance that freedom and flexibility with the need to give a coherent job talk about your research program that centers on a primary theme. If your research projects are too scattered, it might be difficult to paint a picture of your area of interest or expertise. The most important contributions in science often occur when a person is willing to work in one area over a long period with sufficient depth.

We recommend graduate students begin thinking about their program of research right from the start, even as they are coming up with an idea for their thesis project. Although your program of research is likely to change or develop over time, it is important to continue to think about your overall direction. If you have the opportunity to take on a new project, consider how this project relates to your overall research program. How might you talk about it or fit it into the narrative you have already developed? Developing a trajectory is helpful for making scientific progress.

If you have the option to select from different topics or projects, it can be helpful to pick a project that aligns with the research program you have already established. If you do something in a similar area, it is easy to fit this new project into the developing narrative of your research program, and you can more readily draw from your expertise. However, do not let your existing research program stop you from doing projects that are intrinsically interesting or personally meaningful. An important part of graduate school (and research in general) is being able to explore and take advantage of opportunities that come your way.

CONNECTING THE DOTS

Sometimes it takes some work to connect the dots between your various research projects and come up with a narrative that explains your research program as a whole. For example, when Josh was finishing graduate school, a lot of his research seemed disconnected. He had done some work with a professor who focused on the experience of race-related stress in African Americans. His thesis focused on cultural differences in forgiveness. His dissertation focused on religiously accommodative couples counseling, and he had done some other work on religion and spirituality as well. Later in his graduate school career, he started to do more work on humility.

It was a challenge to come up with a coherent narrative that tied all of these different research projects together. This happened partly because Josh did not necessarily have crystal-clear research interests when he got to graduate school. He liked doing research and was eager to learn, but he adopted the opportunist approach: Most of his projects came about because of an opportunity to collaborate. He bounced around a bit before narrowing down what most interested him. This is often the case, and we need to work to connect the dots.

It can be helpful to think about the general areas that might be similar across different research projects. Could these similarities tie your research projects together under one narrative? For example, Josh noticed that a lot of his research had to do with diversity and multicultural issues—this general area could fit his work on race-related stress in African Americans, cultural differences in forgiveness, and religion and spirituality. Josh also noticed that a lot of his research was centered on positive psychology—this general area could fit his work on forgiveness and humility. So, when he went on job talks, Josh framed his research program around the intersection of diversity, multiculturalism, and positive psychology. With this framework, he was able to talk about several of his research studies, as well as his plans in this topic area.

Our experience has been that people generally understand research interests develop and change over time. You do not have to be overly rigid about your program of research. It is not a tightly locked box into which all your projects neatly fit. Most of our research interests are more permeable and flexible than that. Many of us have different research interests that do not fit perfectly with one another. The key is to come up with an overall narrative that can fit your research interests and activities as closely as possible. Take a few minutes and think about your research program. If you had to describe your program of research succinctly, how would you do it? What are the main threads that tie together your research interests and projects?

SCALING UP

As you think about your developing research program, it is helpful to consider how to "scale up" your work over time. In other words, are certain investments more deserving of your time than others? How can you put yourself in a good position for your contributions to build on each other?

Focusing on a particular research program allows you to develop expertise. It could be a topic area: We each put a lot of work into the topic of humility early on in our careers, and now we have some level of expertise in that area. Or it could be a particular type of methodology or statistical analysis. For example, Daryl is an experimental social psychologist with expertise in running laboratory studies. We had a colleague in graduate school who specialized in conducting meta-analyses, which became her area of expertise. The more you can develop an area of expertise, the more opportunities tend to come your way (e.g., invited chapters, opportunities to collaborate).

When deciding whether to focus on a particular topic in your research, it is worth remembering that the most popular areas of research are not always the most fruitful for new researchers. If there have been hundreds (or even thousands) of studies on a certain topic, it may be that most of the low-hanging fruit has been gathered. A less-developed area of research might have more room to explore and do some of the more foundational research. For example, when Josh began graduate school, he was interested in marriage and couples counseling. (He did his dissertation on this topic.) However, the field of couples counseling was mature, with lots of excellent research already completed. Early in his career, he shifted his focus to studying humility, where there was more room to explore and innovate.

Certain investments and types of projects can help your research program scale up over time. One type of investment is trying to get one of your projects published in a top-tier journal. Doing so often requires more work (e.g., multiple studies), but the rewards are often worthwhile. For example, when Josh was interested in cultural humility, he made a commitment to run multiple studies and develop a strong theory; this project ended up getting published in his field's flagship journal, the *Journal of Counseling Psychology*. The paper ended up being highly cited and launched an area of research for Josh and his colleagues.

A second type of paper that has helped to scale up our research programs is a systematic review. A *systematic review* is a paper that reviews all the empirical research on a topic and organizes it in one place. This type of paper tends to get cited quite often because readers appreciate having all the research reviewed in one place. In addition, because you have read much of the research on the area in preparation for writing the review paper, it places you in a position where you have a certain level of expertise. We have also received other opportunities, such as writing invited chapters, after publishing a systematic review.

A third type of paper that has helped us scale up our research programs is one that describes the creation of a new measure. If you are doing research in a new area, there are often not yet good ways to measure the construct of interest. Creating a new measure is challenging, but the payoffs can be huge if your measure becomes the gold standard in the field. For example, Donnie published one of the first measures on general humility, and that paper has been cited quite a bit and established him as one of the key experts in the field.

Jim Collins (2019) talks about the idea of scaling and momentum in his book *Turning the Flywheel*. The idea is that it takes a lot of energy for a flywheel to start moving. But then, little by little, the flywheel starts moving faster and faster. At some point, the flywheel is moving so fast that it takes less effort to keep it going—the momentum is driving it forward. Our experience with research has been similar. It has taken a lot of energy to learn the research process and get our respective research programs off the ground. But at some point, if you keep applying energy to the flywheel, it starts to gain momentum, and you do not have to apply the same amount of energy to keep it moving.

Just as investors benefit from compound interest, research can benefit from a step-by-step process in which prior investments generate leverage and lead to additional opportunities. This type of leverage can also occur at the team level. For example, we have each invested in slightly different areas that have generated leverage for the team. Over their first 10 years working together, Josh made the strongest investment in writing high-quality literature review papers, as well as learning to write books, including some books for popular audiences. Donnie invested especially in developing training structures within his department that promote research training, given his connection to the Center for the Study of Stress, Trauma, and Resilience at Georgia State University. He also recently received two large grants that included funding for two postdocs and nine doctoral students over the next 5 years. He also invested in forming relationships and developing expertise related to testing mechanisms and analyzing longitudinal data. Daryl invested in publishing in top outlets in social psychology (which are competitive), which included advanced skills in experimental methodology, and recently, he also explored working in administrative positions. As a team, we can now develop and lead a broad range of projects.

GRADUATE MENTOR CORNER

We encourage mentors to take a developmental approach to helping students build their research programs, with a particular eye on helping students maintain intrinsic motivation. Students are engaging in a variety of evaluative processes within the first 10 to 15 years, such as passing their dissertations, getting an internship, giving a job talk (and getting a first job), and getting tenure. If they focus too much on these extrinsic factors, they risk getting too far from their reservoirs of intrinsic motivation.

We want to help students negotiate these various evaluative milestones with a heavy dose of agency and self-determination. We do not want them to get underwater, where they are simply dealing with the next deadline. In a special issue on interdisciplinary work, Donnie talked about some of the key challenges for early career professionals (Davis, 2019). To the extent we can help students develop leverage, they can invest in longer term planning and even dreaming. This process is helpful because it provides more room to make career transitions effectively. For example, because he had a head start on publishing, Donnie was able to start making "risky" investments in the 2nd and 3rd year of his faculty position, which made it easier for him to navigate some of the challenges that occurred once he received tenure (e.g., protection for your time goes away, and the expectations for departmental service accrue quickly). It is important to help students make space to let their intrinsic interests guide their exploration.

After people get tenure, they often have more latitude to consider long-term investments. If early career scholars clear the pressure of some of these deadlines, they can start making longer term investments that align with long-term career aspirations. For many academics, this might be the first time they can truly consider longer term investments in a serious way, but we encourage students to start dreaming long before these transitions occur. It is important to keep the big picture in mind.

One thing you can do as a mentor is help reduce the abruptness of some of these transitions. Give your students opportunities to hear the developmental trajectories of a range of scholars as they navigate these common transitions.

For example, Donnie tells stories about how he navigated key transitions, such as writing a first paper, applying for jobs, and navigating the pretenure and posttenure periods. For example, his first major research project required a major shift in structuring time (e.g., spending at least 2 hours per day 5–6 days per week to get his master's thesis finished). To deal with tenure pressure, he set writing goals that clearly surpassed minimal standards, so he could start to shift emotional energy toward his long-term interests sooner in his career. Posttenure, he had to adjust to the organizational demands of organizing a book-length project (which took a lot of trial and error and learning about other people's styles). He also negotiated his teaching roles, designing several project-focused courses that aligned with positive psychology. It feels good when students can use their imaginations to clarify their long-term values and dreams and align their work with these aspirations.

One way we can help our students ride the wave of intrinsic motivation is to model being a lifelong learner. This part of life is caught more than taught. We do not stop training when we finish a training program. To train others in psychological science, we must stay in our network of relationships to ensure our continuing development. This behavior speaks louder than words. We can show students how to keep training at a high level. They can see how we approach learning new tasks. The principle is similar to the suggestion that clinicians seek their own therapy. We only develop our potential as mentors if we also continue to be active in our role as learners. This stance keeps us open to new ways of teaching and passing on knowledge and skills.

UNDERGRADUATE MENTOR CORNER

Students can start dreaming about their long-term goals right away, so one thing we can do is develop a vibrant and supportive culture that promotes initiative and responsibility. Even though most undergraduate students working in a research lab will mainly assist the professor or other graduate students with their research, they can still observe how others are developing their research programs and how the different parts fit together. Also, undergraduate students who do take the lead on their own independent research project (perhaps through an honor's thesis) can start to think about their overall research interests and how this first independent project might fit into that. Many times, the projects that a student is involved in as an undergraduate can shape the mentors they apply to work with or the themes they may consider for their master's thesis. We can also model the flexibility to shift research foci while helping our students see how our work fits together in a broader narrative of interests.

MOVING FORWARD

In this chapter, we discussed how to think about not only single research projects you might conduct but also how those individual research projects fit together into a developing research program. When you apply for jobs, you will need to talk about your research program in a coherent, organized way. But research interests shift and change over time, so sometimes it is tricky to connect the dots. We also talked about strategies to scale up your research program as you get further along in your career. In the next chapter, we consider one of the most helpful and fun ways to scale up your research productivity—collaborating with others.

22 COLLABORATING WITH OTHERS IN RESEARCH

In the previous chapter, we talked about the process of developing your individual research program, including some things you can do to scale up your research. In this chapter, we expand on one of the best ways to scale up your research program: collaboration with other researchers. Specifically, we discuss reasons to collaborate, the keys to good collaboration, and what to do when a collaboration goes poorly. You can certainly do research on your own and be successful. There is no rule that says you have to collaborate with others to be a great researcher. However, our experience has been that research is much more successful (and more fun) when you find a good group of collaborators.

In fact, this book stems from a 15-year working relationship between the three of us. Josh met Donnie in graduate school because they worked with the same research advisor. Donnie entered the program 1 year after Josh did; he even stayed at Josh's apartment for his campus interview. They started to collaborate in graduate school and have worked together ever since. Daryl also went to Virginia Commonwealth University for graduate school; he was in the social psychology program and had a different primary advisor. Daryl first met Donnie in a forgiveness seminar, and then Daryl started attending

https://doi.org/10.1037/0000371-023
The Complete Researcher: A Practical Guide for Graduate Students and Early Career Professionals, by J. N. Hook, D. E. Davis, and D. R. Van Tongeren
Copyright © 2024 by the American Psychological Association. All rights reserved.

our lab meetings because he had research interests in positive psychology (he studied meaning in life). Near the end of our graduate school careers, the three of us began working together more formally and have collaborated quite often over the years.

Not only has the collaborative relationship increased our productivity but we have also been able to do research as a group that we would not have been able to do individually because our skill sets complement each other. For example, Donnie is the "big idea" person in our group. He is good at thinking creatively and outside the box. He often comes up with new ideas and helps us communicate why our research matters to the world. Daryl is the experimental psychologist of the group. His lab is always churning out experiments, and he is able to use experiments to see whether the relationships we find between variables are causally linked to one another. He also aspires to place his work in top outlets in personality and social psychology, which has required him to develop highly rigorous skills associated with linking strong theory to strong research design. Josh's skills are in the area of creating logical arguments for our papers and grant projects. Josh is able to take Donnie's "big ideas" and connect the dots, crafting a step-by-step line of reasoning for our work.

Collaboration has also been a lot of fun. Some parts of research involve lots of tedious and sometimes monotonous steps that require high levels of attention to detail. It is great to have collaborators who are also friends. We work together, but we also have a great time together. Every year since we left graduate school and started our academic positions, we have had an annual "research retreat," where we convene at a desirable destination (e.g., we have been to lakes, mountains, beaches, and even the middle of nowhere in Connecticut) to discuss our collaborative projects and plan for the next year. Our families are engaged in each other's lives, and we have gone on vacations together. Donnie and Daryl were even groomsmen at Josh's wedding. It has been fun to not only work together but also do life together.

Although our collaboration has worked out well, each of us has also had some poor collaborations with other people over the years. Sometimes a collaborator wanted one of us to do more than our fair share of work on a project, and when the project was finished, we realized the collaboration was not worth it. Sometimes we have had interpersonal conflicts or challenges, and the collaboration was stressful and not much fun. Sometimes we have disagreed about authorship or roles on a project. Collaboration, like any work with other people, is not always a smooth process. But overall, we can say that collaboration has definitely been worth it. Even the difficult collaborations have encouraged us to learn new skills and stretch our abilities.

REASONS FOR COLLABORATION

Why should you think about collaborating in the first place? Is it not easier to just do your work on your own? Yes and no. It may appear to be simpler to work by yourself, but adopting a "lone-wolf" model of research has its limitations. Over the years, we have found several benefits to collaboration, including (a) different perspectives, (b) complementary skill sets, (c) the ability to do larger scale projects, (d) increased productivity, and (e) more fun. We describe each of the benefits briefly in the following sections.

Different Perspectives

We each come to the table with our own perspectives based on our cultural and social upbringing. Our individual perspectives are not bad, but they are limited. Josh tends to think about research in a certain way, so if he is working on his own, he only thinks about it in that one way. But if Josh is collaborating with others, they can join their perspectives together. His collaborator might have an idea for a project or a measure based on some of their life experience that Josh might not have (and vice versa). In addition, Josh might have an interesting idea for how to analyze the data that his collaborator has not thought about because they do not have experience with that data analytic technique. The main point here is that collaboration brings more perspectives to the table, which usually results in better research projects. You get to tackle a project from different sides and think about it more holistically when multiple perspectives are involved. What has been your experience with bringing different perspectives to the table when collaborating on research? What benefits have you noticed from having different perspectives? Have you found any challenges with navigating the different points of view?

Complementary Skill Sets

Research is so broad that you cannot be an expert at everything. Solo researchers usually are limited in their contributions unless they have mastered a large number of skills required to do a broad set of projects. Because of this, if you are working by yourself, you tend to do one type of project (what you are good at and most comfortable with). But if you are collaborating with others, you have different strengths in your group that can complement each other and lead to a better overall project. For example, for most of his early career, Josh did not do much qualitative research—he tended to focus on quantitative research. But as his career progressed, Josh felt like his focus on only doing quantitative research was a limitation. Josh wanted to do more qualitative research, but he was not an expert in the area. Josh collaborated with a colleague who was an expert in qualitative research, and they did some qualitative studies together. Josh was able to expand his research repertoire because of his collaborations. What are some of the unique skill sets you bring to the table when it comes to research? What are some limitations or areas for growth that you might be able to "fill in" with other collaborators?

Ability to Do Larger Scale Projects

As time has passed, the standards for what constitutes excellent research have risen. Many top-tier journals require articles to have several studies that programmatically build on each other. Often your paper also needs to have different methodologies that all point toward the same conclusion. You need to be able to test your hypotheses on different types of samples to see if your results generalize. The bottom line is that it is much harder and slower to do all this on your own. To create high-quality research, you often need a team of people working toward the same goal. Collaboration enables you to complete larger scale projects than you can do if you are working by yourself. What limitations have you noticed in doing research on your own regarding your ability to place papers in top-tier journals?

Increased Productivity

Collaboration increases your productivity. At some level, even though we do not like to think about it this way, research success is partially a numbers game. Although quality is preferable to quantity, you will need some volume of papers to establish credibility and earn tenure. How many publications do you have? How many are first authored? How many are in top-tier journals? We all have a limited number of papers we can write. There are only 24 hours in a day, after all. However, if you conduct research using a team-based approach, your productivity can increase because each team member can take the lead on different projects (or parts of projects). We have taken this approach with our research. We work together on quite a few of our projects, each taking the lead on various projects. Also, because of our complementary skill sets, a synergy happens when we collaborate. We are able to accomplish even more than the sum of our parts. In what ways have you noticed your productivity increase when you have collaborated with other researchers?

More Fun

Collaboration can be fun. This factor might depend a bit on your personality—more introverted people may not find it as fun to work with others. But in general, we have found that research and writing can be lonely enterprises. There are a lot of activities (e.g., analyzing data, writing manuscripts) that involve working by yourself for long periods. If you are a social person, this can be boring and tedious. Collaboration helps counteract the loneliness of the research process. Sure, there are still times when you have to work by yourself. But it is balanced by other times when you are engaging with colleagues, working together on projects, and discussing ideas. Like life, research is more fun with friends. Are you more of an introvert or extrovert? What has your experience been like when you have worked on your research alone? What has your experience been like when you have worked on your research in teams?

KEYS TO A GOOD COLLABORATION

Now that we have discussed some reasons to collaborate, what are the keys to a good collaboration? Not all collaborative relationships are created equal. Although we want to encourage collaboration, we would be remiss if we did not point out that some collaborative efforts turn out badly. So, how can we work to develop good collaborative relationships with our colleagues? To organize the keys to good collaboration, we found information by business consultant Patrick Lencioni helpful. In his book *The Advantage*, Lencioni (2012) talked about some key factors for developing a cohesive team. We cover some key factors of good collaboration here, including size, communication, trust, conflict, commitment, accountability, results, and norms.

Size of the Group

How big should a group of collaborators be? The answer to this question obviously depends on the needs of your projects (e.g., larger projects might require more people because more data collection sites are involved or more areas of expertise are needed), but in general, we think a smaller team is better. When your group of collaborators gets above eight or 10 people, it can be tough to get everyone on the same page. It can also be challenging to feel collectively responsible for a particular project when so many people are working on it. With too many people, it is easy to form silos or have people working at cross-purposes. Again, although there is no hard-and-fast rule about the size of your team, we like to keep collaborative relationships fairly small. Groups of between two and five people have worked well for us. We often form teams of two to three for writing projects within our research teams because it optimizes accountability.

Communication

It is important to establish good lines of communication with your collaborators. Being responsive to colleagues is a top priority for healthy groups. It is important to be honest and direct. One way of doing this is to be clear about authorship. Until norms have been set and agreed on, sometimes there can be misunderstandings about who is included as an author and in what order. Before any substantive collaborative work begins, get this clearly spelled out in an email (or in another form of writing) so everyone can reference it in case there are questions. This slight awkwardness for just a few minutes saves potential ruptures in trust or feeling underappreciated or undervalued. Perhaps you will get to a place where norms become more implicit, but that takes time and effort to develop. Start with clear communication and continue to build on it over time. Clear communication involves meeting with the group and openly discussing all aspects of the project (e.g., who is responsible for what), allowing space for questions and discussion. It is often helpful to have regular meetings with collaborators to keep the lines of communication open. Think about a time when you have had to talk with a research collaborator about an issue on one of your projects (e.g., authorship). How did the conversation go? Is there anything you could have done to communicate more clearly?

Trust

When Patrick Lencioni (2012) talks about trust, he is thinking about it slightly differently than most people do. When most people think about trust, we think it means we believe someone will do what they say they will do. Although this kind of trust is important, a deeper level of trust is necessary for collaborative relationships to work well. Teams need to develop vulnerability-based trust, which means team members feel comfortable being honest and transparent about their limitations and faults. Individuals must be able to set aside their egos for the good of the team. You need to be able to apologize and defer to another team member when they have a better idea than you. These actions only happen when there is a high level of trust on the team.

How do you develop trust in a team? One activity that Lencioni (2012) recommended (that we have used with our own research teams) is to have each team member share a little bit about their backstories (e.g., where were you born, how many siblings do you have, where are you in the sibling order, what was the most challenging thing you had to deal with as a kid). It might seem silly, but when Josh shared his struggles of being made fun of growing up for being overweight, it set the stage for vulnerable sharing and building trust. Sometimes we schedule two or three social events (e.g., hiking, bowling) per year to allow people to get to know each other in nonacademic settings.

If you want to develop trust in your collaborative relationships, it is important to lead with trustworthy behaviors. People often hesitate to share vulnerably or admit their mistakes, not knowing how others will respond. You might carry around some fear of criticism or judgment. However, it is important to step into your fear and be the first one to share vulnerably. Usually, people appreciate vulnerability. If you give the benefit of the doubt, seeking to build trusting and mutually beneficial relationships, it will likely encourage vulnerable sharing in your collaborative partner. Then the stage is set, and you can continue building trust.

Of course, being vulnerable and building trust must be accompanied by an awareness of healthy boundaries. Sometimes it can be helpful to share vulnerably in a small way first to see how the relationship goes. We can treat people in a way that gives them the benefit of the doubt, but this does not mean we ignore hurtful behavior. When people consistently act in self-interested ways and do not prioritize the collaboration, we must make necessary adjustments. Think about a relationship you have that has a high level of trust. How did those feelings of trust develop over time? Are there any lessons you could take with you when developing collaborative research teams?

Conflict

Conflict is inevitable in healthy relationships. Conflict occurs because we are different people with our own perspectives. In collaboration, we consider how to put our perspectives together. The challenge is to use conflict to sharpen ideas but manage it in healthy ways, so people do not take disagreement personally nor allow the process to damage trust. Initial attitudes about conflict often develop in our families, where we may have learned some unhealthy habits, such as experiencing conflict as destructive (e.g., name-calling, physical or emotional abuse) or avoiding conflict at all costs. In our adult lives, we may swing from one extreme to the other. For example, we may avoid conflict because it scares us, or we may emotionally erupt and wreck a relationship. Neither way of handling conflict is productive or healthy.

For a collaborative relationship to work, all parties have to be able to be honest with each other, especially when they disagree about something. When group members trust one another, conflict can be viewed as the pursuit of truth or trying to find the best possible answer for the relationship or group (Lencioni, 2012). When group members do not trust one another, however, conflict can become manipulative, as each person tries to convince the other person that their position is correct.

Lean into the fear of conflict. Do not let this fear control your life. Conflict can be uncomfortable, but it does not have to be destructive. Make sure every person on the team is able to voice their opinion. Do not succumb to groupthink, where everyone just goes along with the majority opinion. Be on the lookout for and listen to minority voices. Instill discussions about conflict with humility—encourage people to talk about and listen to the drawbacks of their position. Make sure conflict stays focused on the task at hand. When conflict devolves into mean-spirited personal attacks, it becomes destructive. What has been your experience with conflict? Are you comfortable or uncomfortable with conflict? If you try to avoid conflict, what is one way that you could begin to step into healthy conflict?

Commitment

When everyone has had a chance to voice their opinion and work through conflict, it is time to commit to a plan of action. For commitment to happen, it is important that the foundations of trust and healthy conflict negotiation are in place. People will not be truly willing to commit to a course of action if they have not had the opportunity to voice their opinions and concerns. But if they have had this opportunity, commitment is the next step. When working on a collaborative team, it is important to have specific rather than vague commitments. If commitments are vague (e.g., let us work on a paper together), people are not clear on exactly what they are supposed to do, and the work is likely to falter. To have a successful collaboration, make sure you spend some time working out the details of what each person is responsible for. Clarity is critical—make sure you are clear about what you and others are committing to do and when it will happen.

Accountability

When everyone is crystal clear about the commitments that each person has made, the next step is accountability. Accountability helps to build trust, which occurs when we make and keep our commitments to each other. These are classic team values. Being part of the group means we keep our commitments. If we know we will not meet a commitment, we say something early. We also give each other permission to hold high standards of accountability. Team cohesion and effectiveness drop off quickly when people are not accountable to each other. Often, once accountability falters, relationships are not far from deteriorating, and the collaboration will break down until trust is repaired. We have four key points of advice when it comes to accountability.

First, address your fear of holding people accountable. People often struggle with accountability because they do not want to be viewed as "mean." However, accountability, when it is done well, is a loving action. You are not trying to make someone do something or make them feel bad. The goal is to maintain a high degree of trust in the relationship. We all do best in relationships of high trust and commitment, so you are seeking high accountability because this helps people grow and helps the collaboration succeed. Sometimes people fail to hold a person accountable and then get frustrated and complain about them behind their back or eventually exclude them from the collaboration. This behavior is much less loving than stepping into your fear of holding someone accountable and having an honest conversation.

Second, it is important to practice holding someone accountable early, proximal to when someone does not meet a commitment. Sometimes people fail to hold someone accountable early, and that person learns they can get away with not honoring their commitments. Then things build up. Eventually, you may become so frustrated and angry that by the time you confront the person, it feels like an avalanche of accountability is raining down on them. It is better to start with accountability right from the beginning. Tackle the issue when it is a small problem, and then it does not have the opportunity to grow into something huge.

Third, try to avoid defensiveness when someone else holds you accountable for a commitment you have made. It can feel painful when someone points out a failure on our part to keep a commitment. To avoid feeling this pain, we may get defensive or come up with an excuse for why the commitment was not kept. This usually is not effective. Instead, try to press the pause button when someone holds you accountable. Give the other person the benefit of the doubt, and be careful not to allow yourself to make assumptions about their intentions. This discipline will help you avoid responding in an overly defensive matter. Instead, take some time and think about what the other person said. What are they right about? What can you learn from the accountability opportunity? What can you own? Apologize, if appropriate. Or clarify and renegotiate the commitment. This can go a long way toward building (or rebuilding) a good collaborative relationship.

Fourth, know your limits when it comes to having conversations about accountability. We all eventually can reach a threshold and experience a sense of feeling flooded with stress. When this happens, we may want to ask for some time to think and recover before we come back to a conversation. This step shows we value the relationship and the other person enough to protect the relationship.

What has been your experience with holding other people accountable for their commitments? Do you have any fears or concerns about implementing this practice into your research collaborations? What has been your experience when others try to hold you accountable for a commitment you have made?

Results

The bottom line, when it comes to a successful collaboration, is results. The ultimate goals of the collaboration may vary (e.g., conducting a research study, publishing a paper, obtaining a grant), but for the collaboration to be successful, it must lead to tangible results. For a collaboration to be successful and lead to tangible results, it is important to stay focused on the collective goal of the team. If individual goals become more important than team goals, it is unlikely the collaboration will succeed. You want all members of the collaboration to view the team's shared goal as most important. You do not want your collaboration to look like the U.S. Congress, where members rarely work together and instead work mainly for their individual goals. (Thanks to Patrick Lencioni for this example.)

Norms

Sometimes collaboration does not go well because researchers have different expectations for how the collaboration should go. For example, when Josh includes Donnie and Daryl as coauthors on a paper, they generally return the manuscript with changes within a week. Once, Josh worked with a new collaborator, who did not return a manuscript for several months. Josh was frustrated, but the frustration came about because they had different norms for collaborating on a coauthored manuscript. It is helpful to talk about norms and expectations before beginning the collaborative relationship, so everyone is on the same page.

Norms for collaboration vary widely among researchers, but we thought it might be helpful to share our norms for collaborative research and writing in case they might be helpful for you as well. First, the first author takes the lead in producing a strong first draft of the manuscript. Sometimes they start with an existing data set. Other times, they develop an idea from scratch, refine it with feedback from other experts (on both the idea and research design), and collect the data set. Usually, they run the main analyses (perhaps working closely with the mentor or advanced graduate student).

Next, the first author circulates the manuscript to other coauthors for a line edit. We have guidelines for the role of coauthors that help ward off ineffective coauthor behaviors. As much as possible, coauthors make changes directly to the manuscript using "Track Changes." They are instructed not to leave comments because comments are often ambiguous. Instead, if you want something to be changed, just make the change! The first author can compare the revision with the prior version and make a decision about the suggested change (or try a third option for revising that builds on the coauthor's suggestion). Our norm is also to return manuscripts quickly. With coauthors, the norm is about 5 days (or a business week), and if someone has a time conflict, we often shift the order of reading the manuscript with someone else in the author chain. When the manuscript arrives back to the first author, they can decide which changes to accept, make any other necessary revisions, and then give the manuscript a final proofread before submitting it.

How are these norms helpful for protecting collaborative relationships? One advantage is it balances skill and working styles. The first author can work at whatever pace they are able to, doing most of the work. A mentor can help support the first author in that role. As a result, the time of coauthors is prioritized. It may take a student a year or more to draft a manuscript, but then the coauthors can do their work in a few weeks.

A second advantage is it reduces conflict over authorship. We have a "first-author or bust" norm. Namely, first author matters. In some cases, second author is clear (e.g., if someone helped a lot with analyses). Otherwise, we do not quibble over author order and leave it to the first author to decide. This strategy tends to work well. We have only had a few cases where authorship order required a more extensive conversation.

A third advantage is that the protection of coauthor time makes it easier for people to want to collaborate. This has many benefits. For example, the more opportunities one has to serve as a coauthor, the quicker one learns to write well. Also, the first author gets high-quality feedback on manuscripts, which accelerates expertise development (recall that feedback is one of the major components of expertise).

A fourth advantage is that getting good feedback can increase the odds that the project will get published in a strong journal with fewer revisions. When a paper gets rejected by a journal, it takes a lot of time. In a subsequent submission, the paper will likely be reviewed by different people, and they may find new problems. Thus, it works much better to seek quality feedback to address as many weaknesses as possible during design, analyses, and writing so reviewers find less to critique. (They always find something to critique, but it is great when all they can do is suggest superficial edits because the core of the project is solid.)

A fifth advantage is that good feedback prevents bad coauthor behavior. For example, occasionally, there is an academic with a big ego. They may make a comment that has the potential to generate a lot of work to resolve without putting in the effort to improve the paper themselves. The norm of making the change instead of making a comment creates a level of equity among coauthors. If coauthors have big ideas for revision, they will also generate more work for themselves. It also heads off ambiguity or laziness. It is much easier to leave an ambiguous comment than make the change in the manuscript. But this often creates lots of extra work for someone to clarify what the comment meant and try to resolve it. This is not efficient.

Finally, coauthors sometimes sit on a manuscript for a long time. If someone does not give a timely edit, the first author can simply pull the manuscript back and keep it in circulation. We have had this happen only a few times, and it resulted in one-trial learning.

What has your experience been with collaboration? Have you had any negative experiences? What kind of norms would help you build strong relationships that will stand the test of time and take advantage of the diverse perspectives and personalities of your team? What adjustments will you make when you work with teams with different norms? Are there any boundaries you have that you do not want to compromise, even if other teams have a different working style?

WHEN COLLABORATION GOES POORLY

Collaboration does not always work out well. In general, we are pro-collaboration, and we recommend you work to develop collaborative relationships as you grow in your career. However, we would be remiss if we did not talk about the other side of the coin. Sometimes collaborative relationships break down, which is not a good situation professionally or personally. It could just not be a professional fit. Maybe you thought you would work well together, but the collaboration is not clicking. Or maybe there is an interpersonal problem that is making the collaboration difficult. It is rare, but you might find yourself in a situation where someone is trying to take advantage of or exploit you. If you find yourself in one of these situations, what do you do? How can you move forward when a collaboration goes bad?

Work to Address the Problem

When you start to notice problems in a collaboration, the first step is to work to address them. Sometimes there might be a miscommunication, or something happens that keeps you from being on the same page. It might be possible to address the problem and "right the ship before it goes down." When working to address the problem, be specific. What exactly about the collaboration is not working? What exactly would need to change for the collaboration to work well? Is the other person willing to make the necessary changes? The more specific you can be, the better. Also, try to address the problem as soon as possible. Frustration and anger build up over time. If you wait to address a problem, the relationship may be fractured beyond repair. Even though it is uncomfortable, try to address the problem right away.

End the Collaborative Relationship

Ideally, the person will respond to feedback and work to address the problem. Strong relationships are valuable and worth preserving. But sometimes talking about the problem does not help (Cloud, 2010). Or perhaps the rupture of trust was too severe or the action too egregious. When problems persist or are severe enough, we can adjust our level of trust in the relationship. We do not have to work with the person in the same capacity moving forward. Extending trust despite evidence that the person is untrustworthy is unwise. Do not stay in an unhealthy collaborative relationship because of guilt or the fear of conflict.

Do Not Give Up on Collaboration

Though it might be wise to move on from a collaboration, we think it is important not to abandon collaborating. Even if you have a bad collaborative experience (or two), we encourage you not to give up on collaboration in general. It can take time to find a good set of collaborators. A good collaborative relationship is worth its weight in gold. It will help you conduct high-quality research and enable you to become more productive, and it can be a lot of fun. We may need to develop new norms (or personal boundaries) that will keep relationships in a zone where they feel mutually beneficial. Do not let a few bad experiences sour your energy and excitement for collaboration. When a collaborative relationship does not work out, try not to take it personally—just move on from it as quickly as possible and make note of what worked and what did not. Even negative experiences give us a chance to tweak our approach so we can have more positive and effective collaborations in the future.

GRADUATE MENTOR CORNER

As a mentor, you can help to instill an attitude of collaboration with your graduate students. As advisor, you set the stage for the culture of your research team. Do you meet with the team regularly? When one graduate student takes the lead on a project or paper, do you encourage them to involve other graduate students as collaborators? Do you "take the lead" by including graduate students on your research projects and papers? It is important to set the stage for collaboration by practicing it yourself, both with other faculty members and students on your research team.

Another thing we can do is acculturate students to writing norms that help regulate problematic behaviors. Recall that when you collaborate with others, you often must discuss and negotiate the norms for the collaboration. However, as a mentor, you create the norms for your team. Some common problems include naive trust, unfairly divided work, mismatched anxiety about deadlines, mismatched skills, overcommitment, lack of accountability, lack of vulnerability, lack of commitment, and difficulty with delegation. As discussed earlier in the chapter, our team had specific norms that helped curb problematic behaviors, and we encourage you to develop your own norms for collaboration with your research team. We teach our students to remain flexible when working with other team cultures, but when we are working with other members of the team, we follow the team norms. Having explicit team norms can also help acculturate new members to the good citizenship behaviors of our team.

UNDERGRADUATE MENTOR CORNER

With undergraduate students, collaboration looks different. Sometimes it may be collectively working on a poster for a conference. Other times it is conducting a literature review for a paper or chapter you are writing. And in some cases, you might be cocontributing to manuscripts. In these cases, our main strategy is to involve students in a team-writing approach and set clear boundaries early on. Take note of your position of power and seek to be fair and equitable. Avoid any intimation of exploitation. Often, students will turn to you to set the norms; explain the importance of setting guidelines and expectations early on, and make sure everyone understands the process. Students often thrive with a clear structure and expectations of what is required. When students learn norms early, it helps them feel more comfortable transitioning into a doctoral student role. This confidence can lead to strategic compounding throughout someone's career.

MOVING FORWARD

In this chapter, we talked about the importance of collaboration. In today's world, it is difficult to complete high-quality research by yourself. You need other people who can challenge and sharpen you. And it is a lot of fun to work on projects together. We discussed some of the key reasons for collaboration, as well as the important characteristics of a good collaborative relationship. We also talked about what to do when a collaborative relationship sours. In the next chapter, we talk about some more specific advice for individuals making the transition from graduate student to professor.

23 MAKING THE TRANSITION FROM GRADUATE STUDENT TO PROFESSOR

In this chapter, we cover one of the more difficult transitions in your research career: the transition from graduate student to professor. (We realize many readers may not want an academic career or remain undecided about their career path. Nonetheless, the principles discussed in this chapter are part of learning scientific culture and will thus be helpful context for students with a range of career goals.) One of the difficult things about this transition is that it is a big shift that happens quickly. One year you are a student, taking classes and following your mentor's lead in research. Several months later, you are a professor, teaching classes and expected to lead your own research program (and even help graduate students with their research). For many, this can be an abrupt transition, and it can feel like you are not ready for it. In this chapter, we first talk about applying and interviewing for an academic job, and then we specifically consider the transition to becoming a professor and getting started in research, teaching, and service.

For the three of us, the transition from graduate student to professor was challenging in some ways (e.g., loneliness and adjustment to a new setting), but the transition regarding our research was probably easier than for some

---

https://doi.org/10.1037/0000371-024
The Complete Researcher: A Practical Guide for Graduate Students and Early Career Professionals, by J. N. Hook, D. E. Davis, and D. R. Van Tongeren
Copyright © 2024 by the American Psychological Association. All rights reserved.

because we had each received excellent research mentoring in our graduate program from our research mentors. Because of this, when we made the transition from graduate student to professor, we were ready to hit the ground running. Even with this training in place, it was still a significant adjustment. As we have progressed in our career and talked with other people about their transitions from graduate student to professor, we realized that, unfortunately, our experience was the exception rather than the rule. Many people struggle to make this transition and are left floundering on their own. In fact, this was one of the key motivations for us to write this book—to help people develop their research skills, so they are better able to make the transition to becoming independent researchers.

APPLYING FOR A JOB

Applying for a job in academia can be challenging and stressful. One reason is that the job market varies from year to year. Because of many factors outside your control (e.g., the state of the economy), there may be more or fewer job openings. Another reason applying for a job in academia can be challenging and stressful is that it can be competitive. Especially if you are aiming for an R1 university (high expectations for research activity), there are likely lots of applicants vying for the position, including applicants already in faculty roles (e.g., assistant professors at other universities), postdoctoral scholars, and advanced graduate students. There usually are not many positions open each year, so demand is often higher than supply, and it is challenging to know with whom you might be competing.

One thing to consider when applying for jobs is how broad your job search should be. There are different types of academic positions. Not surprisingly, academic jobs at R1 universities with PhD programs are more focused on research. The pressures to publish and earn grants are higher. You can mentor graduate students and work together on research. The teaching load is lower (usually a 2-2, meaning you teach two classes per semester, or even a 2-1, meaning you teach two classes one semester and one class the other semester).

At the other end of the spectrum, academic jobs at many liberal arts colleges are more focused on teaching than research. They may still want you to publish some of your research, but the demands are usually lower, and there are not the same pressures to publish and get grants. Because there usually is no PhD program, students who work with you will be undergraduates, which is a different type of experience. The teaching load is higher (usually a 4-4, meaning you teach four classes per semester).

There are also different types of academic jobs that fall somewhere in the middle of these two poles. For example, Daryl got a job at Hope College, a liberal arts college focused on research. Daryl's teaching load is a 3-3, and he often finds bright undergraduate students to work in his lab. It is important to think about your preferences regarding how much research versus teaching is prioritized because this will help you narrow down the schools to which you would like to apply. That said, because academic jobs are often competitive, it is a good idea to apply to a range of different schools.

Another avenue to consider is completing a postdoctoral fellowship (i.e., postdoc). You have to apply for postdocs as well, and some can be competitive (although usually not as competitive as a faculty position). A postdoc is a 1- to 2-year position usually funded by a grant. A postdoc is a good option because it enables you to build your curriculum vitae (CV) while getting more research experience, and it ensures that when you are applying for assistant professor positions, you have already completed your PhD. It also sometimes allows people in applied programs to accrue postdoc clinical hours and get licensed. There are benefits and costs to a postdoc: They often pay less than being an assistant professor, but they can allow you the time and resources necessary to strengthen your CV and be more competitive when applying for more research-focused positions. If your life situation allows for it, it may be advisable to apply to both postdoc and assistant professor positions.

Applying for academic jobs is not entirely different from applying for graduate school. The materials required differ depending on the school, but in general, you may be required to submit a cover letter, your CV, a research statement, a teaching statement, a diversity statement, reprints of some articles you have written, and the names and contact information for three individuals who have agreed to provide a letter of recommendation. Remember, academic jobs are competitive, so you want to apply to several places. In what follows, we give some advice for crafting the cover letter, research statement, teaching statement, and diversity statement. However, it is important to remember these are just our thoughts and preferences—your mentor may have other advice or examples to give you. It is also helpful to have your mentor and other graduate students read your materials and give feedback. Finally, positions may have additional or different requirements. As always, read the position description and application instructions carefully and adhere to their guidelines.

Cover Letter

In your cover letter, briefly describe yourself and why you are interested in the position. Succinctly review your educational and professional experience, including research, grants, teaching, service, and mentoring students (if applicable). Try to connect the dots between your interests and experiences and what the university is looking for in the position. It is important to read the job advertisement thoroughly to make these connections and also do some research about the university, department, and program, including their core values. At the end of the cover letter, describe what is included in the application (e.g., different types of statements, CV, reprints, contact information for references). If it fits your personality, do not be afraid to express energy and excitement about the possibility of working in this position. The cover letter is often the first thing a committee will review, so it can be helpful to try to make a connection and impression.

Research Statement

The purpose of the research statement is to briefly describe your program of research, including your most important work to date, as well as where you anticipate your research program going in the future. Crafting this section can take some time and energy to write—the recommendations from Chapter 21 on connecting the dots in your developing research program can be helpful when writing this statement. Also, it can be a good idea to do some research about the university and position and adjust your research statement to reflect their priorities. For example, does the university highly value grant funding? If so, it is probably a good idea to highlight your work on applying for and receiving grants. Is the position focused on research relevant to diversity, equity, and inclusion? If so, make sure you talk about how your research program relates to that priority.

Teaching Statement

Many job applications require a teaching statement, but (if application page limits permit) we recommend going one step further and putting together a comprehensive teaching portfolio, including a statement of one's teaching philosophy, quantitative summaries of teaching ratings, and information on each course taught (e.g., class description, syllabus, exam example, assignment example, qualitative student comments). The purpose of the teaching philosophy is to describe how you think about the purpose of teaching and education, as well as your teaching style. As a graduate student, you may not have thought too much about your teaching philosophy amid all the other pressures of graduate school—this is a good time to reflect on how you are (or who you want to be) as a teacher. More teaching-focused institutions will often want to see a full portfolio and heavily weight this dimension of your application. Similarly, many strongly value teaching experience (both as the instructor of record and as a teaching assistant), so it is helpful to highlight such training in this portfolio.

Diversity Statement

Many colleges and universities are making stronger efforts to improve diversity, equity, and inclusion at their institutions, and they want to ensure that new faculty members have thought about these issues and are committed to working toward these goals. Because of this, many searches request a diversity statement. *Diversity* refers to the goal of seeking faculty members and students with a broad range of perspectives and cultural backgrounds, including those from historically underrepresented and marginalized groups. *Equity* refers to giving individuals and groups fair opportunities to succeed, irrespective of their cultural background or identity. *Inclusion* refers to different individuals and groups feeling welcomed and included in the life and work of the university.

When you write your diversity statement, consider your beliefs and values as well as the cultural norms of the programs to which you are applying. Search committees use this statement to try to get a sense of your values and commitments. Can they trust that you will contribute to the aspirational goals of the program and department you are joining? Keep in mind that every department will have a range of perspectives regarding how to balance the issues involved in serving a diverse and pluralistic public, including addressing problems the university (and the field of psychology) has regarding poor representation from marginalized groups.

Give the program and department a sense of what they can trust you to do as a member of their community according to your values. For example, do not just share jargon. Share your past behavior, such as experiences working with and helping students from underrepresented groups and advocating for social justice. If you are comfortable doing so, you might consider sharing your cultural background and identity, including how you relate to power, privilege, and oppression in your own or others' lives. Stay humble. This is not a multiple-choice test, and no one is perfect or has everything figured out. So, turn down the academic striving and perfectionism. Let your words be sprinkled with grace, gentleness, empathy, caring, and above all, integrity. (Also, it is a good idea to get feedback on your diversity statement from others whom you trust and who know you well.)

THE INTERVIEW

The job interview for an academic position can be a stressful process, but it can also be exciting and fun. The job interview is often a two-step process. First, universities generally invite a larger group of applicants to participate in an interview via phone or Zoom—this is known as the "short list." This is a "screening interview" of sorts, and it helps universities decide who to bring in for an on-campus interview. The first interview is usually short (e.g., 30–60 minutes), and it is usually with the search committee. It is common for six to 12 people to make this short list.

If you make it past the first cut, you will be invited for an on-campus interview. Often, between two to four candidates are flown out to in-person interviews. The on-campus interview is a more in-depth process that usually takes 1 to 2 days. The university will fly you in and arrange a stay at a nearby hotel. You will have several meetings, including with the search committee, other faculty, chair, dean, and graduate students. You will have meals with faculty and/or students. You may be asked to give a research talk or teaching demonstration. At some colleges, you will do both. They might even set you up with a realtor to look around at houses and neighborhoods. The following are a few suggestions for doing well in the interview:

- Do some research on the program you are applying to, as well as the faculty. Try to get a sense of what their priorities are and what they value. Try to make connections between what you offer and what they value. Also, do some homework on the various faculty and their research interests. Try to make connections between your research interests and their research interests. Someone who can collaborate and fit in well with others in the program will be appreciated.

- Throughout the interview process, focus on making connections with everyone you meet. Many people you interact with might not work with you on a project, but they will have to interact with you as a colleague. Everyone wants a relatable colleague with whom they can get along. Also, remember the interview starts from the moment someone picks you up from the airport and lasts until you get dropped off. Everything is part of the interview. Treat everyone kindly and with respect. If something stressful happens (e.g., your luggage is lost), try to take it in stride.

- For the job talk, try to talk about your research program as a whole and walk through several studies if possible. (This is preferable to focusing on just one study, such as your dissertation.) It is fine to get into the details of your studies, but also talk about the big picture and why your research is important. It is a good idea to talk about the future and where you hope to take your research program. You may get some tough questions from the audience. Take a deep breath and respond as best you can. If possible, try to take a collaborative rather than a confrontational stance with the people who ask you questions.

- Some teaching-focused institutions also require a teaching demonstration, where you teach a portion of a class while being observed by faculty members. Be sure to get clarity on what content to cover, the type and size of the class, and how much time you are allotted to cover the material. This is your chance to showcase your instructional skills and put into practice what you said you value in your teaching portfolio. Do not just sit back and read from lecture slides. Be sure to actively engage students in learning that highlights your abilities as a teacher.
- Get clarity on tenure requirements. Ask the chair and dean what the requirements for tenure are. Determine if they are specific and explicit or vague and implicit. Ask yourself, (a) do these match my professional goals, (b) are they realistic, and (c) what do I need to earn tenure? That will frame your negotiation.

THE NEGOTIATION

If you are lucky enough to receive a job offer, the negotiation begins. The negotiation period is when you discuss all the particulars about the job, such as salary, start-up, and lab space, among other things. This process can bring up a lot of anxiety for new faculty members. Negotiation can feel uncomfortable, and you may not want to make the other side angry or frustrated. Perhaps the most important thing to understand about the negotiation is that it is a normal part of the process. It is a regular phase you will go through as you try to sort out your needs and put yourself in the best position possible. Do not shy away from negotiation; if you do not negotiate, it will be unlikely you will get your needs met.

What are some of the different things to think about when negotiating? Probably the most important thing to negotiate is your starting salary. Starting salary is key because your future raises are all calculated relative to your base salary, as is your salary for summer funding when applying for grants. Most universities have some flexibility with their starting salary offers, so it is a good idea to ask for more. If you have more than one job offer, you have leverage and can push harder for a higher starting salary. This should be your primary concern when negotiating.

A second thing to negotiate is your start-up package. Most universities will offer new faculty members a lump sum of money to help with their transition and to set up their office and research lab. The following are some things to consider when negotiating your start-up package:

- **office:** Make sure you have what you need to set up your office, such as a computer, desk, and office furniture.
- **lab:** Equipping your research lab space pretenure is critical. Think about purchases such as computers, software, desks, furniture, and supplies.
- **equipment:** What equipment do you need to do your research? For example, do you need physiological equipment or other equipment to collect data, such as iPads or laptops?
- **participant payment:** It is a good idea to have some money in your start-up funds to pay participants for research studies to enable you to get going on your research and collect pilot data for grant submissions.
- **summer funding:** Most academic jobs are on a 9-month contract. Some universities will allow you to include summer funding for the first couple of years in your start-up package.
- **course releases:** You will have a particular teaching load for your position (e.g., 2-2, which means you teach two courses per semester). Some universities will allow you to have a certain number of course releases (i.e., reassigning your time from one class to do research) to use during your pretenure period.
- **research assistants:** Some universities will fund a research assistant during your pretenure period.
- **travel money:** It is helpful to ask for money to attend conferences and training sessions before you obtain your first grant. Universities typically allocate yearly professional development funds for such travel, but this is an opportunity to request a lump sum to help launch your career and allow you to network with collaborators.

As with salary, it is important to negotiate as much as you can with your start-up package. Start-up packages have quite a range, so it is necessary to make a good case for why you need certain things. For example, a survey of graduate departments of psychology found that the median value of start-up packages for Assistant Professor new hires was $62,736, with a range from $1,500 to $760,000 (APA, 2009). Begin with what you need, add what you dream about, and see how they respond.

A third thing to negotiate is your lab space. Most universities will offer new faculty lab space to collect data and house graduate students, but the size and quality of the lab space vary from place to place. For some institutions, lab space is dedicated to individual faculty members (i.e., only your lab uses it); at other places, lab space is shared. Get clarity on the policies surrounding lab space and make sure you can build a thriving program accordingly. Again, it is important to have a clear idea of what you need and articulate your space needs to your chair or dean. This is the time when you have the power to ask for what you want, so try to get as much space as you need.

A final note about negotiation: If you do not ask, you will not receive it. Many people feel uncomfortable asking, and there can be cultural pressures that fall unfairly on certain groups to be more compliant and resist making a request they need. The chair, dean, and officials from the university know asking is part of the negotiation, so do not shy away from asking. But at a certain point, if you want the job, realize you will be working with many of these individuals, and you do not want to sour the relationship by holding out for every demand. Negotiation is a give-and-take, so do not forget to preserve the relationship while ensuring your needs will be met.

GETTING STARTED IN RESEARCH

When you take up your academic position, there are several things to think about that will help you get your research program up and running, including setting up your research lab, working with students, thinking about tenure and promotion, and developing relationships. In this next section, we offer some thoughts and tips for navigating each of these areas.

Setting Up Your Research Lab

When you get started at a new place, it will take some time to set up your research lab. You will need to set up your space with, for example, computers, furniture, and other equipment. And depending on your research area, you may have other equipment or materials you need to set up and purchase to get your lab ready. This process can take a while and can be challenging because you will have many other tasks that require your attention, such as acclimating to a new place, prepping your classes, and working with students. If you have a research assistant, they can help you with some of these tasks. But in general, expect it to take about 6 months to get your research lab up and going. Make it a priority to set up your space, so you can get moving on your research and start collecting data for your projects.

Working With Students

At most academic jobs, you will be expected to work with students and involve them in your research. Sometimes this mentoring relationship is formal. For example, Josh and Donnie work at PhD programs, where each incoming graduate student gets assigned a research mentor to supervise their research projects. Daryl's situation is a bit different. He works at a liberal arts college where he is expected to involve undergraduate students in his research, but the mentoring is less formal. Students apply to work in his lab, and their tasks vary according to their skill sets and goals.

In general, our recommendation is to be cautious about taking on too many students as a new faculty member who is in the process of transitioning and getting settled. Sometimes there is a temptation to take multiple students to fill out your research lab. Or there might be pressure from your program for you to help by taking on multiple advisees. Taking on students can be helpful in your research, but teaching and training students is a lot of work. In our experience, it is wise to take on new students slowly rather than diving into the deep end. One guideline that has worked well for us is to take on one new graduate student each year. You might even want to go more slowly (e.g., one student every 2 years) if your program allows it.

We have colleagues in much larger programs that sometimes require all faculty to accept three to five doctoral students per year. This kind of situation requires its own form of creativity. Chairing that many dissertations per year is a leadership feat. One strategy is to have your students work on projects in teams so that you are still managing four to five key projects rather than 15 to 20 independent projects on a variety of topics.

We offer one other point before we move on: Sometimes, there is a lot of excitement when a new faculty member arrives, and existing graduate students may want to switch to work with you, especially if they do not have a good working relationship with their current advisor. We recommend caution when thinking about taking on existing graduate students. It is not a hard and fast rule—there may be situations when taking on an existing student would be in your best interests. But it is good to talk with other faculty members about the prospective student and their experiences with them. There may be reasons why the student is having trouble with their current advisor, and you do not want to get stuck with a problematic student right off the bat. Do not succumb to pressure. Less scrupulous colleagues may try to coerce you into accepting a student because it is better for their career than yours. Exercise caution and make sure to make decisions that align with your values.

Tenure and Promotion

One of the more stressful aspects of an academic job is working toward tenure and promotion. At most universities, there are three levels of being a professor. You start out as an assistant professor. Then, after a certain period (usually around 6 years), you go up for tenure and promotion. Tenure gives you job security—you no longer are evaluated yearly, and your job is secure unless you do something unethical or fail to uphold basic job responsibilities (e.g., stop teaching classes to work on your golf game). You also usually get promoted at this point to associate professor. Later, you can go up for full professor. Generally, the timeline is not as exact for the promotion to full professor—you can apply (i.e., "go up") when you think you are ready and meet the requirements set by your department. Generally, the decision to go up for full professor would be made with help from your department chair or a promotion and tenure committee in your department.

When you transition to being a professor, it is important to start thinking about tenure and promotion right away. Your university should have guidelines about what it requires to get tenure—make sure you are clear on what these guidelines are so you can be strategic about how you manage your time during the first few years of the job. For example, when Josh started working at the University of North Texas (UNT), the guidelines stated he had to publish about two to three journal articles per year. Grants were also important—you did not necessarily have to land a big grant, but they wanted to see a consistent record of applying for grants. Having good teaching evaluations was also important. Service was not emphasized too much for pretenure folks. They mostly wanted you to focus on your research, but they did want you to be on a few committees and be a good departmental citizen. Your criteria for tenure and promotion may look like that or may look different. It is critical to determine what is required at your university and make sure you are on track to meet those benchmarks.

Your department should also meet with you regularly during the pretenure period to give you feedback on how you are doing and give you advice if you are falling short in one of the areas of evaluation. For example, at UNT, Josh received a yearly evaluation, as well as a detailed midtenure review after Year 3. Third-year reviews are common and are usually more formal evaluations used in the tenure decision. This feedback helped him to tailor and adjust his activities as he went. For example, one piece of feedback he received along the way was that he needed more first-author publications. He was able to shift gears a little bit and focus more on first-authored papers, so this was not a problem when he went up for tenure and promotion a few years later.

Developing Relationships

We take a deep dive into mentoring in the next chapter, but we want to mention here the importance of beginning to develop collaborative relationships in your research. As we talked about in Chapter 22, collaboration can increase your productivity and improve the quality of the research you conduct. When you make the transition from graduate student to professor, be on the lookout for relationships you can develop regarding your research. For example, there may be a professor at your university who does similar work to you. Or there may be a way your research can complement each other's. When Josh started at UNT, for example, he began to work with a colleague who specialized in doing research on supervision. They did several collaborative projects on the intersection of cultural humility, multiculturalism, and supervision. It is also not a bad idea to keep up your research relationships with people you have connected with in graduate school or at conferences. We were all in graduate school together and have kept up our research collaborations over the years. These relationships helped us quite a bit as we transitioned from graduate students to professors.

GETTING STARTED IN TEACHING

The transition to teaching courses as a professor can feel like a big shift, especially if you did not have many teaching opportunities as a student in graduate school. The process of preparing courses is interesting and labor intensive. There is often a lot of work on the front end: reading the textbook, creating your slides, making your exams, and coming up with discussions or activities to do in class. Some trial and error happens when you teach a class for the first time—some of the things you try may work out well, and others might flop. So, the first time you teach a course, it usually takes a lot of time and energy. But once you have prepped a course, it does not take as much work to teach it again—you can work from what you have and modify from there.

We have a few recommendations about teaching during the transition from graduate student to professor. First, if you have course releases, it is usually a good idea to take them early in the process. This is where the transition is the most difficult because you are in the process of getting your research up and going and prepping new courses. The more you can do to lower your teaching load at the beginning, the better because some of these activities will get easier as you go.

Second, if possible, it is a good idea to teach the same courses over and over during your pretenure period. The more you can teach the same courses, the less work you will have to do to prep new courses and the more you will improve in your instruction while teaching the class repeatedly. See if your department chair will work with you by letting you teach the same few courses each semester and year.

Third, it is not a bad idea to talk with other professors who have taught the same course before and ask if they would be willing to share their syllabi and materials. You do not want to copy the course exactly—you still need to read the textbook and articles and prepare your own slides. But looking at how other people have structured a course can give you a jumping-off point to develop your own course. There is no need to reinvent the wheel. You can start from a skeleton of the course and modify it from there.

Finally, one tip when developing a new course is to see if you can find a regular textbook appropriate for students and then a more detailed text that reviews the course material in a more sophisticated way. If you can find this, one helpful frame to prepping the course is to give the students the regular textbook and then lecture from the more advanced textbook. This avoids the problem of repeating the textbook exactly in your lectures. For example, when Josh prepped his positive psychology course for the first time, he found a regular textbook, which he gave to the students, but he also found a handbook that took a deeper dive into the research on various positive psychology topics. He used the more sophisticated handbook to supplement his lectures.

GETTING STARTED IN SERVICE

When you transition from graduate student to professor, you will have the opportunity to serve on various committees in your department, the university, and the general profession. We recommend being cautious about the service responsibilities you take on during the pretenure period. For most universities, the main thing you need to focus on for tenure are the specifics detailed by your college or university—and they rarely prioritize service alone. You do not want your research to take a back seat because of your service responsibilities. Ideally, your department will protect you from getting too overwhelmed with service responsibilities. For example, at many universities, several committees are not available for pretenured professors to keep their service responsibilities low.

We feel similarly about service to the university and broader profession. If there is a service opportunity you feel passionate about, take it on, but be cautious about taking on too many service responsibilities, especially if they take up a lot of time. As you progress in your research, journals will approach you to review articles or perhaps even to be a member of an editorial board. This is a good experience, and it is a good idea to say yes to these requests, but again, moderation is important. Take on some service responsibilities, but do not let these responsibilities distract you from your focus, which is your research.

Although we recommend caution in taking on too much service early in one's career as a professor, we admit this advice is sometimes difficult to implement. Some departments or programs may not be as cognizant about protecting early career folks from heavy service loads, so there may be pressure from the system to take on a lot of service responsibilities. This pressure may be exacerbated for women and racial or ethnic minorities, who, because of socialization pressures, may feel a responsibility to take on additional service roles. Also, sometimes getting more involved in service may be a way to find support from other like-minded folks. Taking on service responsibilities is an individual decision, but as much as possible, we encourage individuals to make these decisions based on the alignment with their values rather than outside pressure.

GRADUATE MENTOR CORNER

As mentors, we can help our students transition well into their first academic job. This process is like the process of parents "launching" their children. Ideally, we leave plenty of time for students to differentiate and develop independence. We want to cultivate a strong enough relationship so, at any point, they can come back for support, guidance, or perspective. For example, Donnie's meetings with his mentor became fewer and farther between once he left for his internship. When he did ask for a meeting, it often involved key decisions where Donnie wanted to take advantage of his mentor's wisdom (e.g., a key decision about the direction of his research program or interpersonal dynamics within the department).

When we think about Ev's gift to us as a mentor, he did two things well related to navigating systems. (Indeed, a crucial thing we learn in graduate school, which happens between classes and other formal requirements, is how to navigate systems and relationships.) First, he was careful with cynicism. Cynicism is linked to burnout. We can undermine students if we pass on an untrusting and cynical mindset. Even if we are unhappy with a situation or department (and sometimes that may happen because we are human), it is important to have good boundaries. We can share vulnerable feelings that enable connection but not pass along hostility or negativity that will burden our students. In families, parentification can occur when people in authority put too much emotional burden on children (or, in this case, students). A role reversal occurs, requiring students to track alliances and manage competing loyalties, which drains energy from more important tasks.

Second, he was careful with triangulation. All human systems have some conflict. People have different interests, and even when people have a shared goal, they may have different ideas about how to seek their goals. Sometimes faculty agree to keep secrets for students (in the mental health profession, people sometimes confuse their role as faculty with their role as a counselor or psychologist). This can cause dynamics that entrench conflict because, instead of relationship patterns where people discuss conflict with the person with whom they could resolve the issue, they begin to form alliances with others. Essentially, subgroups are formed with different narratives of an offense. It is much harder to address conflict when groups of people are being triangulated into the conflict.

Ev modeled how to steer clear of intractable conflict. His message was clear. It is easy for conflict to escalate. Once this happens, it can take a long time to repair trust. So, often, Ev would work to find a quick path to diffuse conflict. After graduation, several stories got back to Donnie of examples where, in his role as graduate research assistant to the program director, he could have gotten involved in a conflict that was really between faculty within the department. On the basis of his work with couples and families, as well as practical wisdom, Ev acted quickly to keep Donnie out of a triangle position. This modeling helped us all navigate the transition into the complex environment of an academic department.

As mentors, we can provide a secure base (remember the importance of a secure base from attachment theory) for our students as they transition to faculty members. All human systems involve group dynamics, so we do them a huge favor if we can help them develop wisdom as leaders. This enables them to develop the relational skills to avoid unproductive conflict and keep their emotional energy reserved for their primary work, which often has little to do with getting involved in power struggles.

UNDERGRADUATE MENTOR CORNER

The themes of this chapter may seem a lifetime away for many undergraduate students. For example, Donnie started his first academic position when he was 30. So, an 18-year-old college student has a long way to go before needing the specifics of this chapter, and only a small percentage of psychology majors decide to become professors in psychology. Nonetheless, no matter what a psychology major decides to do with their lives, it is helpful to understand the context of scientific culture within psychology. Many of the principles discussed in this chapter apply to other career tracks.

That said, people can acquire wisdom whenever they are ready. We do not need to learn all things the hard way through direct experience. For example, some faculty may make the same mistakes throughout their careers. In contrast, some undergraduate students may pick up some essential wisdom within a year or two of joining a high-functioning and emotionally healthy research team. For example, Josh learned many habits that have served him well throughout his career during the years he volunteered as an undergraduate with Ed Diener (1946–2021), an eminent psychologist within the positive psychology movement. This is the power of professional acculturation.

Accordingly, in the Doctoral Preparation Track at Georgia State University, Donnie surrounds students with layers of mentoring. They have support from a faculty member, a doctoral student, and a group of students who intend to apply to doctoral programs. Science happens in teams, and so does acculturation to scientific culture. Sure, we can get people started with a book, but the contextualization required for real-life decisions involves learning to seek and balance multiple perspectives. So, make room on your team to allow undergraduates to join, learn, and contribute as much as they are ready.

MOVING FORWARD

In this chapter, we discussed the all-important transition from graduate student to professor. A lot is going on with this transition, and it is easy for beginning professors to get overwhelmed with everything they must do. It is important to take a deep breath, take your time, and recognize that setting up your research lab and getting going is a process. It is not going to happen overnight, and that is okay. That said, it is important to understand the requirements of your university regarding tenure and promotion and start moving toward these goals from Day 1. In the next chapter, we take a deep dive into how to develop strong mentoring relationships with your students.

24 MENTORING STUDENTS

One of the most challenging yet rewarding aspects of being a professor and researcher is the opportunity to mentor undergraduate and graduate students and help them start their own research programs and careers. Throughout this book, we have touched on mentoring at the end of each chapter through the Graduate Mentor Corner and Undergraduate Mentor Corner sections. But in this chapter, we take a deep dive into mentoring and talk about some of the key lessons we have learned over the years.

The three of us agree that mentoring is one of the best parts of our job. We each had excellent mentors in our own research training, and it is an honor and privilege to try to teach and collaborate with the next generation of researchers. In fact, our love of mentoring is part of the reason we wanted to write this book in the first place—to provide a resource for graduate students, undergraduate students, and their mentors to help smooth out the process of teaching and learning research skills.

Mentoring is rewarding because you get to see someone else learn the research process and come into their own as a researcher. It is fun to see someone learn new skills and gain experience and confidence. We have felt

---

https://doi.org/10.1037/0000371-025
The Complete Researcher: A Practical Guide for Graduate Students and Early Career Professionals, by J. N. Hook, D. E. Davis, and D. R. Van Tongeren
Copyright © 2024 by the American Psychological Association. All rights reserved.

great pride when one of our students gets an offer for graduate school, does well on a research talk, has an important paper published in a journal, or receives a job offer. Success is measured in part by how we give back and the degree to which we have helped others flourish.

That said, mentoring is not for the faint of heart. Although we have had a lot of positive mentoring experiences, we have also had some mentoring relationships that were challenging. If you have done much mentoring, you will likely have experienced these tough times as well. There might be a mismatch in goals between you and your student. Or perhaps there is an interpersonal issue that is getting in the way. You may have a hard time giving constructive or negative feedback, and this is stalling your student's process. Mentoring is not easy, and there are a lot of pitfalls along the way. We hope that some of the lessons we have learned over the years can help you as you begin your own mentoring journey.

LEARNING HOW TO MENTOR IS A PROCESS

The first lesson we have learned is that mentoring students is a process that takes time. It is a skill like any other skill you want to develop, and that skill is related to, yet different from, the research process itself. In other words, you will not necessarily be a good mentor just because you are a good researcher. The best players do not always make the best coaches. Because of this, do not be surprised if you struggle with mentoring right off the bat. Like any skill, you are unlikely to be good right away. You are only a beginner. Give yourself time to focus on your mentoring skill to improve it. Talk with other more experienced professors about their mentoring experiences and learn from them. You are already investing in the process by reading this book, but do not be afraid to gather other resources about mentoring to help you grow and develop as a mentor. Many of the principles from Chapter 3 on building expertise can be applied to developing skills in mentoring.

MEET REGULARLY

The second lesson we have learned is that it is important to meet regularly with your students, both individually and together as a group. We almost did not include this point—it seems almost too basic—but you would be surprised how many professors do not meet regularly with their students. They might meet with their students "as needed," but irregular meetings tend to slow down a student's progress. Meeting regularly helps students with accountability—they know they will need to talk with their professor at regular intervals about their research progress (or lack thereof). Meeting regularly with your students also helps to build a trusting relationship.

How often should you meet with your students? We know this kind of answer can be frustrating, but there is no one "right" number of meetings you should have. But as a guideline, we recommend meeting once per week or once every other week. For example, Josh meets with all his students individually every other week, and he also meets with his students as a group for a lab meeting every other week. There were also times during his career when he met with his students every week. Daryl holds regular weekly lab meetings for his team and then also meets weekly with students who are conducting an independent study or completing a senior thesis. He finds that the consistency is critical for keeping his team focused and moving on their projects.

RUN EFFECTIVE MEETINGS WITH STUDENTS

The third lesson we have learned over the years is how to run effective meetings. Our general approach is to let students take the lead in meetings and bring up the issues that are most pressing for them. This is a transfer of initiative. We often have a running list of projects or tasks for each student, and we check our notes on the next steps before each meeting. This functions as a checklist. Sometimes, if we know there is a lot to cover, we suggest setting an agenda by making a list to make sure we prioritize appropriately. However, the priority is often clear, and we let the student direct the meeting.

A key part of a meeting is connecting relationally. For psychologists trained as clinicians, these clinical skills come in handy. We focus on process (i.e., the relational dynamics between you and the student), not just content. We want to connect with our students and build trust because they will probably eventually encounter some unexpected difficulties. Life happens in graduate school. Not many people go 5 to 6 years without some kind of transition or disruption. So, building a strong relationship provides a reservoir of trust that helps prepare the relationship for the inevitable ups and downs of graduate school.

A second goal of meeting with students is to think about how to push their research project forward. What would it look like if this project were 1 week closer to completion? What barriers will the student need to overcome to make 1 week's worth of progress? We are tracking the student's affect and attuning ourselves to the student to offer encouragement, support, or affirmation that will build momentum. Sometimes, students build momentum themselves, and we mostly stay out of the way. Other times, we can tell they are stuck and feel discouraged. Perhaps they are putting a lot of pressure on themselves. Many students struggle with perfectionism, so they can get stuck in a self-critical space that drains emotional energy if they get too discouraged. Thus, meetings are contextualized to the student, their personality, motivational style, and current level of energy.

A third goal of meeting with students, which happens over longer periods, is to ask questions to learn about the student's aspirations and dreams for the future. This is more of an identity development process as students begin to think of what kinds of work they find valuable and important. We start to think about projects we could do together to bring these aspirations into the reality of their lives.

BALANCE THE RELATIONAL AND PROFESSIONAL

The fourth lesson we have learned over the years is the importance of balancing the relational and professional when mentoring students. Many professors focus on the professional side of things—after all, that is what many of our interactions with our students are focused on. We talk about the next steps in their dissertation process or degree plans. Obviously, that is the primary focus, but do not forget to tend to the relational side of your student as well. Check in with them about how they are doing and make space for them to discuss personal concerns they want to share as well.

Our students are humans just like us, with a lot of different priorities and responsibilities. School and research are big priorities for them (hopefully), but it is not the only thing they are concerned about (hopefully). If something else is going on in their life that is difficult (e.g., mental health problems, burnout, relationship problems, health concerns), this difficulty will likely spill out into their work and research. For example, you might be confused as to why your student is not making progress on their research, only to find out later that they are going through a divorce or dealing with a physical ailment that requires a lot of their attention.

We let students take the lead in deciding what or how much to share, but we do invite them to let us know how they are doing outside of school. Students will have different boundaries and comfort levels about sharing non-school-related issues, but it is important to let them know that you care about their whole person, not just the researcher part of them.

TEND TO THE RELATIONSHIP

As in the previous point, the fifth lesson we have learned is that it is essential to care for the mentor–student relationship and proactively resolve any ruptures when they occur. Again, you may want to stay focused on the work, but the work will suffer if the relationship between you and your student is fractured.

Sometimes it is hard to know if a rupture has happened in your relationship with a student. Because you have a lot of power over the student's progress in the program, it can be difficult for them to bring up a problem they might have in their relationship with you. Students might fear you will react negatively and decide just to stay quiet.

This is why it is important at the outset of a mentoring relationship to let them know you want to hear about any negative feedback or struggles in your relationship, so you can work together to resolve the issue. It is also a good idea to check in with your student periodically to talk about the relationship and see how it is going. Another sign that the relationship may need some work is if the student's progress slows down or they start missing meetings. These can be more passive ways of telling you something is wrong with the relationship.

What should you do if there is a problem with the relationship? See if you can mend the rupture. If you did something to hurt the student, apologize and make amends. If the rupture was related to communication problems or differences in expectations, see if you can talk it out and come to a common understanding of what happened and what needs to be done to move on. In some cases, it may make sense for the student to begin working with a different advisor, but in most situations, these differences can be worked out.

DEVELOP MUTUALITY

The sixth lesson we have learned is to choose projects that connect with the student's interests as well as your area of expertise. One of the challenges that many professors have when mentoring students in research is striking the right balance between (a) letting them pursue projects that are in line with their interests and (b) directing them to projects that are in line with your areas of expertise. Our advisor Ev used to say that good projects should have "something for you, something for me." What he meant was that good research projects, like good relationships, are mutually beneficial. They involve a mix of the student's interests and the mentor's expertise. This norm prepared us well for forming new collaborations throughout our careers.

There are two main reasons why trying to optimize the investment of both the student and mentor is usually most effective. First, the thesis or dissertation project is a long, difficult task. The student will usually spend 2 years (or more) on this research project. Because of this, the project needs to be something they are interested in. If not, they will lose the motivation to apply sustained effort over a long period. However, it is the professor's responsibility to direct the student toward a project that will likely be a good use of time and resources. If the professor does not know anything about the student's topic, this will be difficult. The student and professor are then in a similar place of not knowing much about the topic. This situation can lead to a failed project or a project that does not make much of an impact. The best situation occurs when a project combines the student's interests and the professor's expertise.

Ideally, these conversations should occur before the student is accepted into the program. Many programs have a mentor model in which each student is matched to a particular faculty member. This means when the student applies to the program, they say what they are interested in researching and how it matches the research interests of one of the faculty members. Ideally, the professor should have a sense of the student's research interests (and the extent to which they are a fit) before the student starts the program. Still, there are situations where this does not happen (e.g., a student changes their interests, a student switches mentors), so it is good to have a clear vision for how to negotiate the topic of a student's project.

INCORPORATE ACCOUNTABILITY AND PROVIDE BALANCED FEEDBACK

The seventh lesson that is critical when mentoring students is to figure out how to incorporate accountability into the working relationship and give critical feedback in a caring way. Many professors make the mistake of failing to help students be accountable and keeping critical feedback to themselves. Sometimes this might come from wanting to be nice or not wanting to cause conflict. But these stances inevitably backfire because you rob the student of an opportunity to develop and improve. And in the end, avoiding the momentary discomfort of sharing difficult feedback can cause significantly more frustration and inefficiencies in the long run.

The best-case scenario is to incorporate accountability and positive and negative feedback throughout the process. Accountability involves asking students to make commitments and helping to track them over time. An easy way to do this is to talk with students at the beginning of each semester and get a sense of their goals for that semester and how they plan to achieve their goals. Then, during the semester, you can check in with your student and ask them how they are doing with their goals and commitments. Accountability is not a punitive process—you are working with the student to help them keep their commitments and reach their goals.

It is also important to incorporate both positive and critical feedback early and often. Make this type of feedback a normal part of the learning process. For a person to improve, they need feedback to adjust and improve their performance. It is best if the feedback is as specific as possible and occurs as close to the behavior as possible. Do not hold back on feedback or wait for a "better time." Give feedback right away and be as specific as possible about what the student needs to do to improve. Do not forget about positive feedback. Sometimes we can get in the habit of giving only critical or negative feedback because that is what the student needs to improve. But it is important to balance critical feedback with positive feedback so students do not get discouraged. John Gottman (1994), who studied marriages, found that healthy marriages had a ratio of 5:1 positive to negative interactions. Try for something similar in your work with students, but make sure it is authentic.

BUILD THE TEAM

The eighth lesson involves team building. Most professors will have several students working with them at any given time. For example, Josh and Donnie generally take one new graduate student per year, so at any time, they might be working with five to six graduate students, as well as a few undergraduate students. Similarly, Daryl usually has four to six undergraduate students working in his lab at any time. Because of this, it can be helpful to think about mentoring not only as a one-on-one activity but as a group activity as well. It can be helpful to set up structures to help your students work together and learn from each other.

Our general recommendation is to set up a developmental structure in your lab in which the older students help mentor the younger students. In Josh's lab, for example, the younger graduate students often go to the more experienced graduate students for help navigating the specifics of the research process, as well as the program as a whole. The graduate students also help mentor the undergraduate research assistants. Often Josh will make these mentoring relationships explicit, for example, by pairing an undergraduate student with a graduate student to prepare a presentation for a conference.

In addition to sharing responsibilities and working together on various projects, you might also think about how you could work on building cohesion in your research team. It can be helpful to spend unstructured time together outside of work; for example, Josh usually hosts a holiday party for his lab, as well as a party at the end of the school year. Similarly, Daryl has invited his lab students to his house for a meal at the end of the academic year. Spending some of your lab meeting time getting to know one another and sharing personal information can help improve team cohesion as well.

CONTEXTUALIZE MENTORSHIP

The ninth lesson we have learned over the years is that mentorship is not a one-size-fits-all approach. Your students are different and unique. They have different personalities, professional and personal goals, motivations, and cultural identities. If you try to engage in the same way with every student, your mentorship style will work well with some students but poorly with others. Instead of trying to force a one-size-fits-all approach with your students, try to get to know them and understand their unique motivations and needs. Then, tailor your approach to fit the individual student.

Sometimes this process of contextualizing mentorship is easier said than done, especially for new professors. You might have had a style of mentorship that worked for you, and you try to do the same thing with your students. Or you might expect your students to be wired like you and be surprised when they have different motivations and needs. You may not have been exposed to different types of students and may not know how to mentor differently. Again, it can be helpful to talk with other professors and get a sense of their mentorship style to see different ways of doing things. It can also be helpful to try and understand your student and observe what motivates them and makes them tick. Are they achievement oriented? Are they competitive? Do they respond well to challenges? Do they need more support? Learning about your student can help you engage with them in a way that sets them up for success.

CONSIDER CULTURE

This 10th lesson builds on the previous one: It is important to consider the cultural background and identities of your student, as well as the intersection between your cultural identities and those of your student. Students with marginalized cultural identities (e.g., racial and ethnic minorities, women, LGBTQ+ individuals, individuals with lower socioeconomic status, first-generation college students) may experience more resistance navigating the university environment. Historically, universities have struggled to offer equal opportunities to graduate students from marginalized groups, perpetuating problems in psychology related to underrepresentation.

Another mentoring issue that sometimes comes up for students with marginalized cultural identities is that they may get targeted to take on more service responsibilities than students with privileged identities. This may come from a benign motivation (e.g., a person in authority might want to make sure racial and ethnic minority students have a voice in a particular organization), but the effect can be detrimental because students feel pressure to spend a lot of time and energy in service responsibilities and thus have less time to make progress on and push forward their own research programs. The recommendations on taking on service responsibilities apply here. Make sure you work with students to balance service responsibilities in graduate school and early career. It is important to teach students how to identify their most important values and priorities and be able to say no to opportunities that fall outside those.

It is important to recognize your own cultural identities and how those may intersect with those of your student. There is already a power differential between mentor and student, given your professional position. Cultural dynamics may exacerbate this power differential (e.g., if you are White and your student is a racial or ethnic minority). You cannot change the power difference (it will be there whether you like it or not), but you can help to empower your student in their relationship with you. For example, work collaboratively on goals and designing the student's progress through the program. Invite feedback and check in regularly with your student about how the mentorship relationship is going. Be humble and understand that what worked for you regarding mentoring may or may not work for your student.

Finally, if a student does have marginalized cultural identities, it can be helpful to connect them with other mentors or groups who share aspects of their identity. Sometimes it can feel lonely if your student is the only person (or one of a few people) with a particular cultural identity. Remember our discussion about communities in Chapter 2. The mentorship relationship is important, but it is not the be-all and end-all. Help connect your student with a variety of groups and mentors so they can receive the support they need.

BUILD CONFIDENCE

The 11th lesson we have learned about mentorship is that it is important to build confidence in your students proactively. Many students struggle with research and get discouraged when the process does not come easily to them.

We have talked about this issue before, but graduate students are often bright and may have had an easy time in school up to this point. Research is often a different experience, however, and even smart students struggle with the research process. If students struggle early on and are not well-supported, they can develop imposter syndrome, which can lead them to doubt their abilities and feel like frauds.

It is important to think about how to build confidence in your students right from the beginning. Setting them up to have some successful experiences in research early on is a great way to build self-efficacy. For example, invite them to join you on presentations and papers early. This enables you to model for them the research process and also allows them to experience some success right off the bat. Giving positive and supportive feedback is another way to help build confidence. Finally, sharing your own failures and struggles as a researcher is a great way to normalize the challenges of research and the developmental process all researchers go through when learning the craft.

GRADUATE MENTOR CORNER

Although this entire chapter was focused on the process of mentoring students, we discuss a few additional ideas in this section. First, it is important to develop realistic expectations as a mentor. Donnie remembers a meeting in his first year or two with Ev. Donnie joked, "It must be nice to have doctoral students to do all your work for you." In Donnie's mind, Ev had an entire team of students to work for him, almost as if he were at the top of a multilevel marketing program. Donnie figured the more people Ev had to work for him, the less work Ev had to do himself, which seemed nice.

Ev chuckled and said, "Talk to me in a few years, after you finish mentoring your first few students. The work is rewarding, but it is time-intensive training and not the easiest way to coauthor a paper."

Early in our careers, we had unrealistic expectations about mentoring. In graduate school, for example, we had several undergraduates, and we tried to have them each run their own project. We thought having more people do more projects would increase our capacity to publish. This did not work out. Most of those projects did not even get started. The key problem was our expectations—we did not realize the students working with us were not ready to take the lead on their own projects. It is not helpful to start with grand expectations of what your students should accomplish. It is better to start where your students are and work from there.

Second, at some point, we noticed strong mentors are focused more on developing leaders than finishing individual projects. Leaning too heavily toward a task-focused leadership style is not the most effective way to develop researchers and writers, which is an area that requires high skill in a range of areas (e.g., project management, research design, analytical and statistical skills). The kinds of students who eventually become independent tend to be hungry for initiative. So, micromanaging is a bad idea—it causes a group dynamic that attracts the wrong members to the team or undermines students' growth. The relationship is not just transactional (i.e., will you do this work for me?). The relationship is focused on a commitment to helping another person develop as a leader who can imagine, manage, and complete multiple projects aligned with their area of interest.

Finally, to help our doctoral students develop as mentors themselves, it helps to transfer the responsibility for research projects to them. This takes practice. If we do too much for our students, we carry the mental load for the project. We do not have enough energy to take responsibility for everyone's projects. However, graduate students come with different levels of leadership experience. Some may have limited experience delegating work and managing the work of others. This skill is complex and requires practice and learning through trial and error. Managing a project requires team accountability. Trust builds as a team gets in the habit of planning during a weekly meeting, anticipating barriers, and clarifying the next steps. Then, the doctoral student and others involved execute short-term goals. The next week, we repeat the process. A team thrives when people gain greater trust in each other's character and competence. Strong leaders will naturally gravitate toward practicing greater levels of initiative and responsibility. Our job is to support this process for people who demonstrate a willingness to lead.

UNDERGRADUATE MENTOR CORNER

Many of the processes of mentoring and running teams with graduate students also apply to undergraduate students. In general, we like to pair undergraduate students with graduate students to help with research projects. Pulling in an undergraduate student to help the graduate student is a good way to scaffold the skills of mentoring. The undergraduate student can even sit in the doctoral student's meeting with us if this would be helpful. A group of three (i.e., faculty mentor, graduate student, and undergraduate student) is stable. The roles are clear. The doctoral student is the first author on a project. Our role is to support the graduate student in making decisions as first author. Having an undergraduate student to assist can provide additional momentum, and sometimes it can even provide a different kind of motivation and accountability. For example, if we have a motivated undergraduate student, we might place them with a doctoral student who is languishing on a project. The energy and motivation of the undergraduate student is something we can use. Most doctoral students will pick up the pace if they see someone else who may not even be in a doctoral program working hard on their project.

Once again, concrete feedback and mentoring are good. In someone's first year or two of conducting research, it helps build self-efficacy to complete concrete tasks. We used to think undergraduate students would want to avoid mundane tasks, such as creating surveys, entering data, or cleaning data sets. However, early on, research feels intimidating and ambiguous. It can feel good to have clear tasks and structure as you are learning new skills. Working closely with a doctoral student can provide an undergraduate student with a chance to develop skills in their zone of proximal development so they build greater confidence and self-efficacy.

MOVING FORWARD

In this chapter, we talked about some of the key things to think about when developing a mentoring relationship with your students. Passing along your knowledge and experience and helping someone else develop their research skills can be an incredibly rewarding experience, but it is not without its challenges. Mentoring is a skill that takes intentional practice and effort over time; give yourself the space to work on this aspect of your professional development. In the next chapter, we broaden our focus and discuss the importance of balancing cohesion and inclusion in teams.

25 BALANCING COHESION AND INCLUSION IN TEAMS

In the previous chapter, we discussed the importance of mentoring. Our discussion mainly focused on one-on-one mentoring with individual graduate students. In this chapter, we continue focusing on mentoring, helping, and giving back but take a step back and broaden our focus to the groups and teams to which we belong. Teams tend to develop a culture of their own, and we want to promote a team environment that helps each member thrive and grow in their strengths. Ideally, the teams we lead would have high levels of cohesion, which often happens when teams have at least some shared values. Shared values facilitate trust, which helps increase commitment. At the same time, we also want teams that cultivate curiosity, flexibility, and humility toward individual and cultural differences. These attributes of teams can help individual members feel like they can belong because their individual and cultural differences are respected and valued. Furthermore, an attitude of cultural humility and respect for differences can facilitate creativity and improve performance because a team can leverage multiple perspectives to improve the quality of feedback it gives team members. Groups that lack cultural flexibility can become rigid and stuck because they do not have the cultural skills to learn from different groups.

---

https://doi.org/10.1037/0000371-026
The Complete Researcher: A Practical Guide for Graduate Students and Early Career Professionals, by J. N. Hook, D. E. Davis, and D. R. Van Tongeren
Copyright © 2024 by the American Psychological Association. All rights reserved.

As you grow and develop in your career, you will have more power to help form the teams of which you are a part, whether it be a research team, a program, or even an entire department. The purpose of this chapter is to consider ways you can invest your growing levels of authority to promote groups and teams that develop a healthy balance of cohesion and inclusion. We give some general suggestions for navigating this balance, but we need to remember we must work these ideas out in our contexts. They are not just abstract suggestions. As leaders, we must get to know our system. Then, we can do things that will generate traction and leverage. We play the long game. We can take risks that are appropriate for our level of professional development. As we do this, we can start to use our influence to make improvements that will strengthen the training environment of our groups and teams.

SUGGESTION 1: FORM COMMUNITIES

First, we must ground ourselves in healthy social bonds that can sustain the complex and challenging situations we face in our careers. Just as community is important for graduate students, as we discussed in Chapter 2, the importance of community continues throughout our careers. The transition into a first faculty position can be lonely. You are transitioning to a new place, and you may or may not know anyone in your program or department. You are also entering an environment where your new peers are in different stages of professional and personal development. For example, when Donnie started at Georgia State University, he was the only assistant professor. In his department, the next person closest to him in professional rank had just gotten tenure. In his program, the next person was at least 15 years ahead of him.

It can take time to get used to a new culture and environment. One guideline is to assume it may take at least a year to start to feel more grounded. Accordingly, even though new professors may feel a lot of pressure to keep their research and writing on track, an important priority is to develop social bonds that will lead to feelings of connection, belonging, and flourishing. Our work is challenging, and we will struggle if we do not have a strong set of relationships and support.

Another reason developing relationships is important is that university departments can be relationally complex and difficult to navigate. Some departments talk about themselves as having "family-like" cultures. It may take a while for a new faculty member to get a sense of that familial culture and the associated relationship dynamics or "how things work." Ideally, a department is healthy enough to protect new members from long-standing power struggles or triangulation, but this is not always the case. It is important to develop some trustworthy relationships to help navigate the murky (and sometimes turbulent) waters.

It is a good idea to form strong relationships within your work environment, such as with your chair and associate or full professors who can provide mentoring and support. Early career professionals can also form broader relationships with different professional communities that promote both security and grounding as well as exploration and growth. They can also stay connected to prior mentors and seek out new mentors. In addition, they can form new collaborations to develop strong teams that provide a balance of encouragement and challenge.

We also caution early career professionals against focusing only on the work environment to meet a broader set of relationship needs. Just as it is important to develop relationships within one's work environment, it is also important to have relational connections outside that environment. Having strong relationships outside of work can provide a psychological buffer. If stress rises within the work environment—such as competition over resources or other processes that might lead to conflict or mistrust—other communities you belong to (e.g., family, friends, church, community groups) can provide sources of relational support and affiliation. You also have more freedom to choose people to spend time with; you cannot choose the coworkers who populate your department or program, but you can choose the friends outside of work with whom you go to a concert or meet for a drink.

SUGGESTION 2: EXPERIMENT WITH NEW WAYS OF LEADING

Second, it can be helpful to experiment with new ways of leading. Beginning graduate students often lack leadership experience and may not have thought much about what it means to be a leader. In the beginning, growing in leadership often involves unlearning some unhelpful styles of leadership. This frequently occurs through trial and error as we engage in a new system. Try to be open to new ways of leading and engaging with groups. Take note of others who seem to be effective in connecting with a wide range of individuals and groups and explore what makes their leadership style effective.

For example, as Donnie started to examine his leadership tendencies, he noticed the need to consider a range of approaches for engaging groups and leadership. He tended to rely on individualistic, direct, analytical, problem-solving approaches, which may work well in small groups that have high levels of trust, engagement, and similar working styles. In more complex groups with different levels of engagement and working styles, however, more work is sometimes needed to build rapport and consensus. Strong leaders think systemically. They facilitate change by moving past content to consider the broader context and process. This approach allows them to look upstream (i.e., beyond the immediate context) to consider ways of generating momentum to sustain long-term changes.

Donnie started to watch and learn from Cirleen's leadership style (Cirleen is his partner and also a counseling psychologist). Cirleen is multiracial—her dad was Belgian American, and her mom is Taiwanese. She is closely attuned to the social harmony of a group. As a multiracial person, she navigates "in-between" spaces well. Cirleen is slow to speak and patient with group processes. She forms trust and often works to form cohesion, even in groups that may not tend to trust each other. Sometimes this way of being causes her anxiety because she can end up in "loyalty binds" as people who trust her want her to prioritize them over someone else who also trusts her. (This experience parallels some of the demands that can be placed on multiracial people regarding their racial and ethnic identities as well.) These skills and ways of being not only accelerated Cirleen's leadership opportunities within the American Psychological Association but also help her "hold space" (i.e., develop norms that allow for psychological safety, despite the presence of differences that have the potential to undermine trust within a group) in multicultural courses or when working to form trust within her research lab, which often includes students with multiple marginalized identities.

As Donnie encountered new situations, he would think of the strengths of other leaders and imagine how they might handle a situation. For example, how might Cirleen use her strengths in building consensus to address the current challenge? Or how would Daryl handle this situation, given his high agreeableness and interpersonal sensitivity? Or how would Josh think about this challenge, given his ability to break complex problems into step-by-step plans that make execution simple and easy for others to track? We encourage you to fully engage the benefits of social learning—trial and error is a necessary part of growth, but we can save ourselves heartache by learning from a group of mentors and colleagues seeking to grow and balance the complex dynamics of leadership and mentoring. By imagining the strengths and creativity of others in difficult situations, we can draw on their wisdom to increase our own psychological flexibility.

SUGGESTION 3: CAREFULLY CONSIDER TEAM NORMS

Third, think carefully about the norms you want to develop in your group and team. Strong teams often have norms that balance cohesion and inclusiveness. The norming process of a team, in which the group begins to form bonds with each other and develop expectations for what will happen in the group, is like the process groups go through in psychotherapy. The leader has a unique role in bringing the group together and helping to negotiate its purpose and norms (Yalom, 1970).

In group psychotherapy, it is important for a group leader to do a good job of "holding space" for a group. In the groups we lead, we are trying to do a similar thing—create a space that allows members to feel connected and bonded with each other yet also respected and honored for their individual and cultural differences.

How can you work to create a group with these norms? Again, a lesson can be learned from group psychotherapy. At the beginning of a psychotherapy group, the leader will often go over a set of guidelines that describe what the group will be about. These can include guidelines about confidentiality, speaking for yourself, or even commitments for group attendance. Similarly, it can be helpful to think carefully about the norms you want to establish for the groups you lead. It can even be helpful to facilitate a group process in which your team discusses and commits to their values. For example, Donnie's research team developed a culture document that describes some of the key purposes of the team, as well as norms related to research, writing, and other issues, such as welcoming and navigating cultural differences.

Importantly, their document reflects a collective process. Third-year students help revise it yearly, so it is a living and active document that reflects the current norms of the team, not just a top-down structure. The norms also indicate how the team relates to the culture of the program and department. As such, team members begin to think of themselves as part of a program that reflects the coming together of a variety of subcultures, the different teams of various faculty.

As a leader, you will need to experiment with your own style of negotiating norms and sharing authority within a research team. That said, we have gathered some thoughts and questions that may help you and your team begin to articulate its norms and ways of balancing cohesion and inclusion.

Encourage Team Values

Your professional and personal values and goals will provide a foundation for your team to work with as you collaboratively develop your team values. Strong teams share many common qualities. For example, Donnie's team values trustworthiness and integrity—making and keeping their commitments. This commitment also involves an action orientation. They make commitments thoughtfully, but when they commit to something, they make sure to track progress with accountability.

Second, they also value humility as they seek to grow and change as a result of high-quality feedback. In a team setting that includes many smart people, it can be easy for folks to get locked into thinking their perspective is the "right" one, which cuts off the opportunity for feedback, growth, and change. They try to keep ego out of the learning process and are quick to take responsibility for problems or mistakes. They are open to each other's perspectives and welcome constructive feedback on research projects or papers.

Third, they invest in a culture of generosity. Their team is not competitive with each other but seeks to develop skills that can be shared freely with each other, which works against the zero-sum thinking that can become prevalent in work settings. They seek to develop expertise through hard work and a positive attitude that encourages team members through example and strong friendships. They are generous with their time and collaborations and share credit for success.

Although these values have worked well for our teams, we do want to share a caveat. Clarifying the values of the team helps the leader to form and protect cohesion in the group, but it is also important to explicitly strengthen values that will help a group grow in its inclusiveness to differences. It is important to recognize that values are culturally influenced, and team members often bring their unique perspectives and worldviews to the table. We want to have some shared values, but we also want team members to feel honored and respected for their unique cultural backgrounds and points of view. This can sometimes be a tricky balance.

For example, suppose one of your values is being able to give one another honest and direct feedback. You value clear communication and expect your team members to do the same. But not everyone shares this value. In some cultures, more indirect communication is the norm. Suppose you have a student who comes from a cultural background that values this type of communication. Are your leadership style and the norms of your group flexible enough to allow this student to feel at home and included in your group, even though their communication style is different from yours? One of the key challenges of leading teams is encouraging team values in a way that is flexible enough that inclusiveness is high.

Protect the Team From Unhealthy Conflict

Conflict is natural for any group or team. Conflict occurs when teams have different perspectives on what to prioritize or how to approach their goals. As a leader, you have a unique role in disrupting threats to cohesion within the group and helping group members navigate conflict in a healthy way. Try not to avoid conflict or think of it as a "bad thing." Conflict is not always damaging, although there are ways of navigating conflict that can be more healthy or less healthy.

Family systems theory (Kerr & Bowen, 1988) highlights some toxic dynamics to avoid. For example, in toxic cultures, triangulation is common. Instead of addressing conflict directly with the person you are in conflict with, seeking a path that preserves the greatest amount of trust possible, people "triangulate" by telling their story to others to gather "support" and form subgroups. This pattern tends to escalate conflict as both sides engage in reputational warfare.

Some organizational systems fall into bad habits related to conflict. For example, sometimes faculty will use stories from students to leverage their perspectives within the department. Triangulation leads to more triangulation. These behaviors are a quick path to professional burnout and lead to patterns that erode trust.

Guard against expressing cynicism to students. As leaders, we have a lot of influence over the climate of our teams. Cynicism is one of the primary ingredients that leads to burnout. When we notice signs of cynicism in ourselves, we can maintain our professional boundaries with students and seek support from outside the system (e.g., family, close friends, counselor).

As team leaders, we have many opportunities to hear stories of frustration and offense. These moments are tests of our character and leadership ability. If we are not careful, we can allow the person talking with us to triangulate us into their conflict. Just like a strong family systems therapist, as team leaders, we can listen to stories about the other person and support our team member in a way that encourages the person to take responsibility for their conflict and does not betray the trust of the person absent from the conversation.

Our mentor Ev was a couples therapist, and one thing we learned from him was to count the costs of ruptures in any relationship. When Donnie was younger, he believed that, in strong relationships, people should address conflict honestly and directly. Over time, he realized this belief was not a good match for all relationships, especially those with lower levels of commitment or those with high levels strain or stress. Handling conflict well requires trust, and conflict can undermine trust. Indeed, even in high-commitment relationships, some ruptures are difficult to heal, especially if one or more people have past relational wounds, and patterns in the current relationship antagonize or even reenact memories of prior hurt.

Ruptures at the group level are especially difficult to repair. Perhaps this is why triangulation is risky; it often leads to "subgrouping" or even scapegoating. Be careful about talking behind people's backs or engaging in "meetings after the meeting" to address conflict. Whereas an individual can apologize or make amends, relational processes are much more complex at the collective level as groups involve various subgroups that vary in their willingness to work toward the repair of trust. Groups cannot easily apologize—perhaps some will speak symbolically for the group, but realistically, groups have members with a range of reactions and ways of engaging conflict. Thus, at the group level, less mature individuals often react with their "worst fears" about the goals and intentions of the other. A downward cycle may occur, in which the least mature members of different subgroups react to each other until conflict seems almost intractable without resorting to cutoff (i.e., emotional disengagement).

Promote Friendship

Part of leading a team involves helping to cocreate a positive vision of what belonging to the team can mean. For us, the highest ideal is one of professional friendship. We build on common values to form a strong bond and commitment to each other. We also leverage these shared values to form a group that can tolerate differences of perspective, not allowing them to devolve into patterns that undermine trust. Ultimately, we want to help each other clarify our sense of purpose and develop leadership abilities, so we can involve others in work that matters. These are admittedly value-laden processes—and it is essential for a team to have conversations to clarify its shared vision.

SUGGESTION 4: LOOK FOR WAYS TO USE YOUR PRIVILEGE FOR THE BENEFIT OF OTHERS

Finally, as you progress in your career, you will move into new levels of power and authority—you will more often have a seat at the table where important decisions are made. Many psychologists feel ambivalent about authority, which can interfere with the process of developing leadership skills. Now is the time to begin exploring behaviors that can empower others and make the path easier for other students and early career professionals. In preparation for this book, we talked with other colleagues in our network to generate a list of possible ideas for ways that tenured (and especially full) professors can use their influence to promote a balance of cohesion and inclusion in their local systems.

Idea 1: Protect Time and Focus

Almost all the ideas in this section involve variations of this first point— protect the time and focus of graduate students and early career scholars.

A wise department will invest in the success of its people. When early career professionals are protected, they can develop strong research programs and integrate their expertise throughout teaching and leadership roles. Strategic compounding occurs, in line with Collins's (2019) work on the flywheel effect (as discussed in Chapter 21). They benefit from an upward cycle in which protection of time allows them to engage in high-quality projects with high-quality teams, which leads to more resources, which enables them to grow stronger teams. Then the entire cycle repeats itself.

In contrast, some departments do not protect the time and focus of early career professionals. In this kind of system, negative strategic compounding occurs (e.g., similar to taking out a loan with a predatory interest rate). For example, some departments will assign time-consuming teaching assignments (e.g., multicultural course, assessment, practicum) or service roles to early career professionals (sometimes even more so for women and faculty of color) without consideration of patterns that lead to the inequitable protection of time and energy. This leads to early career scholars spending more of their time doing things that distract from their unique role as research professors, in addition to the uncompensated and unrecognized labor that such faculty perform.

Idea 2: Engage Positively in Meetings

Meetings set the tone for the culture of a program or department. We all have typical ways of being in groups. As we grow in self-awareness, we may learn the strengths and weaknesses of our natural tendencies. For example, Donnie enjoys group discussions more than most. He likes exchanging ideas, asking questions, and working collaboratively to solve problems. Early in his career, as the only assistant professor in his department, this was fine (e.g., he would often begin comments with, "I'm new here"), but over time, he has learned to temper his enthusiasm. For example, some people are less comfortable speaking up in small group discussions or feel less trust for the group. He had to adjust his group behavior as he had different levels of authority within his department.

As he watched others carefully, he realized people with high trust in the system shared some similar group behaviors. Good citizens stayed emotionally engaged and had a high level of discipline. For example, good citizens made their words count. They were patient and attended to nonverbal cues but spoke with clear intent to aid the group process. Other good citizens in the department engaged with kindness, tact, or even dry humor to help increase rapport. Others used carefully calibrated questions to move the discussion forward. He also noticed good citizens carefully attended to potential gender or racial dynamics or dynamics related to status (e.g., tenure-track faculty, clinical faculty, staff) or relative power within the department (e.g., early career faculty). For example, they might make a follow-up comment to amplify a point by an early career scholar that the group had perhaps not sufficiently engaged. He also saw some faculty who would make sure women and people of color got credit for their work, disrupting any trends to the contrary.

Donnie noticed that stress and impatience are the enemies of positive group dynamics. People tend to become less kind and more self-oriented when they feel afraid of scarce resources. Under stress, it can be easy to talk and share your opinion when it may be better to listen and stay quiet, affirm someone else, or make more space for a colleague. Group dynamics are difficult—sometimes we need to conform, and other times we need to differentiate. It takes time to develop the wisdom to know when to take risks versus going with the flow.

Idea 3: Make Sure the Department Gives Clear Messages About Hiring and Tenure

Sometimes departments do a poor job with boundaries regarding hiring or tenure processes. Sometimes groups may discuss historical dynamics or processes, forgetting new members may not know the history. For example, in Donnie's 1st year, the departmental discussion alluded to information related to his hire. Another faculty member was quick to clarify the insensitive discussion. Over the years, Donnie noticed this faculty member was always vigilant to similar situations. He would consistently go out of his way to diffuse any confusion or awkwardness related to, for example, a discussion about hiring challenges while a recent hire was in the room. The same person also gave clear feedback regarding the promotion and tenure process, which dramatically reduced Donnie's stress during his early career phase. Thus, a little empathy, combined with quick and decisive action, goes a long way to reduce the stress associated with evaluative processes such as hiring, promotion, and tenure.

Idea 4: Make Difficult Structural Decisions

Early in your career, you may choose to avoid decisions pertaining to structures of systems; however, as you gain institutional power and authority, you may find yourself partially responsible for them. There are many ways to leverage your gifts and authority for the benefit of others. A major area of common ground involves creating work environments that support graduate students and early career professionals. This is one of Donnie's favorite things about his department. As long as he has been there, the community has had a strong commitment to protect early career scholars.

This commitment was tested, however, as budget cuts occurred year after year. The department noticed that assistant professors in some programs had less protection of time and energy (because of the administrative needs of programs) than others did. At one point, a colleague who had just finished her 3-year review was under pressure to become a training director. Donnie advocated that the department maintain alignment with its long-standing value, even if it proved costly.

This advocacy eventually led to more disciplined decisions by the department. The next year, the program made a difficult decision. When a new position opened, the program realized they needed someone to do more program administration and teaching, not someone with pressure to publish and get more grants (i.e., tenure-track professor). The department grappled with the decision. Retaining the tenure-track line would require the program to allow a growing number of courses to be taught by adjunct faculty. So, this time, instead of putting an assistant professor in a difficult bind, they hired a clinical assistant professor, so the expectations for the job matched the program's needs. These kinds of structural decisions ease pressure on early career professionals.

Idea 5: Shift Initiative to Early Career Faculty

Movement toward greater inclusiveness is often more about process than content. One example occurred when Donnie's program went through a transition. After over 15 years of having the same training director, Cirleen stepped into the role. As they prepared for an upcoming site visit, the program faced a variety of decisions that required coordination. For example, they needed to clarify training values, revise their comprehensive exam to align with their training values, and make some structural changes to give more support to students that did not have a prior counseling-related master's degree (given a recent change in admissions criteria that allowed students with a bachelor's degree to apply).

One of the faculty members suggested the program form an early career staging committee to develop ideas. He used his influence to promote a shift in initiative within the program. As a result, Donnie worked with other early career professors to coordinate a set of changes to the program. The process helped Donnie and Cirleen take more initiative in the vision of the program. For example, they developed a yearly process that involved the training director meeting with students, conducting a survey based on ideas from cohort meetings, and then convening an end-of-the-year program meeting to set two to three goals for the following year. The important part was process more than content—the program forged new ways of making decisions.

Idea 6: Share the Mental Load

Another thing tenured faculty can do is protect the mental load of early career scholars. They need to protect not just time but also emotional energy. Training programs have much in common with parenting. Students need more than just technical training; they also need high-quality relationships that provide emotional support and responsiveness. Women and faculty of color often carry an inordinate burden to provide such support. This work falls between the lines of what is typically valued within academia (i.e., underrecognized and uncompensated service). Thus, as tenured faculty gain greater power to protect their time, it is important to the health of the system that they look out for the interests of early career scholars.

Donnie and Cirleen have the unique experience, and sometimes the challenge, of being married and tenured faculty within the same program. They also have a 3-year-old son together. They regularly have conversations to seek to balance the mental load between them. This often requires a flexible negotiation of their needs. For example, they change their schedules each semester to accommodate the needs of their family and work. Sometimes in higher education, people from marginalized groups are expected to carry a greater mental load in relationships, including within academic departments. Cirleen and Donnie attempt to divvy up both family and work tasks that speak to their strengths. For example, Donnie is a whiz with spreadsheets, record-keeping, and engaging new technology. Thus, Donnie helps Cirleen with her program director tasks, such as keeping program minutes in meetings and maintaining student records. Also, he now teaches a 1st-year course that gives him much more contact with all students in the program, so students are more likely to feel comfortable accessing him, in addition to Cirleen, as they progress in the program. Cirleen and Donnie have learned their responsibilities are by no means interchangeable, and Cirleen experiences a greater risk of having her work disrupted by her service tasks, but Donnie can engage proactively to soften these dynamics as her partner and colleague.

Idea 7: Minimize the Toll of Dual Relationships

Another thing tenured faculty can do to protect early career scholars is to minimize the toll of dual relationships on women and/or racial and ethnic minorities. Faculty positions often require people to balance different roles and responsibilities. For example, when Cirleen transitioned into the training director role, she also had six students on her research team within the 1st- and 2nd-year cohorts. Cirleen was the first woman program coordinator and the first woman of color program coordinator as well. Her students identified almost exclusively as students of color, including women of color and queer students of color. Thus, she not only served as doctoral advisor to many of the students but also functioned as the primary person convening the program faculty and student representatives. So, she was the primary avenue for addressing student concerns during a series of highly stressful transitions and disruptions in broader society (e.g., the Trump presidency, the George Floyd murder, COVID-19 isolation).

As the program started to orient to the complexities of the students' needs during this period, the program faculty realized it was problematic for Cirleen to carry such a heavy mentoring load while also engaging a major program transition as the new program coordinator. Although her advisor and coordinator roles were not entirely uncompensated or unrecognized, Cirleen's multiple roles amplified the labor that women of color in academia already experience. As the program clarified the complexity of the problem, other faculty worked to add structure to the program to more evenly distribute the work of engaging students. This process took several years and involved creating a student–faculty liaison, adding a process for seeking feedback, setting and tracking yearly program goals, and adding several courses designed to give more structure within the first 2 years of the program. Strong programs share each other's burdens and develop norms that protect the time and energy of early career scholars, especially faculty from marginalized groups that may be particularly prone to service demands that interfere with career progression.

Idea 8: Open Mentoring Networks

Strong departments also support early career psychologists through opening mentoring networks. There is a tendency to work with and mentor people whom you know and are comfortable with. Even in counseling psychology, we see trends that match the rest of psychology and many other industries. The most productive people come from a narrow set of programs. Mentoring matters a lot, and this aligns with what we know about expertise development in other fields. However, if someone was not lucky enough to have good mentoring in graduate school, they can sometimes start a faculty position without strong collaborations or mentoring relationships in place. It is important to help connect early career faculty to relationships that can aid their professional development.

Training networks in psychology involve two dynamics. First, they involve high-quality feedback. For people to grow, they need to keep getting good feedback. Second, they also involve trust networks. For people to succeed in larger research projects and grants, they must join networks. Often it is difficult to get the first grant on your own—you need a mentor or team member who is more experienced to help you. Getting a grant is a little like getting a loan for a house. At first, people may need to borrow on the reputation of others until they establish their own track record. We doubt that we would have received our first large grant on humility if we did not have the mentorship and guidance of our mentor Ev, who had experience and success receiving funding for his research.

So, in this regard, it would be easy for systems to perpetuate unfair access to mentoring networks unintentionally. If you are not thinking about it, it can be easy to continue to work with the people you know and feel comfortable with. This dynamic is something we have discussed among ourselves. We recognize that as three White, heterosexual, cisgender men from middle- to upper-middle-class backgrounds, we have been able to access and maximize multiple types of resources. These advantages helped us get our doctorates, find academic jobs, and achieve tenure and promotion. What can and should any of us do when we realize we have advantages that others do not?

This is a deeply personal (and perhaps even spiritual) question. Yet we suggest two ways forward. First, honor the ways you have benefited from the sacrifice of others, sometimes freely given and other times taken unfairly. For example, Donnie's mother gave up some possible opportunities to homeschool him and his three siblings. She died of ovarian cancer at age 48 while completing a degree in counseling. Her career was cut short at both ends, first by more restrictive gender roles and later by an early and untimely death. After his mom died, Donnie dedicated his work to honoring his mother's life and work. Everything Donnie does is partially in honor of her life and love, which gives him a deep source of motivation. He also remembers his gifts and opportunities are not just for himself. His mom invested her life so her kids would bring good things into the world out of the overflow of the love within her family.

The second way forward is to find ways of expressing generosity and leveraging one's authority and gifts for the benefit of others. As we have become more established in our careers, we have tried to look for ways to share our expertise and time fairly and generously. When it comes to our cultural identities that are more privileged, the goal is to seek healing and integrity so we can live meaningful lives in which we grieve loss, unfairness, and suffering and still seek to express love and generosity that rises to our highest ideals as humans. This process is lifelong and, ideally, infused into everything we do. In fact, this book is one way we can share some of what we have learned with a broader audience.

For us, the solution is not to stop engaging in high-trust relationships. Yet, the socially conscious psychologist knows high-trust relationships have a shadow side. They can keep inequity alive because it is easier to keep collaborating with those you trust, and it can be more challenging to expand the boundaries of your work relationships. For us, the goal is to build a "big tent" and help build structures so others can form high-trust networks. We want to leverage the access trust gives us for the benefit of others. We consider it a privilege to serve, and we want to leave the communities we belong to in better condition than we found them.

GRADUATE MENTOR CORNER

In this chapter, we tackled the difficult challenge of balancing cohesion and inclusion in teams. Although much of the material covered in this chapter applies to professors later in their careers, as they begin to accrue more power and privilege in the environments they serve, some of this material can be applied even earlier. Sometimes graduate students enter a system with the idea they are just a cog in the wheel and believe they have little power. And in many cases, their power is limited. However, graduate students have more power than they think. We often encourage graduate students to experiment with being more proactive in bringing up issues about their research teams, programs, and departments they would like to see changed.

If there are small ways to involve graduate students in leadership opportunities in the groups and teams you are a part of, encourage this involvement. For example, Josh and Donnie have training structures in which their older graduate students take more responsibility for the lab meetings and supervision of undergraduate students. Several of Josh's students have served as the liaison between the graduate students and the program faculty, which gives them a literal seat at the table (at the University of North Texas, the program representative is given one vote in program decisions).

Finally, as you lead by example and through your words, talk through issues related to the balance of cohesion and inclusion on your teams so your students can understand your thought process and how you are weighing these important issues. Help your students check themselves when they express "universal" values that may be culturally specific. Challenge them to be open to individuals who might have different beliefs than they do. Help connect your students to mentors who can help them develop wider collaborative networks—not just your own network.

UNDERGRADUATE MENTOR CORNER

Establishing healthy group norms and working toward inclusion are important parts of any team dynamic, especially among undergraduate students, where the power differential is large. If you work with both graduate and undergraduate students, you can encourage the graduate students to help build the norms of the group for the undergraduates. If you work directly (and only) with undergraduates, modeling healthy group dynamics can prepare them for the transition to graduate school.

When selecting the students to include in your lab, consider your practices for identifying and accepting students. Increasing the diversity of faculty requires addressing the pipeline of people in a profession from underrepresented groups. Progress requires getting a wide variety of students interested and involved in research at the undergraduate level. Be intentional about how you recruit and who you select to ensure you provide opportunities for all students to engage in the research process.

MOVING FORWARD

In this chapter, we talked about some things to keep in mind when leading and participating in the groups and teams you are a part of—your research team, your program, and your department. We also talked through some things to think about as you grow in your degree of power and influence over decisions in the environments you serve. Most of us increase our degree of privilege as we get more experienced—it is important to use that privilege to help others have the space and opportunity to pursue their dreams and goals in an unencumbered way. In the next (last) chapter, we reflect on where we have been and say goodbye.

26 CONCLUSION

Final Thoughts on Growing as a Researcher

We have covered a lot of ground in this book. In Part I, we talked about several important principles and habits to consider when developing as a researcher. The most important tool you have as a researcher is yourself, and investing in your development as a researcher always pays high dividends. We have seen many bright students struggle with research because they had a tough time developing the principles and habits that characterize great researchers. These are the building blocks of personal growth and development you need to engage in to make consistent progress on your research.

Then, in Part II, we walked through how to complete an independent research project from start to finish, step by step. Many bright graduate students struggle to make consistent progress on research because they do not know what they do not know. We hope this section can give a framework to help students and mentors organize and structure the building blocks of the research process. It can also be changed and customized depending on the needs and preferences of the mentor.

Finally, in Part III, we took a broader look at developing your research career. We talked about issues such as leadership, collaboration, the transition to becoming a professor, and mentoring both individuals and teams.

https://doi.org/10.1037/0000371-027
The Complete Researcher: A Practical Guide for Graduate Students and Early Career Professionals, by J. N. Hook, D. E. Davis, and D. R. Van Tongeren
Copyright © 2024 by the American Psychological Association. All rights reserved.

We zoomed out from focusing on completing an individual research project to developing your program of research.

Developing as a researcher is an ongoing journey. We have been doing research for over 15 years now, and sometimes we still do not feel like we have "figured it out." There are days when we get frustrated when studies do not work out or we cannot figure out how to respond to a reviewer critique. On days like these, we need to remind ourselves that developing as a researcher is an ongoing process. The learning does not stop. We hope to continue to grow and learn about research for the rest of our lives (or at least until we retire).

Still, after observing our own process as researchers, as well as training several graduate students in the research process, there are some basic steps that most beginning researchers seem to go through and some common points of struggle. For example, it is important to connect the research process to your values; otherwise, motivation is difficult. There is a science to improvement and developing expertise. Practice does not make perfect, but deliberate practice leads to consistent improvements over time. Setting effective goals that can generate excitement is important. Habits, those things we consistently do, are important predictors of effectiveness. Make sure your research and work habits are dialed in. There is a powerful connection between our thoughts and behaviors—it is important to gather evidence and believe you can do it. Working on your body and getting into a flow state can be helpful for peak performance. Adversity happens to most of us—make sure you have some strategies to take care of yourself. Research can be a lonely process—you can be more effective (and have more fun) working in teams. And do not forget to give back and help those who come after you.

We love helping younger researchers grow and develop their skills and competencies. Research can be an empowering skill—it enables you to ask any kind of question (even big questions) and gather data to try to figure out the answer. When graduate students get the research bug and start to get going, it is amazing to see. The creative juices start flowing, and the sky is the limit. Unfortunately, many students grow to dread research, and some never make it out of their graduate programs because they cannot seem to get the hang of the research process. That is why we wrote this book—to help graduate students who are struggling have a resource they can turn to when starting out. You do not know what you do not know—and that is okay.

In ending this book, we thought it might be valuable to reflect on some of the important lessons we learned along the way that were helpful in our development as researchers but may not have fit neatly into one of the chapters of this book. We hope the following lessons and stories will be helpful and motivating to you as you embark on your research career.

JOSH: SLOW, STEADY, AND CONSISTENT WINS THE RACE

Especially if students are on an academic track, they will often ask me how many publications they need to write to be competitive for a job once they graduate. Of course, this is impossible to answer in any specific way—it depends on the type of job they want, and numbers are not the only thing. Other factors, such as the number of first-authored publications and the competitiveness of the journals, are important to consider as well. Sometimes students have a lot of energy and want to get going on several projects right away. I usually try to settle them down and talk about how being slow, steady, and consistent wins the race.

It is an old story, but the tale of the tortoise and the hare is quite applicable to the research process. Most of you know the story: The tortoise and the hare get ready to race. The hare is fast, so he quickly jumps to what looks like an insurmountable lead. The hare gets far ahead and decides to rest for a bit and take a nap. The tortoise, however, is slow but keeps at it. He keeps plodding along, one foot in front of the other. Eventually, the hare wakes up and discovers more time has passed than he realized. He quickly races to the finish line, but the tortoise is already there!

Often, students are used to working in short bursts. In their undergrad, this process of "cramming" might have worked, but it does not work for research in graduate school and beyond. Graduate students need to make a transition and think about their research work more as a job they do consistently over time. Every day, it is important to come in and put in the hours. Every day, it is important to move your research projects forward a step or two. If you get into this habit of consistent work every day, progress happens over time. When writing a journal article or book chapter, I tell myself I will write one page a day. It does not seem like much, but if I keep that pace up, I can write a 30-page article in a month, which is not too bad. Similarly, when I am working on a book, I tell myself I am going to write one page a day. Again, it does not seem like a lot, but if I keep that pace up, I can write a 300-page book in a year, which, again, is not too bad. Over time, working little by little, like the tortoise, has enabled me to be productive, and I try to instill this attitude in my students as well.

DONNIE: GUARD INTRINSIC MOTIVATION WITH YOUR LIFE

Some students thrive in doctoral studies, while others struggle, seemingly always in a reactive mode and feeling overwhelmed and stressed. A key difference seems to be that students who anticipate threats to intrinsic motivation, one way or another, manage to keep them from stealing their joy. They clarify and regularly reinvest in their internal reservoirs of strength and persistence. Our identity is shaped by what we value and decide to invest our life in, including work. We lose vitality when we trade the intrinsic joy of an activity for external rewards. So, never do this!

Of course, this is easy to say, but it may feel almost impossible to do. Graduate school is a succession of hoops that, if not completed in a timely manner, comes with logical and natural consequences. One will not graduate unless one completes the entire list. So, with such clear external structures, is it even possible to do things for intrinsic reasons?

There are any number of things that may steal your joy in graduate school or beyond: (a) the stakes may feel so high, given that the opportunity costs of not graduating on time are steep—perhaps as high as $100K per year if you have to spend extra time in school instead of getting a well-paying job; (b) sometimes, we may have too many or competing commitments that vie for our primary energy and attention; (c) we may fear rejection or failure in our major goals; (d) we may encounter setbacks in the research process because it never really goes as planned; (e) we may experience self-doubt as we seek to pursue our career goals; and (f) conflict may lead to cynicism and a turning inward in relation to our team and community.

In graduate school, I carefully guarded time for writing so I could devote daily time to refining my craft. As I gained skill, I gained momentum, which allowed me to explore and "waste time" on longer term investments. This gave me the leverage to say to myself, "The university gets part of my intellectual life but not all of it."

If you want to put this idea into practice in your own career, (a) know the "coin of the realm" (e.g., grants and publications), so you can always negotiate some of your interests as you meet the external standards; (b) look for new ways of doing things—always experiment and tweak your approach to maintain and grow intrinsic motivation; and (c) cultivate an active intellectual life. Read widely and build trusting relationships with a broad range of people and communities.

DARYL: PRIORITIZE AND PROTECT

For the past several years, I have had the opportunity to speak to our incoming faculty at Hope College in their presemester professional development program. I sit on a panel about how to develop a productive research program. There, I offer many of the insights from this book, but the one I emphasize the most strongly—and the one that sticks with people the most, weeks, months, or even years later—is to prioritize and protect your research time. Whenever I fill out my calendar for the semester, the first blocks of time I add are my research and writing times. For nearly a decade, this has been every weekday from 7 a.m. to 10 a.m. And I protect it fiercely. Only emergencies or travel typically interrupt this time.

Our life is essentially just time—so how we spend our time matters. Many people feel powerless in the face of their schedules, and there are dimensions of our schedules we cannot control. But as academics, we have considerable autonomy in crafting our weekly rhythms. Thus, because excelling at research is a professional value of mine, I prioritize it with regard to my time. And just as we do not schedule other things during our teaching, we need to protect our research and writing time. Stop giving that up for meetings or viewing it as flexible. Show up, commit to the process, and see the results. When you put in the work, it is remarkable how the changes follow.

JOSH: THE PURPOSE OF FEEDBACK IS TO HELP YOU—DO NOT TAKE IT PERSONALLY

I remember when I was working on my first independent research project in graduate school—the master's thesis. I was working on my literature review, which was challenging. (I have found that the literature review for the first major research project is tough for most graduate students—it is the first major step of the research process, and it is challenging for anybody!) I worked on the literature review all semester and finally turned in a draft to my advisor before I left for winter break.

When I got my literature review back from my advisor, there was A LOT of feedback written all over the document in blue ink. (Ev was old school—he did not use track changes. Instead, he printed out your whole document and wrote on it with pen.) At first, I was overwhelmed by all the feedback and changes. I had thought the literature review was in pretty good shape. I was wrong.

There was one piece of feedback that initially got under my skin. I am paraphrasing, but the comment went something like this: "Right now you are organizing the literature review study by study. An actuary or a librarian could do this. You are not yet doing any real science." No real science? I had just spent 3 whole months working on this project, and I was not doing any real science yet?

Feedback like this can be challenging to receive for the beginning graduate student. Most graduate students are high achievers and used to receiving mostly positive feedback. So, when constructive feedback comes, it can be difficult to sit with and incorporate. But I had to be humble about it. When it came to research, I was a beginner. I was very much a learner. Ev had my best interests in mind—he was trying to help me and make me better.

To grow as a researcher, you must learn not to take negative feedback personally. The feedback loop between mentor and student is important when developing strong research skills and expertise. It is critical to be humble, take in the feedback given, and use it to improve. And this process of receiving and incorporating feedback does not end when you graduate. Whenever I have a journal article, grant proposal, or book proposal rejected and receive feedback about my project, it is an opportunity to grow and learn. I will be honest—sometimes, I still get frustrated and find it hard to take in the feedback. I think that is part of being human—we want to see ourselves in a positive light. But more often than not, I am able to take a step back, take a breath, and learn something from the feedback. And that has made me a better researcher over the long haul.

DONNIE: INTEGRITY HELPS PASS ON VALUES

Many of the themes we discussed in this book involve learning to become a person who makes and keeps commitments to oneself and others. As psychologists, we practice our craft with discipline, persistence, and devotion. We put ourselves in a position to receive high-quality feedback, so we can grow and learn in our areas of developing expertise. We also strive to become people who can involve others in our work. We want to leverage our gifts and opportunities to benefit others, including the many small communities in which we are grounded, as well as the broader society that our institution (i.e., psychology) seeks to serve well.

One of the things we are learning is to leverage our gifts and energy to earn trust across different relationships and communities. We do this by generating margin in our lives, so we have something to give others and model a way of being that adopts an abundance rather than a scarcity mindset—"there is more than enough to go around." We give to others because, somewhere along the way, someone gave us this kind of gift. We know we could never repay such gratuitous generosity—we can only pay the gift forward.

Much of this book was a tribute to our mentor, Ev Worthington, and we all have a group of mentors who make us who we are. Some of my other professional mentors include Hal Stevens, who was always slow to anger and quick to explore. Even though our cultural identities were very different, Hal embodied the core logic of Carl Rogers and engaged me with genuineness, acceptance, and empathy. Deanne Terrell, who was a professor in my master's program, embodied the Martin Luther King Jr. quote—"a threat to justice anywhere is a threat to justice everywhere"—she was nurturing and emotionally trustworthy, no matter what the issue, no matter with whom she was engaged. Cirleen DeBlaere is my life partner—and at the top of my list of heroes. What these people have in common is a deep sense of integrity that is deeply attractive, life giving, and healing.

DARYL: WORK—AND LIFE—ARE MORE FUN TOGETHER

Research can be isolating and lonely. Writing is often done in solitude. And I appreciate some aspects of this individualized work. After all, I am a bit introverted and enjoy having a rich interior life and wrestling with ideas. But it is much more fun to do research with other people. Some of my most enjoyable professional moments have been thanks to my collaborative relationship with Josh and Donnie. It has helped make the long slog of a research career fun and relational. It is what most people hope for in collaborators, and I am incredibly grateful.

But what came as a surprise—and much to my delight—was what great friends we have become. We have walked through the highs and lows of life, sharing plenty of laughter and tears, disappointments and triumphs, disagreements, and too many inside jokes to keep track of. In the shifting world of academia, we have become a close-knit sense of stability for each other. In many ways, we have become like family. That has not only made research more fun but has also been a much richer way to walk through life.

I am not suggesting you must find collaborators who stand up at your wedding, visit you after a family member dies, or take you out for a beer when life feels overwhelming, but it is a good reminder that our research is just one part of life. There is so much more to living a flourishing and thriving life, and nearly everything worth doing in this life involves other people. If you can keep that perspective and be sure to continue nourishing your relationships along the way, you will be healthier and happier. And when the professional and personal mix in mutually beneficial ways, you will consider yourself lucky. I know I do.

MOVING FORWARD

As we wrap up this book, we want to encourage you. Developing as a researcher is a noble and worthy calling. We are excited for you and what you might be able to contribute to the field of science using your research skills. And we realize research is tough, especially at the beginning stages. Like any new skill, it is not easy at first. Research has its own language and norms. It can seem like everyone else "gets it," and you are on the outside looking in. We have all felt like that at some time during our research careers. Stick with it. We hope this book has been helpful for you in connecting the dots to create a picture of what it looks like to become a successful—and complete—researcher. Do not hesitate to reach out to us if you have any questions.

Josh (joshua.hook@unt.edu)
Donnie (ddavis88@gsu.edu)
Daryl (vantongeren@hope.edu)

Appendix

SAMPLE TIMELINES

In this appendix, we have included sample timelines for completing the independent research project (e.g., thesis or dissertation) in graduate school. This is only a guideline—feel free to modify it according to your needs and preferences. We have found, for most students, a 2-year timeline fits best, so we have presented that first. But for others, a 1-year or 3-year timeline may make more sense.

2-Year Plan

Month 1	Choose a topic
Months 2-7	Literature review
Month 8	Project design
Month 9	Method
Month 10	Proposal meeting
Months 11-16	Data collection
Months 17-19	Data analysis
Months 20-21	Results
Months 22-23	Discussion, abstract
Month 24	Defense meeting
Month 25+	Conference presentation, publication

1-Year Plan

Month 1	Choose a topic
Months 2-4	Literature review
Month 5	Project design
Month 5	Method
Month 6	Proposal meeting
Months 7-9	Data collection
Month 10	Data analysis
Month 11	Results
Month 12	Discussion, abstract
Month 12	Defense meeting
Month 13+	Conference presentation, publication

3-Year Plan

Months 1-2	Choose a topic
Months 3-11	Literature review
Months 12-13	Project design
Months 14-15	Method
Month 16	Proposal meeting
Months 17-25	Data collection
Months 26-30	Data analysis
Months 31-33	Results
Months 34-35	Discussion, abstract
Month 36	Defense meeting
Month 37+	Conference presentation, publication

References

Aksnes, D. W. (2003). Characteristics of highly cited papers. *Research Evaluation, 12*(3), 159–170. https://doi.org/10.3152/147154403781776645

American Psychological Association. (2009). *2008–2009 APA survey of graduate departments of psychology: Faculty start-up packages.* https://www.apa.org/workforce/publications/grad-09/report.pdf

American Psychological Association. (2017). *Ethical principles of psychologists and code of conduct* (2002, Amended June 1, 2010, and January 1, 2017). https://www.apa.org/ethics/code/ethics-code-2017.pdf

Appelbaum, M., Cooper, H., Kline, R. B., Mayo-Wilson, E., Nezu, A. M., & Rao, S. M. (2018). Journal article reporting standards for quantitative research in psychology: The APA Publications and Communications Board task force report. *American Psychologist, 73*(1), 3–25. https://doi.org/10.1037/amp0000191

Babauta, L. (2009). *The power of less: The fine art of limiting yourself to the essential . . . in business and in life.* Hyperion.

Bandura, A. (1977). Self-efficacy: Toward a unifying theory of behavioral change. *Psychological Review, 84*(2), 191–215. https://doi.org/10.1037/0033-295X.84.2.191

Bandura, A. (1997). *Self-efficacy: The exercise of control.* Freeman.

Beck, J. S. (1995). *Cognitive therapy: Basics and beyond.* Guilford Press.

Bennett, M. J. (1986). Toward ethnorelativism: A developmental model of intercultural sensitivity. In R. M. Paige (Ed.), *Cross-cultural orientation: New conceptualizations and applications* (pp. 27–70). University Press of America.

Bowen, M. (1978). *Family therapy in clinical practice.* Jason Aronson.

Brooks, A. W. (2014). Get excited: Reappraising pre-performance anxiety as excitement. *Journal of Experimental Psychology: General, 143*(3), 1144–1158. https://doi.org/10.1037/a0035325

Cloud, H. (2010). *Necessary endings.* HarperCollins.

Cohen, J. (1988). *Statistical power for the behavioral sciences* (2nd ed.). Erlbaum.

Collins, J. (2001). *Good to great: Why some companies make the leap and others don't*. HarperCollins.

Collins, J. (2019). *Turning the flywheel: Why some companies build momentum . . . and others don't*. HarperCollins.

Colvin, G. (2008). *Talent is overrated: What really separates world-class performers from everybody else*. Portfolio/Penguin.

Covey, S. R. (1989). *The 7 habits of highly effective people: Powerful lessons in personal change*. Simon & Schuster.

Covey, S. R. (2006). *The speed of trust: The one thing that changes everything*. Simon & Schuster.

Covey, S. R., Merrill, A. R., & Merrill, R. R. (1994). *First things first*. Simon and Schuster.

Coyle, D. (2009). *The talent code: Greatness isn't born. It's made*. Bantam Books.

Csikszentmihalyi, M. (2008). *Flow: The psychology of optimal experience*. HarperCollins.

Davis, D. E. (2019). Response: Why would an early career person ever invest in interdisciplinary work? *Journal of Psychology and Christianity, 38*(3), 172–175.

Doran, G. T. (1981). There's a S.M.A.R.T. way to write management's goals and objectives. *Management Review, 70*, 35–36.

Dweck, C. S. (1999). *Self-theories: Their role in motivation, personality, and development*. Psychology Press.

Dweck, C. S. (2006). *Mindset: The new psychology of success*. Ballantine Books.

Ericsson, K. A., Krampe, R. T., & Tesch-Romer, C. (1993). The role of deliberate practice in the acquisition of expert performance. *Psychological Review, 100*(3), 363–406. https://doi.org/10.1037/0033-295X.100.3.363

Field, A. (2018). *Discovering statistics using IBM SPSS statistics* (5th ed.). SAGE.

Gladwell, M. (2008). *Outliers: The story of success*. Little, Brown and Company.

Gottman, J. M. (1994). *Why marriages succeed or fail*. Simon & Schuster.

Grudniewicz, A., Moher, D., Cobey, K. D., Bryson, G. L., Cukier, S., Allen, K., Ardern, C., Balcom, L., Barros, T., Berger, M., Ciro, J. B., Cugusi, L., Donaldson, M. R., Egger, M., Graham, I. D., Hodgkinson, M., Khan, K. M., Mabizela, M., Manca, A., . . . Lalu, M. M. (2019, December 11). Predatory journals: No definition, no defence. *Nature, 576*(7786), 210–212. https://doi.org/10.1038/d41586-019-03759-y

Hardiman, P., & Simmonds, J. G. (2013). Spiritual well-being, burnout and trauma in counsellors and psychotherapists. *Mental Health, Religion & Culture, 16*(10), 1044–1055. https://doi.org/10.1080/13674676.2012.732560

Harzing, A. W. (2007). *Publish or perish*. https://harzing.com/resources/publish-or-perish

Hayes, S. C., Strosahl, K. D., & Wilson, K. G. (1999). *Acceptance and commitment therapy: An experimental approach to behavioral change*. Guilford Press.

Helms, J. E. (1990). *Black and white racial identity: Theory, research, and practice*. Praeger.

Hook, J. N. (2006). *The effects of individualism and collectivism on forgiveness* [Unpublished master's thesis proposal]. Virginia Commonwealth University.

Hook, J. N. (2010). *The effectiveness of religiously tailored couple counseling* [Unpublished doctoral dissertation]. Virginia Commonwealth University.

Hook, J. N., Davis, D. E., Owen, J., & DeBlaere, C. (2017). *Cultural humility: Engaging diverse identities in therapy*. American Psychological Association. https://doi.org/10.1037/0000037-000

Hook, J. N., Davis, D. E., Owen, J., Worthington, E. L., Jr., & Utsey, S. O. (2013). Cultural humility: Measuring openness to culturally diverse clients. *Journal of Counseling Psychology, 60*(3), 353–366. https://doi.org/10.1037/a0032595

Hook, J. N., Hall, T. W., Davis, D. E., Van Tongeren, D. R., & Conner, M. (2021). The Enneagram: A systematic review of the literature and directions for future research. *Journal of Clinical Psychology, 77*(4), 865–883. https://doi.org/10.1002/jclp.23097

Hook, J. N., Hodge, A. S., Sandage, S. J., Davis, D. E., & Van Tongeren, D. R. (2022). Differentiation of self and cultural competence: A systematic review of the literature. *Practice Innovations*. Advance online publication. https://doi.org/10.1037/pri0000196

Hook, J. N., Owen, J., & Davis, D. E. (2014, August 7–10). *Cultural humility, religious commitment, and therapy outcomes* [Paper presentation]. American Psychological Association 122nd Annual Convention, Washington, DC, United States.

Hook, J. P., Hook, J. N., & Davis, D. E. (2017). *Helping groups heal: Leading small groups in the process of transformation*. Templeton Press.

Kerr, M. E., & Bowen, M. (1988). *Family evaluation*. Norton.

Lally, P., van Jaarsveld, C. H. M., Potts, H. W. W., & Wardle, J. (2010). How are habits formed: Modelling habit formation in the real world. *European Journal of Social Psychology, 40*(6), 998–1009. https://doi.org/10.1002/ejsp.674

Lencioni, P. (2012). *The advantage: Why organizational health trumps everything else in business*. Jossey-Bass.

Levitt, H. M., Bamberg, M., Creswell, J. W., Frost, D. M., Josselson, R., & Suárez-Orozco, C. (2018). Journal article reporting standards for qualitative primary, qualitative meta-analytic, and mixed methods research in psychology: The APA Publications and Communications Board task force report. *American Psychologist, 73*(1), 26–46. https://doi.org/10.1037/amp0000151

Linville, P. W. (1987). Self-complexity as a cognitive buffer against stress-related illness and depression. *Journal of Personality and Social Psychology, 52*(4), 663–676. https://doi.org/10.1037/0022-3514.52.4.663

Llamas, J. D., Nguyen, K., & Tran, A. G. T. T. (2021). The case for greater faculty diversity: Examining the educational impacts of student-faculty racial/ethnic match. *Race, Ethnicity and Education, 24*(3), 375–391. https://doi.org/10.1080/13613324.2019.1679759

Maslach, C., Leiter, M. P., & Schaufeli, W. B. (2008). Measuring burnout. In C. L. Cooper & S. Cartright (Eds.), *The Oxford handbook of organizational wellbeing* (pp. 86–108). Oxford University Press.

Page, M. J., McKenzie, J. E., Bossuyt, P. M., Boutron, I., Hoffmann, T. C., Mulrow, C. D., Shamseer, L., Tetzlaff, J. M., Akl, E. A., Brennan, S. E., Chou, R., Glanville, J., Grimshaw, J. M., Hróbjartsson, A., Lalu, M. M., Li, T., Loder, E. W., Mayo-Wilson, E., McDonald, S., . . . Moher, D. (2021). The PRISMA 2020 statement: An updated guideline for reporting systematic reviews. *BMJ, 372*, n71. https://doi.org/10.1136/bmj.n71

Preacher, K. J., & Hayes, A. F. (2008). Asymptotic and resampling strategies for assessing and comparing indirect effects in multiple mediator models. *Behavior Research Methods, 40*(3), 879–891. https://doi.org/10.3758/BRM.40.3.879

Price, D. D., Finniss, D. G., & Benedetti, F. (2008). A comprehensive review of the placebo effect: Recent advances and current thought. *Annual Review of Psychology, 59*(1), 565–590. https://doi.org/10.1146/annurev.psych.59.113006.095941

Rigg, J., Day, J., & Adler, H. (2013). Emotional exhaustion in graduate students: The role of engagement, self-efficacy and social support. *Journal of Educational and Developmental Psychology, 3*(2), 138–152. https://doi.org/10.5539/jedp.v3n2p138

Rock, I. (1957). The role of repetition in associative learning. *The American Journal of Psychology, 70*(2), 186–193. https://doi.org/10.2307/1419320

Rosen, C. (2008). The myth of multitasking. *New Atlantis, 20*, 105–110.

Rubin, R. S. (2002). Will the real SMART goals please stand up? *The Industrial-Organizational Psychologist, 39*(4), 26–27.

Rubinstein, J. S., Meyer, D. E., & Evans, J. E. (2001). Executive control of cognitive processes in task switching. *Journal of Experimental Psychology: Human Perception and Performance, 27*(4), 763–797. https://doi.org/10.1037/0096-1523.27.4.763

Sadri, G., & Robertson, I. T. (1993). Self-efficacy and work-related behaviour: A review and meta-analysis. *Applied Psychology, 42*(2), 139–152. https://doi.org/10.1111/j.1464-0597.1993.tb00728.x

Schaufeli, W. B., Leiter, M. P., & Maslach, C. (2009). Burnout: 35 years of research and practice. *Career Development International, 14*(3), 204–220. https://doi.org/10.1108/13620430910966406

Schwartz, S. H., Melech, G., Lehmann, A., Burgess, S., Harris, M., & Owens, V. (2001). Extending the cross-cultural validity of the theory of basic human values with a different method of measurement. *Journal of Cross-Cultural Psychology, 32*(5), 519–542. https://doi.org/10.1177/0022022101032005001

Scott, K. (2017). *Radical candor: How to get what you want by saying what you mean*. Saint Martin's Press.

Shults, F. L., & Sandage, S. J. (2006). *Transforming spirituality: Integrating theology and psychology*. Baker Academic.

Simon, H. A., & Chase, W. G. (1973). Skill in chess. *American Scientist, 61*, 394–403.

Sue, D. W., Arredondo, P., & McDavis, R. J. (1992). Multicultural competencies and standards: A call to the profession. *Journal of Counseling and Development, 70*(4), 477–486. https://doi.org/10.1002/j.1556-6676.1992.tb01642.x

Tracey, T. J., & Kokotovic, A. M. (1989). Factor structure of the Working Alliance Inventory. *Psychological Assessment, 1*(3), 207–210. https://doi.org/10.1037/1040-3590.1.3.207

van der Kolk, B. (2014). *The body keeps the score: Brain, mind, and body in the healing of trauma.* Viking.

Verplanken, B. (2006). Beyond frequency: Habit as mental construct. *British Journal of Social Psychology, 45*(3), 639–656. https://doi.org/10.1348/014466605X49122

Vygotsky, L. S. (1978). *Mind in society: The development of higher psychological processes.* Harvard University Press.

Yalom, I. D. (1970). *The theory and practice of group psychotherapy.* Basic Books.

Index

A

Abandoned research projects, 217
ABD (all but dissertation) students, 53, 57
Abstracts, 173–177
    and clinical impact statements, 176
    for conference presentation proposals, 181
    examples of, 175–176
    information included in, 174–175
    mentoring students on writing, 176–177
    in sample timelines, 293, 294
Abundance mindset, 290
Academic positions
    interviewing for, 246–247
    job application process, 242–245
    negotiation period with new, 247–249
Acceptance, manuscript, 195, 196
Acceptance and commitment therapy (ACT), 13, 73
Access, to mentoring networks, 281–283
Accountability
    for building expertise, 43
    of collaborators, 232–234
    in mentorship, 262–263
Acculturation, 29, 256
Achievable goals, 49
Achievement
    goals to elicit, 46–47
    as value, 16, 17
ACT (acceptance and commitment therapy), 13, 73
Actions, beliefs and, 71–73
Advanced graduate student (stage), 203–204, 206
The Advantage (Lencioni), 229

Adversity, 95–104, 286
    example of facing, 96–97, 100–102
    in graduate training and research, 97–98, 103–104
    and knowing your limits, 98–99
    learning from, 101–102
    mentoring students on how to face, 102–103
    preparing yourself for, 97
    strategies for navigating, 100–101
    trust in relationships during, 99–100
Advisors, switching, 250
Agency, 221
Agendas, meeting, 259
Agreement, false sense of, 22
Alcohol use, 89
All but dissertation (ABD) students, 53, 57
Alpha level, 139
American Psychological Association (APA), 25, 156, 180–182, 193, 207
Annotated bibliographies, 127
Anxiety
    about negotiation period, 247
    about paper presentation, 184
    about proposal presentation, 151, 153
    and excitement, 151, 184
    and self-efficacy, 78
APA. *See* American Psychological Association
Approval, IRB, 156–157
Aristotle, xi
Assistant professors, 251, 270, 279. *See also* Early career professionals

Associate professors. *See* Tenured (associate) professors
Associative learning, 166
Assumptions, checking that data meets, 162–163
Attention-check questions, 159
Authenticity, 208–209
Authority, ambivalence about, 276
Authorship, in collaborative research, 230, 235
Automatic data collection scheduling, 158
Automaticity, of habits, 58, 66–67
Avoiding conflict, 231, 274–275

B

Babauta, Leo, 51
Bad collaborations, 236–238
Balanced feedback, 37, 210
Batching similar tasks, 62
Beall's List, 193
Beginning graduate student (stage), 203, 206, 289–290
Behavior. *See also* Habits
  alignment of values and, 13
  relationship of beliefs and, 71–73, 286
Behavioral psychology, 34
Beliefs, 47. *See also* Positive beliefs
Beneficence, 156
Benevolence, 16
Bimodal distribution, 163
Boundary setting
  in collaborative relationships, 231, 238
  on leadership and service commitments, 203, 204, 207
  and rainy-day planning, 97
  with students who work to deadlines, 152–153
Brainstorming sessions, 134, 170
Breaks, 62–63, 88–89, 91–92
Brevity, 176
Broad goals, 50
Brooks, Alison, 184
Buffers, 97, 271
Burnout, 31, 98–99, 254
Business cards, 185

C

Caffeine, 89
Career development stages, 203–205, 213
Career goals, 12, 33

CBT (cognitive behavior therapy), 72–73, 78
Center for the Study of Stress, Trauma, and Resilience, 220
Challenges, as opportunities, 80
Chance, in publication process, 196
Charts, summary, 109, 120
Chase, W. G., 36
Chunks
  breaking goals into, 47–48
  splitting tasks into, 61–62
Clarity
  in collaborative writing, 236
  in commitment to collaborate, 232
  in communication, 210, 230, 278
  of feedback, 210
  of goals, 54
  on inclusion and exclusion criteria, 118
  in messages about hiring and tenure, 278
  on motivation, 19
  on research interests, 218
  on research topic, 116–117
  on tenure requirements, 247
Clinical impact statement, 175, 176
Clinically-oriented careers, 126
ClinicalTrials.gov, 143
Coaches, 37
Coauthors, 82, 234–236
Coding, in literature review, 122
Cognitive behavior therapy (CBT), 72–73, 78
Cognitive model, 72
Coherent research programs, 215–218
Cohesion, team, 269
  and accountability, 233
  promoting, 264, 276–283
  and trust, 272
Collaboration, 225–239
  after bad experience, 237–238
  benefits of, 225–229, 239
  break downs in, 236–238
  building expertise through, 42
  on data analysis, 166
  on data collection, 159
  with faculty committee, 148
  on goal setting, 54
  key factors in good, 229–236
  mentoring as form of, 257, 261
  mentoring students on, 238–239

and networking at conferences, 185, 186
opportunist approach to, 216–218
program-based considerations in, 216
on research study design, 134
Collaborative relationships, 229–236
accountability in, 232–234
break downs in, 236–237
building, 229, 252
conflict in, 231–232
ending, 237
size of, 229–230
vulnerability and trust in, 230–231
Collins, Jim, 209, 220, 277
Commitment(s)
to collaboration, 232
honoring, 54, 208, 233
renegotiating, 96, 99, 100, 102–103, 233
to take care of yourself, 99
team, 269
Communication
about renegotiating commitments, 99
in collaborations, 230, 237
of expectations, 43
within groups, 274
Community building, 21–32
balance of dwelling and seeking in, 28–29
at conferences, 186
by early career professionals, 270–271
and facing adversity, 101, 103
mentoring students on, 29–31
with multiple communities, 24–26
patience in, 26–27
for personal growth, 27–28, 31–32
prioritizing, 23–24
Compensation, participant, 140, 158, 248
Competence
demonstrating, 148
operating at the edge of, 98
Competency building, 201
Complementary skills sets, of collaborators, 227–228
Conclusion, overall, 123
Conclusion paragraph, 170
Concrete roles, for students, 212
Conditional effect, 122
Conference(s)
dissemination of work at, 179–180, 186, 187
experience at, 186
networking at, 181, 185, 186
selecting, for presentation, 180–181
undergraduate attendance of, 187

Conference presentations, 179–187
acceptance of poster for, 82
example of, 186
mentoring students on making, 186–187
pairing up students for, 206, 263
paper presentations, 182–184
poster presentations, 184–185
rationale for making, 179–180
in sample timelines, 293, 294
submitting proposals for, 181–182
Confidence, 101, 265–266
Confidentiality, 156, 157
Conflict
in collaboration, 231–232
in mentorship, 255, 261
in teams, 274–276
and trust, 275
Conformity
freely chosen values vs., 14
in periods of dwelling, 28–29
resisting, 32
as value, 16
Connecting the dots
in cover letter for job application, 244
to explain research process, 82
to explain research program, 218–219, 223
Connections with others, 246, 259
Consensus, 22, 272
Consistency
in deep practice, 43
to form habits, 67, 287
and productivity, 287
in sleep patterns, 88
Construct, defined, 191
Constructive feedback, 289–290
Construct validity, 141
Consultants, in research design phase, 133
Context switching, 62
Convenience samples, 138
Convergent validity, 141
Core beliefs, 73
Core values, 16–17, 20
Correction mode, 77
Correlations between variables, 163–164
Corresponding authors, 197
Course preparation, 252–253
Course releases, 248, 252
Cover letters
job application, 243–244
manuscript submission, 194

Covey, Stephen, 216
Cramming, 4, 69, 88, 287
Creativity, 130–131, 134, 174
Critical feedback, 262–263
Critiques, reviewer, 194–196
Cronbach's alpha, 141–142
Cross-sectional studies, 168–169
Csikszentmihalyi, Mihaly, 90
Cultural considerations, in mentorship, 264–265
Cultural humility, xi, 269
Cultural identity development, 29–30
Cultural span, 22
Cultural upbringing, 22
Cultural values, 26
Culture(s)
   departmental, 270–271
   of generosity, 274
   in research lab, 211–213, 222
   of rewarding initiative, 212–213
   team, 42, 211–213, 222, 269
Culture document, group, 273
CV (curriculum vitae), 180, 204, 243
Cynicism, 254, 275

D

Data analysis, 161–166
   analyzing hypotheses in, 164–165
   data cleaning and checking in, 162–163
   exploring descriptive information in, 163–164
   mentoring students on, 165–166
   in meta-analyses, 123
   in sample timelines, 293, 294
Databases, key word searches of, 118–119
Data checking, 162–163
Data cleaning, 162–163
Data collection, 155–160
   budgeting time for, 155, 158–159
   example of, 158–159
   mentoring students on, 159–160
   preparing for, 157–158
   process of, 155–156
   in sample timelines, 293, 294
   study design to maximize, 131–132
   and submitting study proposal to IRB, 156–157
Data entry errors, 162
Data exclusion rules, 138

Data quality, 159
Deadlines, 152–153, 171, 186
Dead person's goals, 51
Deep (deliberate) practice, 35–41, 43, 286
   at edges of ability, 38
   engagement required for, 38–39
   intentional design of, 37–38
   with mentors, 41–43
   repetition of, 40–41
Defense meetings, 147n1, 153, 293, 294
Defensiveness, 30, 151, 233
Delegation, 267
Deliberate practice. *See* Deep practice
Delivery of proposal document, 150–151
Demographic information, on participants, 138
Department(s)
   clarity of messages about hiring/tenure in, 278
   leadership opportunities in, 207
   pretenure feedback from, 251
   protection of time and focus by, 276–277
   relational complexity of, 270–271
Department handbook, 148–150
Descriptive information, 163–164
Descriptive statistics, 162
Designed deep practice, 37–38
Destabilization of existing relationships, 28–29
Difficulty level of task, 91, 92
Disagreement, 195, 232
Disappointment, 83
Disciplinary conferences, 180
Discriminant validity, 141
Discussion section, 167–172
   areas for future research in, 169–170
   conclusion paragraph in, 170
   identifying limitations of study in, 168–169
   mentoring students on writing, 171–172
   outlining implications/applications of research in, 170
   overview of, in abstract, 174, 181
   reviewing main findings in, 168
   in sample timelines, 293, 294
   of systematic literature review, 124
Dissemination of work
   at conferences, 179–180, 186, 187
   via publication, 187, 189, 197

Dissertation
   in advanced graduate student stage, 203–204
   conference presentation based on, 181
   expertise necessary to complete, 33
   journal articles based on, 189–190
   literature review for, 117, 125
   method section of, 137–140, 142, 143
   proposal meeting for, 107
   research study design for, 130, 131
   strategy for completing, 3–4
   with tight deadline, 171
   topic selection for, 111
Distraction(s)
   and deep practice, 39–40
   and flow state, 90–91
   goal setting as, 53–54
   mentor as source of, 92–93
Diversity
   defined, 245
   of perspectives, 227, 231, 276
   prioritization of, 28
   purposeful engagement with, 22
   of self-concept, 24–25
Diversity statement, 245
Doctoral program, 3, 99. *See also* Graduate school
Documentation, of literature search, 119–120, 124
"Do not disturb" hours, 92–93
Doubt, extending benefit of the, 102, 231, 233
Drive, of leaders, 209
Drug use, 89
Dual relationships, 280–281
Dweck, Carol, 79, 80, 83
Dwelling, in community, 28–29

E

Early career professionals. *See also* Assistant professors; Transition from graduate student to professor
   advising by, 4
   career development stage of, 204–205
   community building by, 270–271
   dual relationships for, 280–281
   leadership opportunities as, 202
   long-term planning by, 221
   open mentoring networks for, 281–282
   proposal meeting guidance for, 152
   protecting the time and focus of, 276–277
   sharing mental load of, 280
   shifting initiative to, 279–280
   structural decisions that support, 278–279
   topic selection guidance by, 111–112
Edges of ability, 38, 47
Editorial board, 208
Effect size, 122, 123, 139
Ego, 194, 236
Email
   batching tasks related to, 62
   in collaborative projects, 230
   task switching to answer, 91
   treating, like a task, 63–64
   unplugging from, 88
Emotional needs of undergraduates, 31
Emotional state, changing, 77–79
Empirical papers
   abstract of, 173–177
   discussion section, 167–172
   introduction section of, 126, 190–191
   method section of, 137–145
   as prerequisite for dissertation, 111–112
   results section of, 161–162, 165, 166
   systematic literature review vs., 120, 121
   thesis or dissertation as basis for, 190–192
Empowerment, 265, 276, 286
Encouragement, 76–77
Engagement, 38–39, 277–278
Enjoyment, 229, 257–258, 291
Environment
   for habit formation, 67
   for improving self-efficacy, 82
Equipment, in start-up package, 248
Equity, 245
Ericsson, K. A., 36
Ethical principles, 156–157
Excitement, anxiety and, 151, 184
Exclusion criteria, 118
Exercise, 87, 88
Expectations
   about collaboration, 234–235
   about conference attendance, 187
   about literature review, 115–116, 126
   about mentoring, 266
   about proposal meetings, 153
   about publication, 196
   communicating, 43
   of student's abilities, 82
   when planning research studies, 144
Experience, self-efficacy and, 71–72, 74–75

Experimentation, 80, 271–272
Experiment management websites, 158
Expertise
   in collaboration, 227–228
   in data analysis, 161
   of faculty committee members, 149
   matching student's interests and mentor's, 261–262
   in mentoring, 258
   methodological, 131, 166, 219
   scaling up program to build, 219
   sharing, 282–283
   statistical, 131, 166, 219
   topic selection and mentor's, 110–112
Expertise in research and writing, 33–43
   deep/deliberate practice for, 35–41, 43
   growth mindset for, 34–35
   hard work and, 34
   mentoring students on, 41–43
   of mentors, 82
Exploratory data analysis, 132
External validity, 134
Extroverts, 229

F

Faculty committee, proposal meeting, 147–151
Failure
   in early leadership roles, 202
   in holding others accountable, 233
   sharing stories/resume of, 75, 82, 266
Family-like cultures, 270–271
Family members, health scares for, 96–97, 100–102
Family of origin
   attitudes about conflict in, 231
   destabilization of relationship with, 28–29
   values of, 22, 23
Family systems theory, 275
Fear
   of conflict, 232
   of holding people accountable, 233
Feedback
   on abstract, 174–175
   balanced, 37
   building confidence with, 266
   in collaborative writing, 235–236
   constructive, 289–290
   critical, 262–263
   on data analysis, 165
   in deep practice, 37, 40–41
   encouraging, 77, 82
   on goals, 54
   in graduate training and research, 98
   honest, 210
   immediate, 37, 263
   from mentor, 42, 82, 258, 262–263, 290
   negative, 210, 262–263, 289–290
   positive, 262, 263, 266
   during pretenure period, 251
   on proposal document, 153
   purpose of, 289–290
   with rejection of manuscript, 194
   on research study design, 133, 135
   from reviewers, 194–197
   specific, 37, 263
   from student, on mentoring, 261
   supportive, 210, 266
   in training networks, 282
Fellowships, 82, 110, 133, 243
Field, Andy, 165
File-drawer studies, 119
First authorship
   in collaborative writing, 234–235
   as requirement for tenure/promotion, 251
   for undergraduates, 197, 202
First-year graduate students, 24
Fit, in mentorship, 261–262
Five S's of habit formation, 67–69
Fixed mindset, 34–35, 79, 80, 83
Flow state, 85, 89–93, 286
   defined, 86, 90
   difficulty level of activity and, 91, 92
   distractions and, 90–91
   focusing on a single task in, 91
   for graduate students, 92
   peak time for, 90
   physical health and, 90
   rest and, 91–92
Flywheel effect, 220, 277
Focus
   for deep practice, 38–39
   for goal setting, 51–52
   narrowness of, 109, 189–190
   on outcome, 80–81
   protecting team members', 276–277
   on a single task, 61, 91
Focused work, breaks in, 63, 91–92
Forgiveness, xii, 109
Forms, proposal meeting, 150
4-4 teaching load, 242

Free association, to identify values, 14–15
Freely chosen values, 14, 18
Friendships
  with collaborators, 291
  deepening of, 26–27
  destabilization of existing, 28–29
  professional, 276
  support in, 23–24
  with team members, 271, 276
Frustration, 286
  with collaborators, 233, 234, 237
  with team members, 275
Full professors
  career development stage of, 205
  promotion to, 251
  team cohesion and inclusion promoted by, 276–283
Funding. *See also* Grants
  open science practices for, 144
  summer, 247, 248
  topic selection based on, 108, 110–111
Funeral exercise, 15
Future research, areas for, 169–170

G

Generosity, 274, 282–283
Goal orientation, 45
Goals
  in abstract, 174
  accountability for achieving, 263
  career, 12, 33
  characteristics of, 46–47
  of collaboration, 234
  habits and, 57
  laser-focus on, 23
  leadership opportunities that fit, 212
  mismatch between mentor and student, 258
  negative, 50–51
  realistic, 49, 55, 130
  of research, 129
  and Schwartz's values, 16
  values vs., 13–14, 46
Goal setting, 45–55, 286
  breaking big goals into chunks, 47–48
  and characteristics of goals, 46–47
  as a distraction, 53–54
  of health-related goals, 93

mentoring students on, 54–55
  positive framing for, 50–51
  and positive reinforcement, 52–53
  simplifying focus for, 51–52
  with SMART goals, 48–50
  as work habit, 70
Good collaborations, 229–236
"Good enough" method for literature review, 116, 125–126
Good to Great (Collins), 209
Google Scholar, 119
Gottman, John, 263
G*Power, 138
Graduate school
  admission to, 31
  adversity in, 97–98, 103–104
  clarifying motivation to attend, 19
  developmental progression of cohort in, 24
  leadership roles in, 202
  prioritizing physical health in, 86–87
  research program development in, 215
  stressors in, 87, 95, 97, 103
Graduate students. *See also* Transition from graduate student to professor
  abstracts written by, 176
  advanced stage, 203–204, 206
  advisor-switching by, 250
  aiding in transition for, 254–255
  beginning stage, 203, 206, 289–290
  building of habits by, 69
  challenges with research projects for, xv–xvi, 3–4, 79
  collaboration with, 238
  community building by, 21–24, 29–30
  conference presentations by, 186
  consistent work by, 287
  cultivation of positive beliefs by, 81–82
  data analysis by, 165–166
  data collection by, 159–160
  developing leadership skills of, 210–212, 267
  encouraging, 76–77
  experimentation with leadership styles by, 271–272
  expertise building by, 41–42
  first steps into leadership for, 201–203, 283
  flow state for, 92
  goal setting by, 45, 54
  intrinsic motivation for, 287–288

leadership and service opportunities for, 203–204, 206, 208
learning from other, 76, 82, 156, 171, 206, 263
literature review for, 117, 126–127
perfectionism for, 80
periods of adversity for, 102–103
planning and drafting of method section by, 144
practical wisdom for, xii
proposal meeting for, 147, 152–153
protecting the time and focus of, 276–277
publication for, 196–197
recommendations for mentoring, 266–267
research program development for, 217, 221–222
research project timelines for, 293–294
research study design by, 133–134
self-efficacy for, 71–72
sleep deprivation for, 88
starting to work with, 250
structural decisions to support, 278–279
team cohesion and inclusion issues for, 283
topic selection by, 111–112
undergraduate assistants for, 267–268
values of, 18
views of research by, 286
writing of discussion section by, 171
Grants
with open science requirements, 144
and tenure/promotion, 251
topic selection influenced by, 108, 111
trust networks and awarding of, 282
winning, as motivation, 82, 133
Gratitude, xii
Grief, 101, 102
Grouping similar tasks together, 62
Group psychotherapy, 273
Groups and teams, 269–284
brainstorming areas for future research with, 170
and community building, 270–271
data collection by, 157–158
deep practice with, 37
discussing research study design with, 131
dissertation projects in, 250
experimenting with leadership styles for, 271–272
goal setting in, 46–47
mentor as member of, 4
mentoring students on leading, 283–284
mentoring within, 263–264
norming process for, 272–276
processing learning in, 83
promoting cohesion and inclusion in, 276–283
reviewing main findings with, 168
scaling up research programs with, 220–221
size of, 229–230
writing in, 133
Groupthink, 232
Growth mindset, 79–81, 83
benefits of, 79
to build expertise, 34–35
defined, 79
modeling, 83
process for developing, 80–81
Guilt, 59

H

Habits, 57–70, 286
defined, 55, 57, 58
as factor in success, 53
mentoring students on, 69–70
research, 59–66, 70
and self-efficacy, 79
strategies for forming, 67–69
time required to form, 66–67
of undergraduates, 256
Handouts, conference presentation, 183, 184
Hard work, expertise and, 34
Harm, protecting participants from, 156
Harzing's Publish or Perish program, 119
Health. See Physical health
Hedonism, 16
Hiring, 278, 284
Holding space, 272, 273
Holistic approach to mentoring, 92
Honesty, 210, 232
Honors thesis, 112
Hook, presentation, 183
Hope, xii
Humility, 32, 109
about feedback, 290
about research experiences, 75–76
cultural, xi, 269

in diversity statement, 245
intellectual, xi
of leaders, 209
as team value, 274
Hypotheses, 164–165, 191–192

I

Identity development, 260
Immediate feedback, 37, 263
Impact factor, 193
Implications, of findings, 167, 168, 170
Important tasks, 60–61, 64–65
Imposter syndrome, 80, 266
Inclusion
  defined, 245
  in groups and teams, 276–283
  values that promote, 274
Inclusion criteria, 118, 122
Independent research project(s)
  and career development stages, 203–204
  as challenge for graduate students, xv–xvi, 3–4, 79
  connection between values and, 17–18
  habits and progress on, 57, 69
  methods of organizing, 6
  narrowing focus of, for publication, 189–190
  setting goals for, 45–48
  steps in completing, 285
  timelines for, 48, 50, 293–294
  training students to take on, 42–43
  for undergraduate students, 6–7, 112, 222, 266
  variability in organization of, 107, 108
Informed consent, 157
Initiative
  of independent students, 267
  promoting, 212–213, 222
  shifting, to early career professionals, 279–280
  transfer of, in meetings with mentors, 259
In-person data collection, 157
Institutional review board (IRB), 156–157
Instrumental motivation, 17
Integrity
  in community, 27–28, 30
  of leaders, 208–209
  modeling, 290–291
  as team value, 273
Intellectual humility, xi
Intellectual leadership, 127

Interests
  matching mentor's expertise and student's, 261–262
  shifts in, 217, 218, 223
Internal consistency, 141
Internalization of values, 14
Interpersonal problems, 236, 258
Interrater reliability, 141
Interviews, job, 246–247
Intrinsic motivation, 221, 222, 287–288
Introduction section
  of journal article, 126, 190–192
  of systematic literature review, 121–122
Invitations, faculty committee, 149–150
IRB (institutional review board), 156–157
Iterative processes
  clarifying literature review topic, 117
  deep practice, 40–41
  topic selection, 113

J

Job applications, 215, 242–245
Job interviews, 246–247
Job openings, academic, 242
Job search, 242
Job talks, 153, 216–218, 246–247
Journal(s)
  choosing target, 192–194
  reporting standards for, 161–162
  requirements of, 173–174, 193
  service opportunities with, 208, 254
  top-tier, 219, 228
Justice, 156–157

K

Key word searches, 118–119
Kindness, 101
King, Martin Luther, Jr., 291
King, Stephen, 66
Kurtosis, 163

L

Lab meetings, 131, 259, 264
Lab space, 248, 249
Lally, Phillippa, 66
Large-scale projects, 228

Large tasks, splitting, 61–62
Leaders
   negotiating of group norms by, 273
   qualities of good, 208–210
Leadership, 201–213
   graduate students' first steps into, 201–203, 283
   of groups and teams, 270, 283–284
   intellectual, 127
   in meetings with mentors, 259–260
   mentoring students on, 210–213
   at stages of career development, 203–205, 213
   types of opportunities for, 206–208
Leadership skills, 4–5, 267
Leadership structure, 211–212
Leadership styles, 271–272
Learning
   from adversity, 101–102
   associative, 166
   to be a mentor, 258
   breaking down, into small steps, 81
   focusing on, 81
   group processing of, 83
   to lead, 211
   lifelong, 222
   as motivation, 13
   from other graduate students, 76, 82, 156, 171, 206, 263
   social, 272
Learning objectives, for conference presentation, 182
Leisure time, prioritizing, 59
Lencioni, Patrick, 229, 230, 234
Letters to the editor, 195
Leveraging opportunities, 220–221
Liberal arts colleges, 242–243
Lifelong learning, 222
Limitations
   and areas of future research, 169–170
   of literature review, 124
   of research study, 168–169
Limiting beliefs, 70
Limits, knowing your, 98–99, 101, 209, 234
Listservs, 119, 180
Literature reviews, 115–128
   alternatives to systematic, 125–126
   clarifying inclusion and exclusion criteria for, 118
   clarifying your topic for, 116–117
   conducting and documenting search, 118–120
   and discussion section, 171
   example of, 124–125
   feedback on, 289
   to focus research question, 108
   functions of, 128
   for journal article, 190, 191
   mentoring students on writing, 126–127
   in research process, 115
   and research study design, 129–130
   in sample timelines, 293, 294
   selecting type of, 117–118
   summarizing studies in a chart, 120
   writing sections of, 120–124
Literature search
   conducting and documenting, 118–120, 125
   methods section on, 122
Loneliness, 21, 229, 265, 286, 291
"Lone-wolf" model of research, 227
Love, xiii
Loyalty binds, 272

M

Main constructs, 126, 191
Main findings, 167, 168, 170
Manual data collection scheduling, 158
Manuscript submission, 190, 192–194
Marginalized identities, people with
   amplifying voices of, 278
   dual relationships for, 280–281
   mental load for, 280
   mentoring, 264–265
   motivation for research benefiting, 17
   representation of, 245, 265, 284
Margin for unexpected events, 97, 99, 100
Maslach Burnout Inventory, 98–99
Master's thesis, 107
   in beginning graduate student stage, 203
   conference presentation based on, 181
   journal articles based on, 189–190
   literature review for, 124–125
   method section of, 137–140, 142, 143
   proposal meeting for, 152
   research study design for, 130, 131
   topic selection for, 110–111
Mastery, 36
Mean (arithmetic), 163

Measurable goals, 49
Measurement strategy, 133–134
Measures
　creating new, 220
　describing, in literature review, 123
　inclusion/exclusion criteria based on, 118
　in method section, 140–142
　study limitations related to, 169
Mediators, 121–123
Meetings
　with collaborators, 230
　at conferences, 185, 186
　defense, 147n1, 153, 293, 294
　with faculty committee members, 149–150
　lab, 131, 259, 264
　with mentors, 30, 254, 258–260
　positive engagement in, 277–278
　proposal, 107, 147–153, 293, 294
Mental health
　community and, 23–24
　physical health and, 85–86
Mental load, sharing, 280
Mentor(s)
　feedback from, 42, 82, 258, 262–263, 290
　as part of community, 271
　passing on values of, 290–291
　relationship of faculty committee members with, 149
　topic selection influenced by, 108, 110–111
　work habits of, 69
Mentoring networks, 281–283
Mentoring skills, 258, 266–268
Mentoring students, xvi–xvii
　on abstract writing, 176–177
　on building a research program, 221–222
　on collaborating, 238–239
　on community building, 29–31
　on conducting a literature review, 126–127
　on core values, 18–19
　on data analysis, 165–166
　on data collection, 159–160
　on developing research and writing expertise, 41–43
　on developing research habits, 69–70
　on facing adversity, 102–103
　first steps in, 202
　and framework for planning research project, 6
　on goal setting, 54–55
　on leadership, 210–213, 283–284
　on making conference presentations, 186–187
　on physical health issues, 92–93
　on planning/writing a method section, 144–145
　on positive beliefs, 81–83
　on proposal meetings, 152–153
　on publication, 192, 196–197
　on relational and professional issues, 260
　in research labs, 211
　on research study design, 133–134
　in teams and groups, 269
　on topic selection, 111–112
　on transition from graduate student to professor, 241–243, 250, 254–256
　undergraduate students, 6, 7, 267–268
　on writing a discussion section, 171–172
Mentorship (generally), 257–268
　accountability and feedback in, 262–263
　building confidence with, 265–266
　contextualizing style of, 264
　cultural considerations in, 264–265
　deep practice in, 37–38, 41–43
　effort associated with, 266, 268
　helping students develop skills for, 266–268
　improving self-efficacy with, 75
　as intentional practice, 268
　layers of, 256
　as leadership opportunity, 204
　learning process for, 258
　with mutually beneficial research projects, 261–262
　regular meetings for, 258–259
　rewards of, 257–258
　running effective meetings for, 259–260
　team building in, 263–264
Mentor–student relationship
　attending to, 102–103, 261
　challenges in, 258
　deeper knowing in, 18
　differentiation in, 18
　observing successful experiences in, 75–76
　productive, 4–6
　as source of support, 29
Meta-analyses, 117–118, 122, 123.
　See also Systematic literature review

Methodological expertise, 131, 166, 219
Method section, 137–145
  data collection details in, 160
  emphasizing open science/
    preregistration in, 143–144
  literature search details in, 119
  measures section of, 140–142
  mentoring students on planning/
    writing, 144–145
  overview of, in abstract, 174, 181
  participants section of, 137–140
  planned analysis section of, 142–143
  procedure section of, 140
  research design section of, 142
  in sample timelines, 293, 294
  of systematic literature review, 121–123
"MI-50" project, 45
Micromanagement, 267
Midwestern Psychological Association, 187
Mind–body connection, 85–87, 93
Minimal missing data, 162
Miscommunication, in collaborations, 237
Missing data, 122, 162
MITs (most important tasks), 60–62
Modeling
  of cohesion and inclusion promotion, 283
  of collaboration, 238
  of flow state, 92
  of good work habits, 69, 70
  of growth mindset, 83
  of integrity, 290–291
  by leaders, 208–210
  of lifelong learning, 222
Moderators, 122, 123
Momentum, building, 220, 288
Monocultural perspective, 30
Mood, 85–87
Most important tasks (MITs), 60–62
Motivation, 286
  assessing level of, 12
  goals and, 45, 46, 50–51
  instrumental, 17
  intrinsic, 221, 222, 287–288
  in meetings with mentors, 259–260
  in mutually beneficial research projects, 262
  undergraduate students', 268
  values as source of, 12–14, 19–20
Mozart, Wolfgang Amadeus, 35

Multimethod approaches, 134
Multiple communities, 21, 24–26
Multitasking, 38, 39, 61, 91
Music Academy of West Berlin, 36
Mutually beneficial projects, 237–238, 261–262

N

Narrative, for research program, 216–219
Narrative reviews, 117–118, 125, 126.
    See also Systematic literature review
Negative correlation, 164
Negative feedback, 210, 262–263, 289–290
Negative goals, 50–51
Negotiations, new job, 247–249
Nervousness, about presentations, 183–184
Networking
  for advanced graduate students, 204
  at conferences, 181, 185, 186
  in professional organizations, 207
Nonmaleficence, 156
Nonurgent tasks, scheduling, 60
Normal distribution, 163
Normality, 163
Norms
  collaboration, 230, 234–236, 238, 239
  group and team, 272–276, 284
  proposal meeting, 148–152
  publication, 196
Novel contribution, 129, 130
Nutrition, 87–88, 90

O

Observation, of successful experiences, 75–76
Office space, 248
On-campus job interview, 246
One-size-fits-all approach to mentoring, 264
One-tailed test, 139
Online data collection, 157, 159
Open-ended questions, 132
Openness to new opportunity, 27, 28
Open science, 143–145
Open Science Framework, 143
Opportunist approach to research program, 216–218
Opportunities, viewing challenges as, 80

Opportunity costs, 203, 288
Optimization
　in mutually beneficial research projects, 262
　of physical health, 87–89, 93
Organizational skills, 159
Outcome of search, in methods section, 122
Outliers, 162–163
Overall conclusion, 123
Overall effect size, 123

P

Page limitations, journal, 190
Pain, bearing witness to others', 102
Paper presentation, 182–184, 206
Parallel structure, 165
Parentification, 255
Parenting, improving self-efficacy in, 74–75
Participants
　describing, in literature review, 123
　method section on, 137–140
　study limitations related to, 169
Passion, 110
Past research, 168, 191
Past success, 72, 74–75
Past theory, 168
Patience, xii, 26–27
Peak time, 90
Peer-review process, 194–196, 204, 208, 254
Peers, discussing study design with, 131
Perfectionism, 80, 260
Performance, self-efficacy and, 74
Perseverance, xii
Persistence, 104
Personal growth
　community building for, 27–28, 31–32
　at edge of competence, 98
　goals to elicit, 46–47
　for graduate students, 29–30
Perspectives, diversity of, 227, 231, 276
Phronesis, xi–xii
Physical activity, 63, 88, 101–102
Physical health, 85–93
　and facing adversity, 101–102
　and flow state, 89–93
　health scare as source of adversity, 96–97, 100–102
　mentoring students on, 92–93

and mind–body connection, 86–87
optimizing, 87–89, 93
and self-efficacy, 78
of undergraduate students, 93
Placebo effect, 86
Plan for improvement, 41
Planned analysis section, 142–143
Planning fallacy, 60
Plans of action, 107, 232
"Poisons," physical health, 89
Positive beliefs, 71–83
　about research skills, 74
　about self-efficacy, 73–79, 83
　and growth mindset, 79–81, 83
　mentoring students on, 81–83
　relationship of actions/behaviors and, 71–73, 286
Positive correlation, 164
Positive emotions, building on, 68
Positive feedback, 262, 263, 266
Positive framing, for goals, 50–51
Positive mood, self-efficacy and, 77–78
Positive reinforcement, 52–53, 77
Postdoctoral fellowships, 243
Postdoctoral positions, 204
Poster presentations, 82, 182, 184–186
Power
　of graduate students, 283
　of mentors, 261
　using, to benefit others, 276–283
　as value, 16
Power analysis, 138–140
Power differential, 265, 284
Power level, 139
The Power of Less (Babauta), 51
PowerPoint presentations, 150, 183
Practical applications of research, 170
Practical goals, 81
Practical wisdom, xi–xii
Predatory journals, 193
Preferred Reporting Items for Systematic Reviews and Meta-Analyses (PRISMA) guidelines, 120, 122
Preliminary searches, literature review, 117
Preparation. *See also* Rainy-day plans
　for data collection, 157–158
　to face adversity, 95–97
　for paper presentations, 182–184
　for poster presentations, 184–185
　for proposal meetings, 148–152
Preregistration, 132, 143–144

Presentations
   conference. *See* Conference presentations
   proposal meeting, 148, 150–151
   by undergraduate students, 153
Prestige, of target journal, 193
Pretenure period
   research responsibilities in, 249–252
   service responsibilities in, 253–254
   teaching responsibilities in, 252–253
Primacy effect, 177
Prioritization
   of community building, 23–24
   of physical health, 86–87
   of the process, 80–81
   of research and writing, 92–93, 288–289
   of self-care and relationships, 29
   of tasks, 64–65
   of work over play, 59
PRISMA (Preferred Reporting Items for Systematic Reviews and Meta-Analyses) guidelines, 120, 122
Privilege, using, to help others, 276–284
Problems in collaboration, addressing, 237
Procedures
   method section on, 140
   study limitations related to, 169
Productivity
   of associate and full professors, 205
   collaboration to improve, 228
   consistency for, 287
   in flow state, 90
   and physical state, 96
   and task switching, 61
Profession, leadership in, 207–208
Professional development funds, 248
Professional friendship, 276
Professional goals, basing MITs on, 60
Professional growth, 98
Professional identity, integration of, 27–28
Professional issues, mentoring on, 260
Professional organizations, 203, 204, 207
Professors. *See also* Transition from graduate student to professor
   assistant, 251, 270, 279
   full, 205, 251, 276–283
   research challenges for, xvi–xvii
   tenured/associate, 205, 221, 251
Program leadership, 207
Progress
   goals for tracking, 46, 48, 49
   meeting with mentor to ensure, 259–260
   slowing down, when facing adversity, 100, 102–103
Progressions of studies, 132, 228
Promotion, 251
Proposal document, 150–153
Proposal meeting, 107, 147–153
   example of, 152
   mentoring students on, 152–153
   preparing for, 148–151
   purposes of, 148
   in sample timelines, 293, 294
Proposals
   conference presentation, 181–182
   submitting, to IRB, 156–157
ProQuest Online, 119
Psychology of Religion and Spirituality Preconference for the Society for Personality and Social Psychology, 207
PsycInfo, 119
Publication, 189–197
   choosing target journal for, 192–194
   of collaborative writing, 235–236
   as goal of research study, 129
   for job applicants, 242, 287
   mentoring students on, 196–197
   narrowing project focus for, 189–190
   poster presentations prior to, 186
   of recent literature review on research topic, 116
   rejection in, 76
   as requirement for tenure/promotion, 251
   responding to reviewer critiques for, 194–196
   revising paper for, 190–192
   in sample timelines, 293, 294
   scaling up research programs with, 219–220
   submitting manuscript for, 194
   of systematic literature review, 125, 128
Publication bias, 119, 123
Public significance statement, 175, 176
p value, 139

Q

Qualitative data, 132
Qualtrics, 157

R

R1 universities, 242
Racial disparity, of faculty and graduate students, 30
Radical Candor (Scott), 210
Rainy-day plans, 97, 99
Realistic expectations, 82, 144, 266
Realistic goals, 49, 55, 130
Reference sections, reviewing, 119
Registered reports, 143–144
Regular mentoring meetings, 258–259
Rehearsal, presentation, 150, 183
Reinforcement schedule, 52–53
Rejection, 76
 of manuscript, 193, 194, 196
 of paper presentation proposal, 182–183
 sharing stories of, 196–197
Relational issues, mentoring students on, 260
Relational nature of research, x, xii, xiii
Relationships. *See also specific types*
 prioritizing, 29
 ruptures in, 261, 275–276
 when facing adversity, 99–100
Relaxation, 88–89
Relevant goals, 49–50
Reliability, measure, 141
Religious community, 25–26
Remote work, 100
Repetition, 40–41, 66–67
Research
 adversity in, 95, 97–98, 103–104
 connection between values and, 286
 crowding in field of, 109
 developing expertise in. *See* Expertise in research and writing
 prioritizing, 204–205
 in transition from graduate student to professor, 241–242, 249–252
 values related to, 18
Research assistants
 data collection by, 157–158, 160
 lab setup with, 249
 in start-up package, 248
Research career, developing, 285–286

Research design
 describing, in literature review, 123
 inclusion/exclusion criteria based on, 118
 method section on, 142
 study limitations related to, 168–169
Researcher(s)
 competence for, 7
 development process for, 285–286
 leadership roles for, 201–202
 personal attributes of, 5
 virtues of successful, xi–xiii
Research habits, 59–66, 70, 286
 completing your MITs first, 60–61
 focusing on a single task, 61
 grouping small tasks together, 62
 practicing time management, 59–60
 prioritizing important nonurgent tasks, 64–65
 prioritizing work over play, 59
 splitting large tasks into chunks, 61–62
 taking small breaks, 62–63
 treating email like a task, 63–64
 writing a little every day, 65–66
Research lab
 culture in, 211–213, 222
 leadership opportunities in, 204, 206, 211–212
 rewarding initiative in, 212–213
 setting up, 249
Research process
 alignment of values with, 11, 18
 assumptions about students' knowledge of, 92
 changes in best practices in, 107
 explaining, 82
 literature review in, 115
 practice activities to learn, 42
 resources on, 4–5
Research program, 6, 215–223
 connecting the dots to explain, 218–219, 223
 discussing, in job interviews, 246–247
 for early career professionals, 204
 evolution of, over time, 217
 literature review before launching, 127
 mentoring students on building, 221–222
 process of developing, 215–217
 strategies for scaling up, 219–221
Research question, 108–109

Research skills
  improving, 3–5, 33, 41, 201, 203
  mentoring skills and, 258
  mindset about, 41, 79
Research statement, 244
Research study design, 129–135
  creativity in, 130–131
  to develop methodological/statistical expertise, 131
  examples of, 132–133
  feedback on, 135
  literature review as guide for, 129–130
  for maximizing data collection efforts, 131–132
  mentoring students on, 133–134
  for progression of studies, 132
  in sample timelines, 293, 294
  taking a medium-sized step forward with, 130
Research talk, 246. *See also* Job talks
Resilience, 24–25
Respect, 157
Responsibility(-ies)
  culture of, 222
  helping one another cover, 99–100
  progression of, 211–212
  in transition from graduate student to professor, 249–254
Rest periods, 63
  and flow state, 91–92
  for physical health, 88–90
  when facing adversity, 103–104
Results, of successful collaborations, 234
Results section
  analyzing hypotheses in, 165
  of empirical papers, 161
  helping students write, 165, 166
  organization of, 161–162
  overview of, in abstract, 174, 181
  and review of main findings, 168
  in sample timelines, 293, 294
  of systematic literature review, 121, 123, 126–127
Resume of failure, 75, 82
Retreats, taking, 63, 131
Review articles, 108–109, 115, 126
Reviewer critiques, 194–196
"Revise and resubmit" response to manuscript, 195, 196
Revisions
  of abstract and introductory paragraph, 176–177

  for publication, 190–192
  requested by IRB, 156, 157
  requested in proposal meeting, 151
  in response to reviewer critiques, 195–196
Rewards, 52–53, 70
Round-robin studies, 132
Ruptures, in relationships, 261, 275–276

S

Sabbath rest, 63, 88
Salary negotiations, 247
Sample
  inclusion/exclusion criteria based on, 118
  in research design phase, 133
Sandage, Steve, 28
Scaffolding experiences, 42–43, 127, 212, 267
Scaling up research programs, 219–221
Scheduling
  of attentionally demanding tasks, 39
  of data collection efforts, 158
  to develop new habits, 68
  of meetings at conferences, 185
  for peak time, 90
  of proposal meetings, 150
  to protect your time, 289
  of time for responding to email, 64
  of time for writing, 70
  as time management tool, 59–60
Schwartz, Shalom, 15–16
Scott, Kim, 210
Screening interviews, 246
Search, literature, 118–120, 122, 125
Security, 16, 28
Seeking, in community, 28–29
Selectivity of journals, 193
Self
  differentiation of, 22–23, 27–28
  focus on, 201
Self-care, 29, 60, 78, 99
Self-concept, diverse, 24–25
Self-control (self-regulation), xi
Self-determination, 221
Self-direction, 16
Self-efficacy, 73–79, 83
  building, with mentor, 266, 268
  changing state to improve, 77–79
  defined, 71, 73

encouragement to improve, 76–77
experiencing success to improve, 74–75
methods of improving, 74–79, 82–83
observing successful experiences to improve, 75–76
for undergraduate students, 82–83
Self-interest, 231
Self-report measures, 169
Service, 286
    at career development stages, 203–205
    as requirement for tenure/promotion, 251
    by students with marginalized identities, 265
    in transition from graduate student to professor, 253–254
Shallow practice, 36–37
Shame, 103
Shared values, 26, 269, 274, 276
Shirking, 159
Short list, for academic position, 246
Siloing, 229
Simon, H. A., 36
Simple goals, 51–52
Single-tasking, 61, 91
Skewness, 163
Sleep, 85–88, 90
Slides, presentation, 183
Small changes, making, 68
Small problems, accountability for, 233
SMART goals, 48–50
Smoking, 89
Social events, 231, 264
Socialization, 254
Social learning, 272
Social media, 22
Social modeling, 76
Society for the Psychology of Religion and Spirituality (Division 36), 25, 180, 207
Society of Counseling Psychology (Division 17), 25, 180
Sona Systems, 158
Specificity
    of commitments, 232
    of feedback, 37, 263
    of goals, 48–49
    of habits, 67–68
    of literature review, 116–117
    of research topic, 109
Spiritual needs, 31

Standard deviations, 163
Starting salary, 247
Start-up package, 248
Statistical analysis
    expertise in, 131, 166, 219
    of hypotheses, 164–165
    in meta-analyses, 117
    in planned analysis section, 142–143
    in power analysis, 138
Statistical methods, encouraging learning of new, 134
Stimulation, 16
Strategic compounding, 277
Strengths, discussing study, 169
Stress
    community support to deal with, 31
    in graduate school, 87, 95, 97, 103
    meeting behavior under, 278
    staying active during periods of, 101–102
Structural decisions, difficult, 278–279
Structured supervision, 128
Student representative to program faculty, 207, 283
Study description, 123
Study skills, 69
Study type, inclusion/exclusion criteria based on, 118
Subgroups, 275–276
Substance use, 89
Successful experiences
    improving self-efficacy with, 72, 74–75, 82
    observing vicarious, 75–76
    for undergraduates, 82
Summary
    in annotated bibliography, 127
    in discussion section, 168
    in literature review, 124
    for poster presentation, 185
Summary tables, 109, 120, 124
Summer funding, 247, 248
Supervision, 27–28, 128, 283
Support
    community as source of, 21, 27, 28, 271
    for habit formation, 68–69
    from leaders, 210
    in mentor–student relationship, 103
    in service roles, 254
    for students with marginalized identities, 265

during transition from graduate student to professor, 254, 255
for undergraduate students, 212–213
Supportive feedback, 210, 266
Survey Monkey, 157
Syllabi, of previous professors, 253
Symposia, 182
Synergy, in collaboration, 228
Systematic literature reviews, 115–128
    alternatives to, 125–126
    clarifying inclusion and exclusion criteria for, 118
    clarifying topic for, 116–117
    conducting and documenting search for, 118–120
    as guide for research study design, 129–130
    narrative reviews vs. meta-analyses, 117–118
    publication of, 190
    summary chart for, 120
    writing, 120–124
Systematic review, 220

T

Target journal, selecting, 192–194
Task assignment, 38
Task-focused leadership, 267
Task switching, 39, 61, 91
Teaching assistantship, xv
Teaching demonstration, 246, 247
Teaching evaluations, 251
Teaching load, 242, 248, 252
Teaching philosophy, statement of, 244
Teaching portfolio, 244–245
Teaching responsibilities, 252–253
Teaching statement, 244–245
Team building, 263–264. *See also* Groups and teams
Team culture, 42, 211–213, 222, 269
Technology, for conference presentation, 183
Templates
    for abstract, 176
    for discussion section, 171
    for method section, 144
    for posters, 184
    for results section, 165, 166
10-year rule, 36
Tenure, 247, 251, 278
Tenured (associate) professors, 205, 221, 251

Tenure-track faculty positions, 204
Test–retest reliability, 141
Texas Psychological Association, 180
Textbook selection, 253
Text messages, 91
Theory
    consistency of research with, 168
    discussing, in good-enough approach, 126
    discussing, in systematic literature review, 121–122
    presenting, in introduction section, 191
Thesis. *See* Master's thesis
Third-year reviews, 251
Time
    budgeting, for data collection, 155, 158–159
    to form habits, 66–67
    for leadership and service activities, 207
    protecting team members', 276–277
    protecting your own, 288–289
Time management, 59–60
Time-oriented goals, 50
Title page, manuscript, 194
Tolerance, 89
Topic
    abstract on, 174
    clarifying literature review, 116–117, 125
    defining, in good-enough approach, 126
    narrowness of focus on, 109, 113
Topic area
    building expertise in, 219
    of target journal, 192–193
Topic selection, 107–113
    example of, 110–111
    mentoring students on, 111–112
    narrowing down process for, 108–110, 113
    research program development and, 215
    in sample timelines, 293, 294
Top-tier journals, 219, 228
Toxins, 89
Tradition, as value, 16
Training
    leveraging opportunities related to, 220–221
    for research assistants, 157–158, 160
Training networks, 282
Transactional relationships, 267
Transformation of nonnormal variables, 163

Transition from graduate student to
    professor, 241–256
  abruptness of, 241
  applying for a job, 242–245
  community building in, 270–271
  job interview process, 246–247
  mentoring students on, 221–222,
    241–242, 254–256
  negotiation period, 247–249
  research responsibilities in, 241–242,
    249–252
  service responsibilities in, 253–254
  teaching responsibilities in, 252–253
Transitions
  in graduate school, 95, 97
  into leadership roles, 201–205
Travel money, 180–181, 248
Treatment description, in literature
    review, 123
Triangulation, 255, 270, 275
Trust
  during adversity, 99–100
  between collaborators, 230–233, 237
  and conflict, 275
  honoring commitments to build, 54
  and leadership, 210–211, 267
  in mentor–student relationship, 30,
    102, 259
  in relationships, 26
  shared values and, 269
  team cohesion and, 272
Trust networks, 282, 283
Trustworthiness, as team value, 273
Turning the Flywheel (Collins), 220
2-1 teaching load, 242
2-2 teaching load, 242, 248
Two-tailed test, 139

U

Uncertainty, xii, 97, 101
Undergraduate students
  abstracts written by, 176–177
  acquisition of wisdom by, 256
  building of habits by, 70
  collaboration with, 238–239
  community building by, 30–31
  conference presentations by, 187
  cultivating positive beliefs for, 82–83
  culture of initiative and responsibility
    for, 222
  data analysis by, 166
  data collection by, 160
  expertise building by, 42–43
  goal setting by, 55
  improving self-efficacy of, 74
  independent research projects for, 6–7,
    112, 222, 266
  leadership of, 202
  literature reviews by, 127–128
  mentoring of, 263, 267–268
  open science practices for, 144–145
  periods of adversity for, 103
  physical health of, 93
  presentations by, 153
  in publication process, 197
  pursuit of values for, 19
  research study design for, 134
  rewarding initiative of, 212–213
  starting to work with, 250
  team cohesion and inclusion issues for,
    284
  topic selection by, 112
  working with, at liberal arts colleges,
    242, 243
  writing of discussion section by, 171–172
Unexpected challenges, 95–97
Universalism, 16, 17
Unpublished studies, 119, 179–180
Urgent tasks, 58, 64

V

Vague goals, 48–49
Values, 11–20
  alignment of behavior and, 13
  connection between research and,
    17–18, 286
  defined, 13–14
  and diversity statement, 245
  goals vs., 13–14, 46
  identifying your, 14–16
  mentoring students on, 18–19
  passing on, 290–291
  shared, 26, 269, 274, 276
  as source of motivation, 12–14, 19–20
  team, 273–274
Vicarious successful experiences, 75–76
Virtues, xi–xiii, 109
Vulnerability
  about research experiences, 75–76, 82
  in collaborative relationships, 230–231
  deepening relationships with, 26

in mentorship, 254–255
modeling, 83
Vygotsky, Lev, 38

W

Walking, to change state, 78
Widespread missing data, 162
Winsorizing, 162
Wisdom, xi–xii, 256
Withdrawal, 89
Word limits, 174, 190
Workaholism, 59
Writing
of abstracts, 173–177
collaborative, 234–235, 238–239
consistency in, 287
as daily habit, 59, 65–66
developing expertise in. *See* Expertise in research and writing
and dictation while walking, 78
of discussion section, 167–172
engagement in, 39
in groups and teams, 133
of introduction section, 190–191
of literature review, 120–127
of method section, 137–145
of results section, 161–162, 165, 166
scheduling time for, 60, 70, 288
splitting large tasks related to, 61–62

Z

Zero, correlation of, 164
Zone of proximal development, 38, 42, 268

About the Authors

Joshua N. Hook, PhD, received his doctorate in counseling psychology from Virginia Commonwealth University. He is a professor of psychology at the University of North Texas and a licensed clinical psychologist in the state of Texas. His professional interests include humility, religion/spirituality, and multicultural counseling. He has published more than 300 journal articles and book chapters, as well as eight books, including *Cultural Humility: Engaging Diverse Identities in Therapy* (American Psychological Association [APA]). He has also received several grants from the John Templeton Foundation for his research and received the early career awards for APA Division 17 (Society of Counseling Psychology) and Division 36 (Society for the Psychology of Religion and Spirituality). In his free time, he enjoys blogging (https://www.JoshuaNHook.com), cheering on the Chicago Bears, trying not to get injured doing CrossFit, and hanging out with his wife and daughter.

Don E. Davis, PhD, is a professor of psychology at Georgia State University. Donnie did undergraduate work at Yale and his doctorate at Virginia Commonwealth University. He completed his psychology predoctoral internship at Clemson University and is currently licensed in the state of Georgia. A member of the Ken Matheny Center for the Study of Stress, Trauma, and Resilience, Donnie has worked on more than 30 grants, many with the John Templeton Foundation. His research and clinical interests are in the area of positive psychology. His work focuses on humility and related virtues such as forgiveness and gratitude. He also does work on the role of religion/spirituality in character development. He has published more than 275 articles or chapters. He has also written books on several of these themes. He is the associate editor of *The Journal of Positive Psychology*. Donnie has a wife and three kids,

Catherine (age 14), Adam (age 9), and Emerson (age 3), and enjoys biking, hiking, and other outdoor activities—and he loves reading.

Daryl R. Van Tongeren, PhD, is an associate professor of psychology at Hope College. A social psychologist, he has published more than 200 scholarly articles and chapters on topics such as meaning in life, humility, religion, relationships, and well-being. His research has been covered by numerous media outlets, including *The New York Times, Chicago Tribune, The Washington Post*, National Public Radio–affiliated radio stations, *Scientific American*, and *Men's Health*. This is his third book, having authored *Humble* in 2022 and coauthored *The Courage to Suffer* (with Sara A. Showalter Van Tongeren) in 2020. His work has been supported by numerous grants from the John Templeton Foundation, and he was won national and international awards for his research. He was named a 2016 Rising Star by the Association for Psychological Science, won the Margaret Gorman Early Career Award for APA's Division 36 (Society for the Psychology of Religion and Spirituality) in 2022, and won the Early Career Contributions Award from the International Society for the Science of Existential Psychology. Currently, Daryl is an associate editor for *The Journal of Positive Psychology* and a consulting editor for *Psychology of Religion and Spirituality* and *The Journal of Social Psychology*. He enjoys running, biking, and hiking near where he lives with his wife, Sara, in Holland, Michigan.